The
Canon EOS Digital
Rebel T1i/500D
Companion

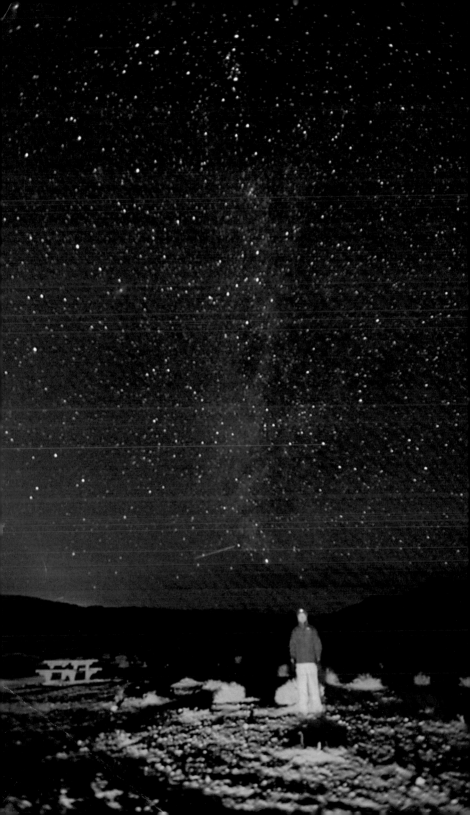

The
Canon EOS Digital
Rebel T1i/500D
Companion

BEN LONG

O'REILLY®

Beijing · Cambridge · Farnham · Köln · Sebastopol · Taipei · Tokyo

The Canon EOS Digital Rebel T1i/500D Companion
by Ben Long

Copyright © 2009 Ben Long. All rights reserved.
Printed in Canada

Published by O'Reilly Media, Inc. 1005 Gravenstein Highway North, Sebastopol CA 95472

O'Reilly books may be purchased for educational, business, or sales promotional use. Online editions are also available for most titles (*safari.oreilly.com*). For more information, contact our corporate/institutional sales department: (800) 998-9938 or *corporate@oreilly.com*.

Editor: Colleen Wheeler
Proofreader: Genevieve d'Entremont
Technical Editor: Derrick Story
Interior Design: David Futato, Ron Bilodeau
Indexer: Denise Getz
Cover Designer: Monica Kamsvaag
Photographer: Ben Long

Print History: July 2009, First Edition.

ISBN: 978-0-596-80363-6
[F]

Contents

Acknowledgments

Ask anyone who knows me and they'll probably say that it's not a good idea to be around when I'm working on a book, because I'll invariably ask to make a photographic example of you. This book was no exception, and I'd like to thank Konrad Eek, Rossitza Jekova-Goza, Emily Clinton, Jeanne Phyllis Verity Parkhurst, Hans Wendl, Rick Poland, Regina Saisi, Joanna Silber, and Marz the cat for standing (or laying) there while they were turned into example images. A very special thanks to Janine Lessing for doing some boring grunt work that made the writing of this book much easier, and to Flavio Salazar for modeling for the cover.

Thanks, too, to the grandmothers of GAPA—Grandmothers Against Poverty and AIDS—an amazing NGO in South Africa composed of grandmothers who are trying to hold their families and communities together in the face of the AIDS pandemic while simultaneously raising their own grandchildren and fighting to improve the lives of people in townships all over South Africa. Some images of them (and their grandchildren) appear in Chapters 8 and 12. Check out *www.gapa.org.za* to learn more about this amazing organization.

Derrick Story did a fantastic job of tech editing this book, and many things that you will learn in these pages will be easier to understand thanks to his help. Finally, thanks to Colleen Wheeler for concocting the idea in the first place and for being so helpful in bending it into its current shape.

Preface

Before we get to how cool your Rebel T1i/500D is, I want to clear up an important issue: Why in the world do you need this book? This camera comes with a very detailed manual, so you might be wondering why you should slog through another big batch of pages.

If you've already looked at the manual that came with your camera, then you've probably discovered that it details each and every button in reasonably clear language and that it's well-organized, leading you from simple features to more advanced ones. However, knowing what each button on your camera does won't necessarily mean you can shoot great pictures. Personally, I know the basic concept of a paintbrush, but I can't paint a decent painting to save my life. To use a creative tool well, you must understand both the technique and the craft of the tool, as well as have some sense of artistry when you use it.

That's the idea behind this book. While the automatic systems in the Rebel T1i/500D mean you can shoot snapshots that are almost always properly exposed and possessed of great color, if you want to go further and create images that express something more than a simple documentation of an event, then you need to know something of the art of photography. This book is intended to serve as a full-on photography class, one that covers everything, including technical matters and exposure theory, composition theory, and how to find images and expand your visual sense. However, unlike a regular photography class, the lessons in this book are built specifically around the T1i. That means every concept is presented in terms of the T1i/500D's controls and features.

By the way, for those of you outside the United States, please excuse my T1i-centric terminology in this book. Unfortunately, Canon gives the same camera different names in different parts of the world. So, in the United States, it's the Rebel T1i; in most other parts of the world, it's the EOS 500D; and in Japan, it's the Kiss X3. For the sake of readability, we decided not to refer to the camera as the T1i/500D/Kiss X3, because that's simply too cumbersome and distracting. So when you see *T1i*, *Rebel T1i*, or *Rebel* in this book, know that I'm still talking about your camera (assuming you have a Canon Rebel T1i/EOS 500D/Kiss X3—oops, I was trying to avoid that).

Automatic cameras are great because they do a lot of the work for you, but sometimes you must take manual control and make decisions on your own. This Rebel T1i companion will walk you through all the basic photography theories that apply to any camera—whether film or digital—and that you need to understand to fully exploit the capabilities of the T1i.

So, by the time you're done with this book, in addition to knowing how all of the T1i's controls function, you'll also know how to recognize a good photo and how to use the T1i's controls to represent that subject as a compelling image. In other words, you'll be a better photographer, whether you're shooting simple snapshots or aiming for something more.

I realize once you start using this camera, you probably won't be able to resist taking lots of pictures. This is a good thing; one of the great advantages of digital photography is that it doesn't cost you anything to shoot. Because your storage media is reusable and because there's not an expensive chemical process, you can shoot for free, making it easy to practice and experiment. The freedom to practice will do more to improve your photographic skill than anything else. This book has been great fun to write, largely because the T1i is a fantastic camera. At one time or another I've had my hands on just about every digital SLR made, and I own several that I shoot with all the time. The camera's image quality is top-notch, and the compact design and excellent interface make it a lot of fun to work with. The T1i's ability to shoot in low light means you don't have to stop shooting when light levels dim. This is a camera that delivers a tremendous amount of imaging power right out of the box, and with this book, you'll learn how to get the most from it.

For More Information

You can address comments and questions concerning this book to the publisher:

O'Reilly Media, Inc.
1005 Gravenstein Highway North
Sebastopol, CA 95472
(800) 998-9938 (in the United States or Canada)
(707) 829-0515 (international or local)
(707) 829-0104 (fax)

We'll list errata, examples, and any additional information at:

http://oreilly.com/catalog/9780596803636

To comment or ask technical questions about this book, send email to:

bookquestions@oreilly.com

You can also find more information by going to O'Reilly's general Digital Media site:

digitalmedia.oreilly.com

CHAPTER 1

Getting to Know the Rebel T1i

SHOOTING SNAPSHOTS USING AUTO MODES

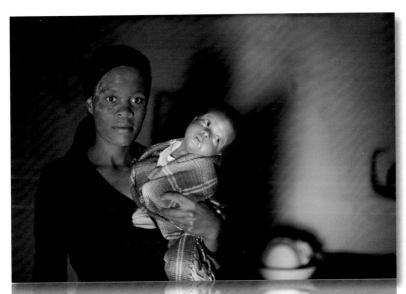

If you're new to the Rebel T1i, you're probably much more interested in shooting than in reading a book. So, in this chapter I'm going to quickly get you up to speed on the camera's automatic features so that you can get out the door right away and start using the camera. One of the great things about the T1i's design is that you can start out using it just like a point-and-shoot camera and then activate more sophisticated controls as you need them. This first chapter explains the fundamental concepts of the camera and photographic technique that we'll build on through the rest of the book.

BEFORE YOU CAN SHOOT WITH THE REBEL T1i

If you haven't yet set up your camera, you need to do a few things before you can shoot with it. Fortunately, the T1i's manual is very good, and you can learn everything you need to know about setup by reading the following sections of the manual:

- The camera battery may have a little charge when you first unpack the camera, but t's best to give it a good refueling before you head out to shoot. Read pages 24–26 of the Rebel T1i manual to learn about charging and installing the battery.

- You'll need a Secure Digital (SD) memory card for your camera. The Rebel T1i does not ship with a card, so you'll need to buy one. Any photography store or electronics store should carry them. You can learn how to install and remove the card on pages 31–32 of the T1i manual.

- A lens must be attached to your camera. If you bought the Rebel T1i kit, then you probably got an 18–55mm lens. If you bought the body-only package, then you should have bought a lens separately. You can learn how to attach and remove a lens on pages 33–34 of the T1i manual.

- The power switch on the top of the camera powers up the camera (as long as you have a charged battery installed). If it's the first time you're turning the camera on, then the camera will prompt you to enter the date and time. Page 29 will walk you through setting the date and time, and page 30 will show you how to set the language that you want to use in the camera's menus.

- Finally, the camera includes a shoulder strap. The best way to ensure that your camera doesn't get damaged is to attach the shoulder strap and use it! The camera will be more secure and easier to carry if you have the strap attached. Page 23 of the T1i manual shows how to attach the strap.

From left to right, the Rebel T1i's media slot, lens mount button and reference dot, and battery.

If you've shot only with a point-and-shoot camera, then you'll find much to like about working with an SLR. The bright, clear viewfinder, the ability to change lenses, and the advanced manual controls will give you far more creative power than you probably had on your point-and-shoot camera. If you're an old-school SLR film shooter, then the switch to digital will bring you huge improvements in workflow, image editing, and overall image quality.

Obviously, with all the power packed into a camera like the Rebel T1i, you have a lot to learn. However, since the camera also has advanced auto functions, you can get started shooting with it right away and, to a degree, use it just like you used your point-and-shoot.

The best way to learn your camera is to use it, so before we look at the specific parts and components of your T1i, you should do a little snapshot shooting just to get your hands on the camera and get a feel for the general control layout.

Resetting the Camera's Defaults

If you've already been playing with your T1i, you might have made some changes to some of the internal settings. To ensure that your camera behaves the way that I'll describe in this book, reset to the camera's defaults:

1. Set the Mode dial to P, then press the Menu button.

2. Press the right arrow button on the back of the camera until the second-to-last menu is selected.

3. Press the down arrow to select "Clear settings".

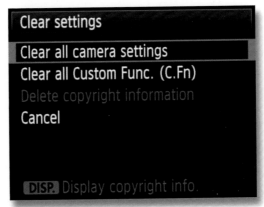

From the Clear settings menu, you can reset the camera to the factory defaults, which will make it easier to follow along with the instructions in this book.

4. Press the Set button to execute the "Clear settings" command, then select "Clear all camera settings" and press Set.

5. The camera will ask you to confirm the operation. Select OK and press Set.

6. Then, choose Clear all Custom Func. and reset those as well.

Snapshot Shooting in Full Auto Mode

The Rebel T1i has full autofocus and autoexposure features that can make all of the necessary photographic decisions for most situations. When in Full Auto mode, all you have to do is frame the shot and press the shutter button, and the camera will automatically figure out just about every other relevant setting. However, you need to know a few things to get the most out of Full Auto mode.

On the top of the T1i, on the right side of the camera, is a Mode dial. The mode you choose determines which functions the camera will perform automatically and which will be left up to you. So, if you want more creative control, then you'll want to select a mode that offers less automation and leaves more power in your hands.

For snapshot shooting, Full Auto mode will be your best bet and will make your T1i function much like a simple point-and-shoot camera—but one that delivers the superior image quality of an SLR. To select Full Auto mode, set the Mode dial to the green box (□).

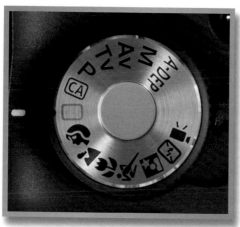

Set the camera's Mode dial to the green box to select Full Auto mode.

If you haven't done so already, take the lens cap off the camera. You don't have to worry about accidentally shooting with it on, because if the lens cap is on, you won't see anything in the viewfinder. Make sure the switch on the lens is set to Autofocus, not Manual.

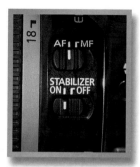

The 18–55mm lens kit includes an autofocus switch, and most other lenses will have a similar switch. Make certain it's set to AF.

Framing Your Shot

This next part you probably already know: look through the viewfinder and frame your shot. If you have a zoom lens attached to your camera, you can zoom to frame tighter or wider. For now, we're not going to worry about composition, because we'll be discussing that in detail later.

Autofocus, or "How to Press the Shutter Button"

With your shot framed, you're ready to shoot. However, although pressing the shutter button may seem a simple thing, there are some important things to understand about it, because it's your key to the camera's autofocus feature.

Once you've framed the shot, press the shutter button *halfway*. When you do this, the camera will analyze your scene and try to determine what the subject is.

The camera can analyze nine focus points. Once the T1i has determined the subject (or what it thinks is the subject), it will light up the focus point that it thinks is correct. If more than one point sits on the plane of focus, it will light up them all.

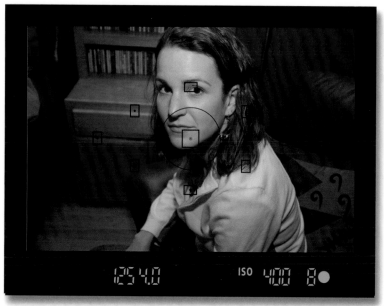

When you half-press the shutter button to autofocus, the XS will light up the focus spots that it thinks are correct for your subject.

Very often, several potential subjects sit on the same plane (that is, they're all the same distance from the camera). The T1i will show you all the focus points that it considers in focus. As long as one of them is on your subject, then it has focused correctly.

When the T1i has achieved focus, it will beep and show a green circle on the right side of the viewfinder status display. (You can see this in the previous figure.)

This half-press of the shutter is a *crucial* step when using the T1i (or any other autofocus camera). If you wait until the moment you want to take the shot and *then* press the shutter button all the way down, you'll miss the shot, because the camera will have to focus, meter, and calculate white balance before it can fire, and these things take time.

WARNING: Don't Zoom After Locking Focus

Once the camera has locked focus, don't adjust the zoom control. Focusing at a specific distance is a function of your current focal length. If you change focal length (that is, if you zoom in or out), you'll throw your image out of focus.

REMINDER: "My flash popped up!"

In Full Auto mode, the T1i will decide whether it needs to use the flash. If it decides that it needs it, the flash will automatically pop up and will be fired when you take the shot.

Take the Shot

Once the camera has told you that it's focused and ready to shoot, gently squeeze the shutter button. If you jab at the button, you might jar the camera, resulting in a potential loss of sharpness in your image.

OOPS!

ARE YOU IN AUTOFOCUS?

If your camera doesn't beep or flash the confirmation light when you half-press the shutter, your lens might be set to manual focus mode. Somewhere on the body of the lens should be a switch for changing from auto to manual focus.

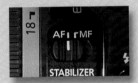

Your lens should have a way to change from auto to manual focus. If the lens provides stabilization, there will be a switch for turning stabilizing on and off.

Make certain it's set to AF or Auto.

- If your autofocus light blinks but doesn't lock focus, it's because the camera can't find a subject that has strong contrast. As we'll see, strong contrast is necessary for autofocus to work. You'll learn how to compensate for this problem later.

- If the focus beep repeats rapidly, then the camera has locked onto a moving subject and is tracking it. Shoot as normal.

After you shoot, the camera will display the image for two seconds, giving you a moment to review. When you're ready to shoot again, follow the same procedure. It's very important to remember to do a *half-press* of the shutter to give the camera time to autofocus.

TIP: Flash Shooting

In a low-light situation, you may see some strange flashes coming from the flash when you press the shutter halfway. These flashes serve to help the camera's autofocus mechanism "see" when the light is low. Once focus is locked, the camera will beep, indicating that you can press the button the rest of the way, whenever you're ready, to take your shot.

Those are the basics of shooting. Compose your shot, press the shutter button halfway to focus, and then squeeze the shutter button. This is the process that you'll use no matter what mode you're shooting in. Spend some time shooting in Full Auto mode to get a feel for the shutter and basic camera controls.

The Viewfinder Status Display

When you press the shutter button halfway down, several things happen inside the T1i's viewfinder. As I already mentioned, the camera shows you which focus points it has selected for autofocus. It also uses the readout at the bottom of the viewfinder to tell you about its exposure choices and to give you some additional status information. The content of this readout will vary depending on the mode you're in.

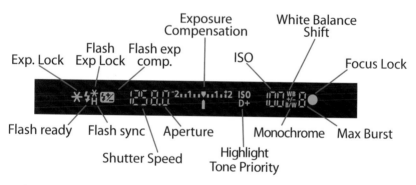

The Rebel T1i's viewfinder shows all the settings you need access to while shooting.

From left to right, the readout includes the following:

• If the camera has chosen to use the flash, it will display the flash icon. The flash icon will blink on and off, and the word *busy* will be displayed, until the flash unit is charged and ready to go. If your battery has a good charge, this shouldn't take very long.

- Next, the camera displays its chosen shutter speed and aperture. You'll learn more about these in Chapter 5.

- The Exposure Compensation display is shown next. It has a range of -2 stops to +2 stops.

- Next comes ISO choice. For now, all you need to know is that the higher the number is, the grainier your images will be. Don't worry about this now; we'll discuss it in more detail later.

- Finally, you'll see a number showing how many shots you can shoot before you will have to wait for the camera's buffer to empty. The camera has enough onboard RAM to shoot nine images when in Full Auto mode. Although this may not sound like much, remember that as soon as you shoot, the camera immediately starts writing its buffer out to the storage card.

    So, if you're not shooting too fast, you'll never come close to overrunning the buffer. If you're shooting bursts of images—at a sporting event, say—then you might fill up the buffer and have to wait a moment before you can shoot again. You don't have to wait until all nine images are available. As long as the number reads at least 1, you can still shoot.

- Finally, at the far right of the display is a green dot that appears whenever the camera has locked focus and is ready to shoot. When you press the shutter button halfway, you can press the rest of the way once this green dot appears.

As you can see, the status display includes a few other indicators, which you'll learn about in later chapters.

The LCD Status Display

In addition to the in-viewfinder status display, the T1i also shows a lot of status information on the rear LCD. What's displayed on the screen varies depending on what mode you're in, simply because in some modes you don't have as much manual control and so don't need as much status feedback. In Full Auto mode, your screen should look something like the image on the next page.

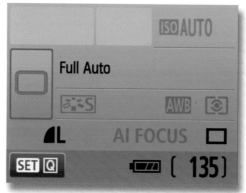

In Full Auto mode, the LCD screen should look something like this.

As you can see, you can easily tell how many shots are remaining, how charged the battery is, and the image format that you're shooting in. The camera also shows what light-metering mode you're using, which, to be honest, is kind of strange, because you can't actually change this when shooting in Full Auto.

When you half-press the shutter button to tell the camera to focus and meter, it displays its chosen shutter speed and aperture at the top of the status display. We'll explore what these mean in later chapters.

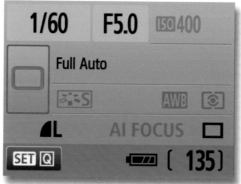

After you half-press the shutter button, the status screen will show your shutter speed and aperture.

Just below the viewfinder, you can see a small black window. This is a sensor that detects when you have the camera held up to your face. As you raise and lower the camera, the T1i automatically disables and enables its LCD screen, so that it doesn't distract you while shooting. You can also turn the display off completely by pressing the DISP button. Pressing it again reactivates the screen.

Shoot some more in Full Auto mode and get comfortable with the camera's controls. Even though the camera has a lot of other buttons and dials, you don't really need to worry about them right now.

> **TIP:** If the Viewfinder Is Not Sharp
>
> If you wear glasses and like to remove them when shooting, you can use the *diopter control*, the small knob next to the viewfinder, to compensate for some near- or farsightedness. Turn the knob until the nine autofocus boxes inside the viewfinder are sharp. Note that the diopter may not be able to completely compensate for extremely bad vision. Also, you'll have to change it again if you put your glasses back on. If the viewfinder ever inexplicably goes out of focus, it might just be that you bumped the diopter knob. Turn it until focus is restored. If the diopter does not offer enough correction, you'll want to look at Canon's replacement diopters.

Viewing Your Images

As you've seen, the T1i displays your image for a brief time after you shoot. As you'll see later, you can extend this time by changing a menu setting. But when it comes time to review your images, you'll want to use the camera's playback mode.

To review your images, press the Play (■) button on the back of the camera (obviously, the camera needs to be powered on for this to work).

The camera displays the last image that you shot, along with some status information. (If you don't see the image number and format information, press the DISP button once.)

The left and right arrow keys on the back of the camera let you navigate forward and backward through your images. Playback mode has a number of other features that you'll learn about in Chapter 3.

At any time, you can press the Play button again or give a half-press to the shutter button to return to shooting mode. Note that the T1i can change between shooting and playback modes very quickly, much faster than most point-and-shoot cameras, meaning you don't have to worry about missing a shot because the camera is locked up in a playback mode.

Shutter Speed   Aperture   Folder # File #

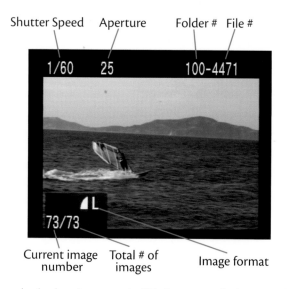

Current image   Total # of
number   images   Image format

*When you play back an image on the T1i, the camera displays some important
status information along with your image.*

Using Scene Modes

Now you've seen how the T1i's Full Auto mode works. Since Full Auto mode takes
care of all the critical decisions regarding camera settings, it's an ideal mode for
snapshot shooting and for getting used to the camera. Before you go off shooting,
though, let's take a quick look at some other auto features that you might find
useful while getting started.

On the Mode dial, you'll see a bunch of little icons underneath the Full Auto option. These are the T1i's scene modes.

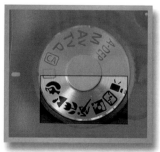

*These options on the Mode dial are scene modes, which bias the camera's decisions
under specific conditions so that it calculates more appropriate exposures.*

Scene modes are also fully automatic, but each one biases some of its decisions in a certain way to make it more appropriate to particular types of shooting.

Portrait mode Portrait mode is ideal for shooting—you guessed it!—portraits. What makes a portrait different from any other type of shot? Typically, in a portrait you want the background blurred out to bring more attention to your subject. Portrait mode biases its exposure decisions to attempt to blur the background.

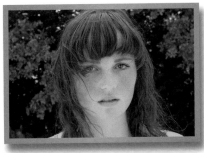

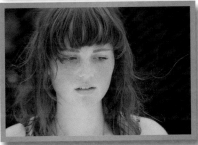

In the upper image, I shot with deeper depth of field to reveal details in the background. In the lower image, I shot with shallow depth of field to blur the background out and bring more focus to the subject.

TIP: For Softer Background in Portraits

If you want a really soft background, try to position your subject away from the background as much as possible.

Landscape mode Landscape mode can help your landscape shots because it will choose settings that attempt to maximize the amount of your scene that will be in focus. It's basically the opposite of Portrait mode.

☘ **Close-up mode** Close-up shots of flowers or small objects (what is traditionally referred to as *macro* photography) are made easier with Close-up mode.

🏃 **Sports mode** When shooting fast-moving subject matter such as moving wildlife or a sporting event, opt for Sports mode. Sports mode biases the camera's exposure so that fast-moving objects will be sharp and clear.

When using Sports mode, make sure the center focus point is on your subject when you press the shutter button halfway. Unlike other modes, you won't hear a beep when the camera has locked focus. Instead, the camera will begin beeping continuously to indicate that it is now *tracking your subject!* Yes, Sports mode uses the Rebel T1i's Servo focus feature to track a moving object and keep it in focus.

Press the shutter to take a shot. If you keep the shutter button held down, the camera will continue to shoot.

Night Portrait mode One of the biggest mistakes people make when shooting with flash is that they assume a flash can light up an entire scene, just as if it were daylight. But the flash on any camera has a limited range. It's usually enough to light up your subject but not your background, leaving you with a subject that appears to be standing in the middle of a dark limbo.

> **REMINDER:** Night Portraits Require Still Subjects
>
> When shooting with Night Portrait mode, the flash will fire, but the camera's shutter will *stay open* for a bit. So, it's important to tell your subject not to move until after you say so. (And it's just as important for you to stay still until the camera is done, too.)

Disabling Flash mode Flash photography is not always allowed. Museums, performances, and other public venues often prohibit flash photography. Set the mode dial to Disabling Flash mode, and the T1i will never use its flash.

When shooting without the flash, you may find that some of the numbers inside the viewfinder blink. When this happens, the camera is informing you that light is low, so you need to be extra careful to hold the camera steady. Also, be aware that when the numbers are flashing, there's a good chance that your resulting image will be too dark.

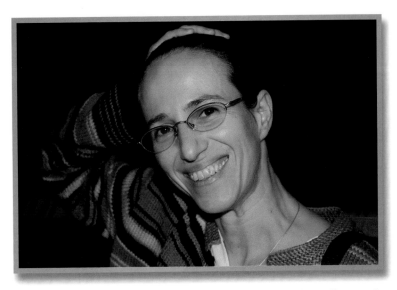

At night, if you take a flash picture, you'll usually end up with a well-exposed subject on a background of complete black. This is because the range of the flash is only about 10 feet. Objects beyond that will not be illuminated by the flash.

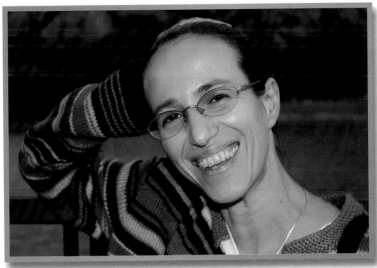

Night Portrait mode uses the flash and a longer shutter speed so that both your subject and background are well-exposed.

Also, when shooting in low light without flash, any moving subjects will likely be blurred, so if you're trying to shoot a portrait, be sure to tell your subject to sit very still.

> **QUESTION:** What about Movie mode?
>
> The final Scene mode icon on the dial is the Movie mode option, which we'll cover in Chapter 9, "Specialty Shooting."

Snapshot Tips

While the rest of this book is going to cover just about every aspect of shooting in great detail—from holding the camera to processing images—you can do a lot with what you've already learned about the Full Auto capability. Since the camera is taking care of most of the technical issues for you, it's a good time to practice handling the camera and composing shots.

We're going to talk about composition in great detail in Chapter 8. For now, consider the following tips when shooting snapshots.

Watch That Headroom: Fill the Frame

When shooting a portrait or candid snapshot of someone, you usually do not need a lot of headroom, unless you want to show something about the environment they're in.

For example, in the top image on the facing page the extra headroom doesn't add anything to the picture. In fact, it's kind of distracting and takes up space that could be used to show a larger image of the person. In the bottom image, we fill the frame with more of the person. We can see a better view of him, but we still get enough background detail to get an idea of the environment he's in.

"Fill the frame" is one of the most important compositional rules you can learn, no matter what type of image you're shooting. Don't waste space in the frame. Empty space in your image is space that could be used to provide a larger, better view of your subject.

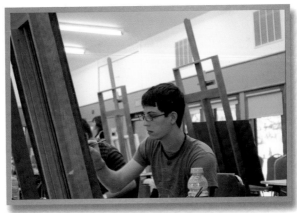

The extra headroom doesn't contribute anything to the image.

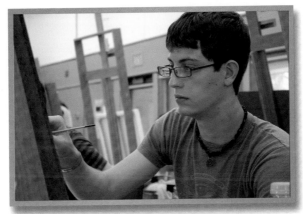

In this image we've filled the entire frame, which lets us see a larger view of our subject.

Don't Be Afraid to Get in Close

Another portrait tip: you don't have to show a person's entire face or head. Don't be afraid to crop them and get in close for a very personal shot.

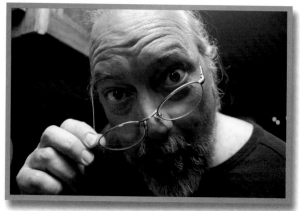

When shooting portraits, don't be afraid to get in close. You don't have to show a person's whole head. It's fine to crop.

You can get close either by standing physically close to the person or by standing farther away and zooming in. However, as you'll see in Chapter 6, these two options produce very different images, so you'll want to think about which approach is right for your subject.

Remember That Your Knees Can Bend

It's easy to forget about that third dimension that you can move in, and shoot all of your shots while standing up. Don't forget that you can bend your knees (or even lie on the ground) to get a different angle. Getting down low is especially important when shooting children and animals, since it puts you at a more personal, eye-to-eye relationship with them.

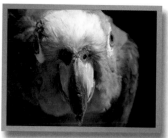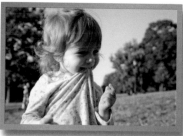

Often, the best pictures of animals and children occur at their altitude.

Lead Your Subject

When shooting a portrait of someone who's looking off-frame, consider *leading* the subject. When someone is looking out of the frame, we're more interested in the space that's in front of them than the space that's behind them. Even if we can't see what it is they're looking at, we still want to feel the extra space that sits in the direction they're looking.

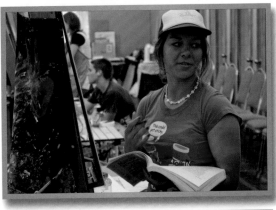

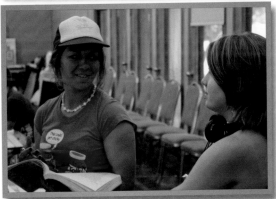

When your subject is looking off-frame, it's almost always better to "lead" them. Frame the shot so that we can see in the direction they're looking—even if what they're looking at isn't in the frame.

Watch the Background

Don't pay attention just to your subject; remember that they're also standing in front of something. Make sure there's nothing "sticking out" of their head or juxtaposed in a distracting way.

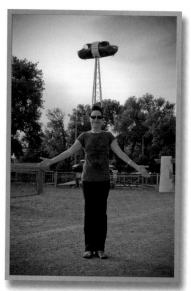

Pay attention to the background in your image.

Watch Out for Backlighting

This is loosely related to the previous tip. Be careful about shooting your subject in front of a brightly lit background, such as a window, or shooting into the sun. Although sometimes you can use such an approach to great effect, for simple snapshots you'll get better results keeping a close eye on the backlight in your shots. If you find yourself shooting someone in front of a window or bright light, try to move them or yourself so that the light is not directly behind them.

The problem with bright lights in the background of a shot is that they confuse the camera's light meter. When a bright light appears in the background, the camera meters to properly expose that bright light. This usually means the foreground is left underexposed and appears too dark.

In Full Auto mode, the Rebel T1i should recognize such a situation and automatically pop up the flash. The flash will serve to light up the foreground, creating a more even exposure with the background.

You'll learn more about metering, as well as other strategies for handling backlighting, in Chapter 7. For now, even if you aren't sure exactly how to handle such a situation, at least start learning to recognize when you're shooting in this type of difficult lighting condition.

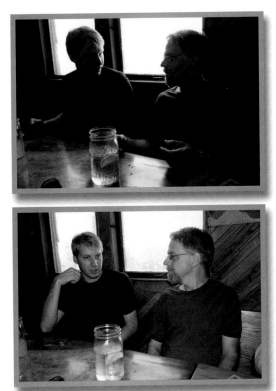

The window is throwing off the camera's meter. Shooting with flash helps illuminate the foreground and evens out the exposure.

Understand Flash Range

While the flash on the T1i can do a good job of illuminating a subject, you have to remember that it has a limited range. Anything beyond about 13 feet from the camera will fall out of the flash's range and not be illuminated at all. So, if you're standing at night across the street from a person or building and you shoot a picture with the flash popped up, you'll probably get a shot that's completely black.

For this situation, flash is not the answer. Instead, you'll need to employ some low-light shooting strategies, which we'll discuss in Chapter 7.

> **TIP:** Use Night Portrait Mode
>
> As you saw earlier, flash range can also impact the background of your scene. If your subject is in range of the flash but your background isn't, you can end up with people standing in totally black limbo environments. See "Night Portrait mode" earlier in this chapter.

Cover Your Shot, or "One Shot Is Rarely Enough"

There's one mistake that all beginning photographers make: they think an expert photographer sees a scene or subject, determines how to best frame and expose it, and then takes a picture of it. If you describe this process to an "expert" or "professional" photographer, they'll most likely laugh.

The fact is, even the most accomplished photographer rarely gets it right the first time and so rarely shoots only one exposure of a subject. Instead, they *work* their subject—something we'll be talking about a lot through the rest of this book.

Very often, the only way to find the best composition or angle on a shot is to move around. Get closer and farther, stand on your tiptoes, squat down low, circle the object—and look through the viewfinder the whole time, and shoot the whole time.

If you like, review your shots and try again. Often, photography is like sculpture. You can't see the finished shot right away. Instead, you have to "sculpt" the scene, trying different vantage points until you find the angle that makes for the most interesting composition and play of light, shadow, and color.

> **REMINDER:** Keep Moving!
>
> When a subject catches your eye, the chances you happen to be standing in the very best spot in the world and that you happen to be the perfect height to photograph it are pretty slim. So, go out now and practice shooting broad coverage of some scenes. Stay moving, play with distance and angle, and notice the difference in what you see in the viewfinder, what you recognize while you're shooting, and what the final results look like on the camera's screen.

You may be surprised to find that the final images you like best are the ones that are very different from what you originally envisioned.

CHAPTER 2

Anatomy of the Rebel T1i

LEARNING TO HOLD AND CONTROL YOUR CAMERA

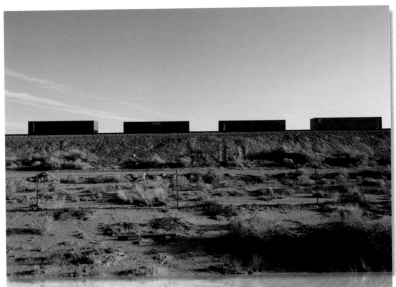

In the previous chapter you saw how you can use the Rebel T1i's automatic features for easy snapshot shooting. Before we go on to learn about its more advanced shooting features, we're going to take a tour of the camera and learn its parts. The T1i is a complex tool, and the better you know its workings, the more easily and effectively you'll be able to make it do what you want.

What Is an SLR Anyway?

The Rebel T1i is an *SLR* camera, a term you may have come across when you were shopping. SLR stands for *single lens reflex*, and those words tell you some important things about how the camera operates.

As the name implies, a *single* lens reflex camera has only one lens on it. If you're wondering why a camera might have two lenses, consider a point-and-shoot camera. On the front of a lot of point-and-shoot cameras, you'll see two lenses, one that is used to expose the image sensor and a separate lens that serves as a viewfinder. Because it's very simple to engineer and doesn't take up much space, a point-and-shoot camera can be made very small.

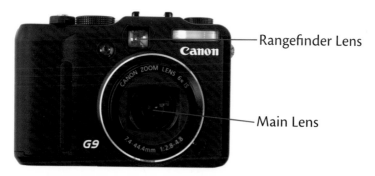

Rangefinder Lens

Main Lens

Unlike an SLR, this point-and-shoot camera has two lenses, one that exposes the image sensor and another that serves as a viewfinder.

The downside to this setup is that when you look through the viewfinder, you're not necessarily seeing the same thing the camera's image sensor sees. You're not seeing the effects of any filters or lens attachments you might be using, and because you're looking at your scene from a slightly different vantage point, the cropping you see in your viewfinder might be slightly different from what the camera actually shoots (this problem is referred to as 2).

When you look through the viewfinder on an SLR, you're actually looking through the same lens that is used to expose the image sensor. As in a film camera, the image sensor in a digital camera sits on the *focal plane*, a flat area directly behind the lens. In front of the sensor is the shutter, a mechanical curtain that opens and closes very quickly when you press the shutter button. The shutter lets you control how long the sensor gets exposed to light. Obviously, because there's an image sensor and a shutter sitting directly behind the lens, you can't easily get a clear view through the lens without some work, with the shutter and image sensor in the way.

DEFINITION: Parallax

The easiest way to understand parallax is simply to hold your index finger in front of your face and close one eye. Now close the other eye, and you'll perceive that your finger has jumped sideways. At close distances, even a change of view as small as the distance between your eyes can create a very different perspective on your subject. A camera that uses one lens for framing and another for shooting faces the same problems. Parallax is not a problem at longer ranges, because the parallax shift is imperceptible.

Take a look at the profile of your camera and note that the lens is actually sitting much lower than the viewfinder. If you could take a cross section of your camera, you would see that the image sensor and shutter are directly behind the lens. In *front* of the shutter sits a mirror set at a 45° angle. This mirror bounces the light from the lens *up* into a complex optical arrangement called a *pentamirror*, an array of mirrors that bounces the light back out through the viewfinder. Thanks to this system of mirrors, you can see out the lens. Of course, since the mirror sits between the lens and the focal plane, there's no way that the image sensor can see out the lens. This is where the *reflex* part of "SLR" comes to play.

When you press the camera's shutter button, the camera flips the mirror up so that it's completely out of the way of the focal plane. Then the shutter is opened, the sensor is exposed, the shutter closes, and then the mirror comes back down. Part of the distinctive sound of shooting with an SLR is the sound of the mirror going up and down.

You can actually see the mirror itself any time you take the lens off your camera. It sits inside the *mirror chamber*. If you look toward the top of the mirror chamber, you can see where the light gets bounced up into the pentamirror.

SLRs have many advantages over point-and-shoot cameras, and the fact that you and the sensor look through a single lens is a very big one. It means that what you see through the viewfinder is much more accurate than what you typically find with the optical viewfinder on a point-and-shoot camera. Also, because they're larger than point-and-shoot viewfinders, SLR viewfinders are usually much brighter, clearer, and easier to see.

Of course, on a point-and-shoot camera, when you use the LCD screen as a viewfinder, you're looking through the same lens as the sensor. But the optical viewfinder on an SLR still offers advantages. They're visible in bright daylight, and as you'll see, present you with a view of more of the colors and tones in your image.

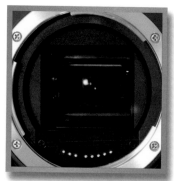

If you take the lens off your camera, you can see the mirror and look up into the pentamirror assembly.

Finally, many photographers prefer SLR viewfinders because they like to block out the rest of the world with the camera so that they can fully concentrate on the image in the viewfinder. This is much harder to do with the inferior viewfinder or LCD viewfinder on a point-and-shoot camera.

> **TIP:** Watch the Mirror Move
>
> With the lens off and the power on, you can press the shutter button and ac-tually see the mirror flip up and, if you're quick, see the shutter open behind it. *However*, before you do this, know that shooting the camera with the mirror off will expose your sensor to dust. Don't do this outside or in a dusty room (or at all, if you don't want to take chances). Better still, if you have a friend with an SLR, try it with his camera when he's not looking.

Cleaning and Maintenance

At a fundamental level, all cameras are the same: a lens focuses light onto a re-cording medium. Because the recording medium is light-sensitive, it must be kept in a lightproof box. A shutter in front of the recording medium allows for control of when the sensor is exposed and how long the exposure will last. Cameras have worked this way since the beginning of photography in the 1850s, and while all sorts of new technologies have come along—everything from light meters to sta-bilized lenses to self-timers, color film, and autofocus—the basic principles of a lens that focuses light onto a light-sensitive medium held in a lightproof box have remained the same.

Of course, the significant change in a digital camera is the recording medium that's being exposed. Rather than a piece of celluloid covered with light-sensitive chemicals, a digital camera employs a silicon chip covered with light-sensitive bits of metal. And, where a film camera needs a bunch of mechanics to move the film in and out of the roll, a digital camera needs an onboard computer and storage device to process and store the images that it captures.

Other than this change, though, your Rebel T1i is similar in design to a traditional 35mm SLR. The camera body is the lightproof box that houses the image sensor, shutter, and viewfinder. Of course, it also has lots of other things, like the shutter button, controls, LCD screen, battery, media card, tripod mount, pop-up flash, and more.

The Rebel T1i is *not* weatherproof, meaning that Canon has not engineered it for handling harsh environments. The various openings on the camera—the lens mount and assorted doors—are not sealed against sand and moisture. So, if you're planning an extended stay in the Sahara or a float trip down the Amazon, you might want to think about taking a sturdier camera. That said, there's no reason you can't go shooting with the camera in drizzle or light rain. A little water on the body won't hurt anything; just wipe off the camera and keep shooting.

The T1i Battery

Your camera requires a battery to power its onboard computer, light meter, image sensor, and other components. If you were following along in the previous chapter, then you've already charged and used the battery, so we're going to cover some battery tips here:

- With a new battery, you should find that you can get about 500 shots off of a single charge. As the battery ages, this number will go down, but the included battery should be good for a couple of years of shooting before you need to replace it.

- Note that, in general, you do not need to worry about completely draining the battery before recharging it. You can "top it off" at any time without harming the battery itself.

- However, for the first few charges, drain the battery completely and then give it a full charge. After that, you can "top it off" anytime you like.

THE T1i AND BAD WEATHER

While the Rebel T1i can handle light rain, it's not going to do so well in heavy rain, or submersed in water. If you accidentally submerge your camera, take it out of the water immediately and *don't* turn it on. Remove the battery and media card and let the camera sit for several days to dry out. To speed drying, place the camera in a bowl and cover it with dry, uncooked rice. The rice will act as a desiccant and can help speed drying.

After a few days, try powering up the camera. If it works—and the viewfinder isn't too dirty—then there's no reason not to start shooting. If it doesn't work, then you'll need to send the camera in to Canon. You can find instructions for getting your T1i reparied at Canon's website, *www.canon.com*. From the repair page, you can easily set up a mail-in repair request. My experience with Canon's service center is that it's very speedy, so you shouldn't be without your camera for very long.

If you're shooting in extreme heat or cold, be aware that the LCD screen on the back of the camera may not work. Canon officially rates the operating temperature of the T1i as 32 to 104°F (0 to 40°C). You can probably go a little beyond these temperatures, but if you do, you will be risking a hardware failure. At extreme temperatures, small parts and circuits expand and contract and can break.

If you're shooting in very cold, damp weather, you must be careful when returning indoors, because condensation inside the camera can cause the lens or viewfinder to fog. When shooting in cold, take a Ziplock bag with you. Before you return to a heated room, turn off the camera and place it in the bag. Zip up the bag and leave it zipped until the camera has had time to warm up. Once the temperature inside the bag has equalized with the temperature outside, you can open the bag without fear of condensation.

- If you plan on an extended trip away from power, or if you tend to shoot a *lot*, then you might want to invest in another battery. For less than $100, you can get a second battery and charge it up before you leave. You can easily swap out the battery as needed.

- You might also consider some alternate chargers, such as a charger that can work off a car cigarette lighter or a small, inexpensive solar charger, which will provide you with a way to charge your camera battery (as well as a cell phone or iPod) any time you have access to sunlight. See *www.completedigitalphotography.com/cameracharging* for more details.

TIP : International Charging

The battery charger that comes with the T1i can adapt to voltages around the world, so you don't have to worry about finding a different charger for international travel. However, you will need a plug adapter to make it fit into foreign outlets. You can get these at Radio Shack or in many airports.

The Media Card

As you already know, your Rebel T1i uses a Secure Digital (SD) card. The T1i is also compatible with SDHC, a newer format that has the same form factor as SD but comes in higher capacities and offers speedier transfer. Note that you'll need an SDHC reader for SDHC cards. Fortunately, an SDHC reader will read normal SD cards, so you need only one reader to read both formats.

When shopping for media cards, you'll find a wide range of capacities and vendors and a correspondingly wide range of prices. What's the difference between a 2 GB card that costs $19 and one that costs $49? Nothing at all, in terms of the number of images it will hold. However, that $49 card is probably much faster, which means your camera will be able to dump images to it more quickly.

As you already learned, the number on the right side of the viewfinder status display shows how many images the camera can currently fit in its internal buffer. As you shoot, the buffer fills, and the number goes down. It takes time for the camera to dump these images to the card, and while the camera is performing this transfer, you may not be able to shoot at all or to shoot a full burst of images. So, with a speedier card, the camera will be able to dump its images more quickly, freeing up buffer space for more shots. How much this will matter to you depends on the type of shooting you do. If you plan on shooting sports or other action shots, where you'll typically be shooting bursts, then you will want a speedier card.

Another way to look at it is that if you want to ensure the best chance that the camera will always be able to shoot, then get a speedier card. A 133x card (or faster) will deliver a very good level of performance in the T1i. If you find that those cards cost more than you'd like to spend, then go for something less expensive, but understand that sometimes the camera might be tied up with storing images and so won't be able to shoot.

The T1i has some additional media considerations, though, because of its ability to shoot video. While a video frame doesn't use the camera's full resolution, cranking out dozens of them per second requires a speedy card. In general, if you're planning on shooting video, you should get a Class 6 SDHC card.

TIP: Know Your Speed Class

SDHC is a newer derivative of SD cards. Offering higher capacities and speedier transfer than regular SD, SDHC cards will work fine in your Rebel T1i. However, whereas SD cards use a multiplier rating—133x, for example—SDHC uses a speed class rating. The multiplier used on regular SD cards indicates how much faster the card is when compared to a standard speed CD-ROM drive. SDHC cards come in three classes, Class 2, 4, or 6. Class 2 cards can transfer 2 MB per second, whereas Class 4 or 6 can transfer 4 or 6 MB per second, respectively.

Body Parts

As you work through the rest of this book, you will become well-versed in all of the T1i's controls. Let's take a quick look at the different interface elements on the T1i so that you understand what controls I'm referring to as you work through the rest of the book.

Camera Top

You should already be familiar with the power switch and Mode dial on the top of the camera. We'll be exploring all of the mode options throughout the rest of the book.

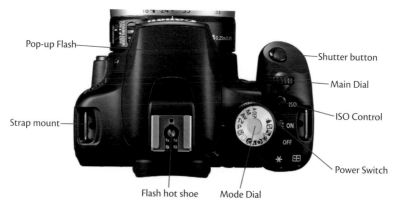

On the top of the camera you'll find several essential shooting controls.

- If you've been shooting, then you also already know where the shutter button is and understand that it has two positions, a half-press position for focusing and a full press for taking a shot.

- Just behind the shutter button is a Control Wheel. You'll use this for changing parameters such as aperture and shutter speed.

- Behind the Control Wheel is the ISO button, which is used for setting the ISO speed of the camera. You'll learn about this in Chapter 6.

- Finally, just above the viewfinder is a hotshoe for mounting an external flash unit.

Camera Front

The front of the T1i has minimal controls, but the few buttons that are there are ones you'll use often.

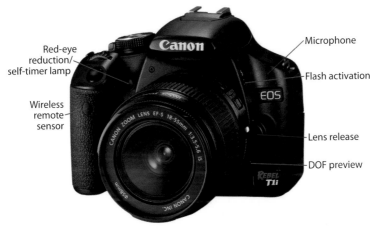

The front of the camera has a few simple but important controls.

- The Flash button pops up the camera's internal flash. In Full Auto mode, the flash pops up automatically whenever the camera thinks you need it. In most other modes, *you* decide when to use the flash and press this button to activate it.

- Note the position of the microphone, which is used during video recording. You'll want to be very careful not to cover this with your fingers while shooting.

- You'll press the lens release button any time you want to remove the lens from your camera. Press and hold the button while twisting the lens counter-clockwise.

- The depth-of-field preview button is used to get an idea of how much of your image will be in focus. We'll explore it in Chapter 7.

- On the front left of the camera is a sensor for Canon's optional RC-1, RC5 wireless remote (or a compatible third-party remote). The camera communicates with the remote through the sensor on the front of the hand grip. In addition to wireless remotes, the T1i is also compatible with Canon's RS-60E3 wired remote.

- The red-eye reduction/self-timer lamp serves two purposes. When shooting with the flash in red-eye reduction mode, this lamp flashes to try to reduce red eye. When shooting with the self-timer, the lamp flashes to indicate that the camera is counting down to firing.

> **WARNING:** Don't Block the Lamp
>
> If you're using the red-eye reduction flash, be sure your fingers don't block the red-eye reduction lamp when you're holding the camera.

Camera Sides

The left side of the camera (if you're looking at it from behind) holds a rubber door that covers three ports.

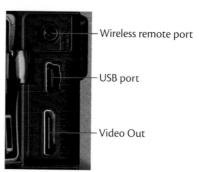

The left side of the camera holds the USB port, which is used for transferring images, a port for a remote control, and the video out port, for connecting the camera to a TV.

These ports are used for connecting your camera to a TV to play back images, for connecting a wired remote, and for attaching your camera to a computer. We'll look at all of these options in more detail later.

The port cover doesn't snap closed; instead, you kind of have to mash it into its receptacle until it stays.

On the right side of the camera is the media slot cover, which you should already have used when inserting your media card.

Note that just below the media slot cover, on the rear of the camera, there's a small light. Any time the camera is reading or writing data, this light will illuminate. If you open the door when an image is being written, the camera will beep and post a warning on the screen.

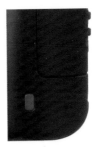

This lamp lights up whenever the camera is writing to the card. Removing the media card while this lamp is lit could wreck the images stored on the card.

WARNING: Do Not Remove Card When the Light Is Lit

Wait until the camera is completely finished writing before removing the card. If you remove the card before the write is completed, you not only will lose the images that are being written, you might also corrupt images that have already been stored on the card.

Camera Back

Obviously, it is the back of the camera where the bulk of the controls are housed, alongside the LCD screen.

Above the LCD screen are the Menu and Display buttons, which are used to control what is shown on the camera's LCD screen.

To the right of the screen is a circular array of controls, along with exposure compensation and and Live View buttons. These are the controls you'll use in everyday shooting to change shooting parameters.

In Chapter 1, we covered the diopter control, which allows you to adjust the viewfinder to compensate for your glasses prescription.

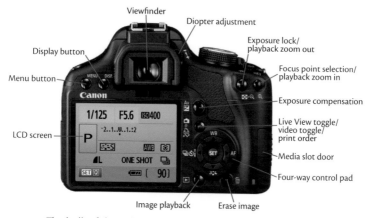

The bulk of the T1i's controls are on the back of the camera.

On the upper-right side of the camera are two additional buttons, which are used to change focus point selection and to control exposure lock.

These controls also have blue magnifying glasses beneath them. Blue icons indicate playback mode functionality. So, when reviewing your images, these two buttons turn into zoom in and zoom out controls. (Similarly, the Live View button does double duty as a Print button.)

Finally, at the bottom of the camera, you'll find the Play button, which you should have used already, and the Delete button, which we'll cover in Chapter 3.

Camera Bottom

The bottom of the camera doesn't have any controls, but it does have two important features. There's the battery compartment, which you've already used, and there's the tripod mount.

The Rebel T1i Menu System

Many of the Rebel T1i's features are accessed through the camera's menu system. When shooting in a rapidly changing environment, such as a sporting event, busy street, or birthday party, you'll want to be able to quickly change camera settings, so it's important to be able to use the camera's menus speedily and efficiently. Fortunately, the T1i has a very good menu layout, so with just a little practice, you should find that you can get to any option you want very quickly.

The contents of the menus change depending on what mode you're in. In Full Auto mode, the menus contain a smaller subset of the camera's full menuing options. In the other modes, you'll find a complete selection of items.

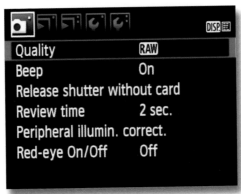

In Full Auto mode, the first page of the menu system looks like this.

In this section, we're going to look at menu navigation so that you'll know how to go to a particular menu item—something you'll be doing a lot of throughout the rest of this book.

For the sake of this example, change the camera's mode to P so that you can see the full assortment of T1i menus.

To activate the menu, press the Menu button on the back of the camera. You can do this whether you're currently shooting or viewing images.

In Program mode, the T1i displays eight different menus, and the most recently visited menu is always the one that is currently active when you enter the menu system.

Each menu is represented by a tab at the top of the screen. The current menu is brightly lit, and bounded by a white box, while the others are slightly faded. Each menu contains a different set of options, but no menu contains more options than can fit on one screen, so you don't ever have to worry about scrolling up and down to find a menu item.

When the menu is activated, the four semicircular buttons on the back of the camera function as arrow keys.

To change from one menu to another, use the left and right arrow keys. To select an item in the menu, use the up and down arrow keys.

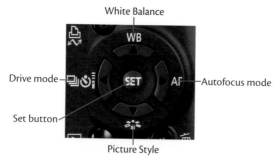

White Balance

Drive mode

Set button

Autofocus mode

Picture Style

The four-way control pad on the back of the camera allows you to navigate menus, as well as configure several essential functions.

The menus are grouped by function. The first two menus contain shooting functions, and so they sport camera icons on their tabs. The next two contain playback functions.

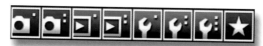

Left to right, the tabs on the menu page are two Shooting menus, two Playback menus, three Tool menus, and the Custom menu.

The next three menus are tool menus. They contain various utility functions, such as setting date and time, formatting your media card, and other options. I'll be referring to these menus as "tool menu 1," "tool menu 2," or "tool menu 3."

Finally, there is a custom menu called My Menu, where you can define your own custom set of options. We'll explore this menu in Chapter 12.

Once you've selected the menu item that you want to access, press the Set button. What happens next will depend on the feature you've chosen, which we'll be covering throughout this book.

So, if I tell you to access the Auto Rotate feature in tool menu 1, you'd press the Menu button to activate the menu, then use the left or right arrow key to navigate to the first tool menu, use the down arrow key to select Auto Rotate, and then press the Set button to execute the feature. In the case of Auto Rotate, a submenu will appear, which offers three different options. (Note that you can also use the Main dial to cycle through the menus. This might be speedier for you than using the buttons.)

WARNING: Visible Menus Are Context Sensitive

If you press the Menu button and don't see any tool menus, it's because you're in a mode that doesn't support these menus. Change to Program, Tv, Av, or M mode and try again.

Camera Status

With the menu active, you can press the Disp button on the back of the camera to get a view of some important camera statistics.

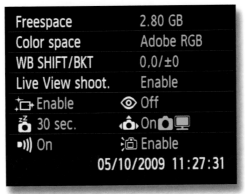

Pressing the Disp button at any time gives you a simple status readout of the camera's current settings.

There's nothing on this screen that you can't learn by going and looking at the settings of the individual parameters, but it can be a nice way to quickly get a look at some vital settings. You'll learn more about each of these settings later.

Holding the Camera

Holding the T1i might seem like a fairly obvious procedure, but good photographic "form" can mean the difference between a sharp image and one that's blurred from camera shake. Observing a few simple guidelines about camera grip and posture will improve your chances of getting stable, sharp images.

The Grip

Obviously, your right hand goes around the camera's grip, with your forefinger positioned on the shutter button. To guarantee the most stable hold, your left hand should go underneath the lens barrel, where it connects to the camera.

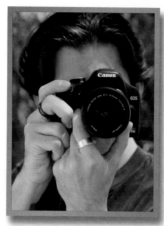

Support the lens with your left hand to ensure a more stable hold on the camera.

Cradling the camera this way makes it easier to hold the camera for long periods of time and will help you hold the camera steady. With your forefinger on the shutter release, you should be able to easily reach the control buttons on the back of the camera with your thumb.

Feet, Elbows, and Neck

When standing, your most solid, secure stance is to have both feet firmly planted on the ground, about shoulder-width apart. Obviously, depending on the terrain, this may or may not be possible. The best way to ensure a stable hold is to always remember to *keep your elbows touching your sides.*

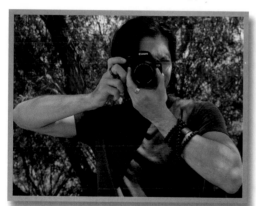
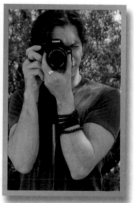

Elbow position is critical to achieving a stable, shake-free camera hold. Remember: your elbows should always be touching your sides.

"Elbows in" gives you a very sturdy platform for holding the camera. If you get in the habit of keeping your elbows against your side, eventually it will simply feel wrong to not have them pressed against you when shooting. In most cases, even if you're on uneven terrain and have to change your foot position, you can still keep your elbows at your side. Elbows in also holds true when you're seated.

When switching from landscape to portrait orientation, you *still* want to keep your elbows at your side to ensure a more stable position.

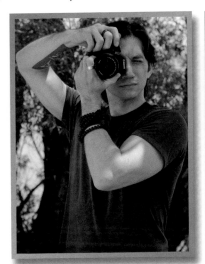
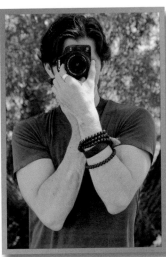

The elbow rule holds for vertical shooting as well. The image on the right shows a much more stable position than the image on the left.

Finally, lift the camera all the way to your face. This may sound strange because you probably think you are, but many people lift the camera partway to their face and then push their neck forward to close the gap. In addition to giving you bad posture (and probably contributing as much to back pain after a day's shooting as that heavy camera bag on your shoulder), it's a much less stable position.

Q U E S T I O N : Does Stability Really Matter?

When your camera is shooting at 1/1000th of a second (or faster), you may think stability doesn't really matter. If you're a stickler for sharpness, though, even a tiny bit of motion can make a difference. If you blow things up a lot, or if you're shooting with a long telephoto lens, trying to shoot more stably is very important. Besides, there's nothing difficult about these techniques, so there's no reason not to learn them.

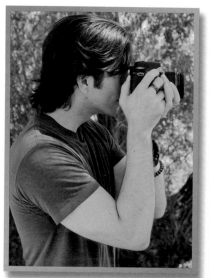
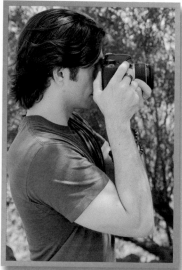

You'll get a more stable shot, and have less neck pain, if you bring the camera all the way to your eye, rather than pushing your neck forward.

The Lens

One of the great things about an SLR like the Rebel T1i is that you can remove the lens and replace it with another. Interchangeable lenses allow you to build a lens collection tailored to the way you like to shoot. For example, if you're a nature shooter who likes a long reach, you can invest in telephoto lenses; if you're a landscape shooter, you might want to weight your collection toward wide-angle lenses. Because you can remove the lens, you can choose to upgrade lenses later and improve the quality of your images without having to replace the entire camera. Removable lenses also give you the option to add specialty lenses, such as fisheye lenses for creating stylized pictures or tilt/shift lenses for architectural work.

Depending on the configuration you purchased, your Rebel T1i may or may not have come with a lens. If you bought the Rebel T1i kit, you probably have an 18–55mm zoom lens or an 18–200mm. You should already be practiced at mounting and unmounting a lens, as detailed on pages 33–34 of your Rebel T1i manual.

Ideally, you want to leave the camera body open for as little time as possible. As you learned in the previous section, just inside the body is the mirror that reflects light up into the viewfinder, and behind that is the shutter and image sensor. You don't want to get dust or dirt on the image sensor, because any type of debris on the sensor will show up on your images as dark splotches. The less time you leave the camera body open, the less chance dust will get inside.

If you have more than one lens, you'll find that, over time, you will work out a coordination that allows you to remove one lens, hold it, and get the other lens on with minimal exposure of the camera body. Obviously, you have to be careful not to drop anything. Keeping the camera around your neck with the included strap will free up your hands enough to manage a lens change.

> **WARNING:** Manage Those Body Caps
>
> Every lens has a body cap that covers the end of the lens that attaches to the camera. Unfortunately, a lot of people stick these caps in their pocket, where they get covered with lint, and then put the cap directly onto the lens when they're changing lenses. This is a great way to get dust and lint on your lens, and that debris can get transferred directly to your image sensor when you mount the lens on your camera. So, clean those body caps before you put them back on your lens!

Understanding Focal Length

If you wear glasses, you are probably already familiar with the idea that a thicker lens provides more magnification. The same is true for your camera lenses—a longer lens provides more magnification.

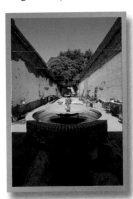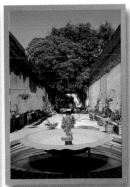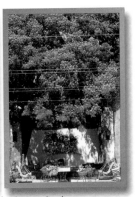

The image on the left was shot with a short lens, while the image in the center was shot with a very long lens. Obviously, the image on the right is more magnified.

FOOD FOR THOUGHT

35MM EQUIVALENCY

If you're coming from a 35mm film camera background, then you might already have certain ideas about focal length. For example, you probably think of a 50mm lens as a "normal" lens, that is, a lens with a field of view that's roughly equivalent to the human eye.

In turn, you probably think of anything longer than 50mm as being telephoto and anything shorter as being wide-angle. To you, a 16mm lens is probably a super-wide angle, while a 400mm is a long telephoto.

The image sensor in the Rebel T1i is smaller than a piece of 35mm film. All lenses project a circular image onto the focal plane, and a rectangular crop is taken from that to create the final image. But because its sensor is smaller, the T1i cuts a smaller crop out of that circle.

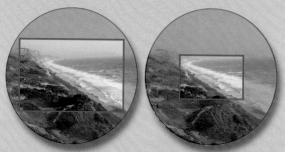

On the left, you can see what a piece of 35mm film cuts out of the image projected by a lens. On the right, you can see the image that the T1i captures. It has a much narrower field of view, as if you were shooting with a more telephoto lens.

In practical terms, this means that, for any given focal length, the field of view of a lens on the Rebel T1i will be narrower than that same focal length on a 35mm camera.

To put it another way, on the Rebel T1i, a 50mm lens has the same field of view as an 80mm lens on a 35mm film camera.

To calculate the 35mm equivalency of any lens you put on the T1i, simply multiply the focal length of your lens by 1.6. So, if you have an 18–55 mm lens—a lens that would be an ultrawide to normal lens on a 35mm film camera—you can think of it as a 28.8 to 88mm lens in 35mm terms.

Another way of thinking about magnification is to pay attention to the field of view. In the figure on the previous page, the center image has a much narrower field of view than the left image. As focal length increases, the field of view captured—that is, the distance from left to right—gets narrower.

On lenses, the "thickness," or length of a lens, is measured in millimeters and is referred to as the lens *focal length*. A longer focal length means a more telephoto lens, which means more magnification and less field of view. So, a 300mm lens will be more telephoto than an 80mm lens. We'll be speaking about focal length a lot throughout the rest of this book.

Types of Lenses

In general, lenses fall into two categories: *prime lenses* and *zoom lenses*. A prime lens has a single, fixed focus length. A zoom lens lets you change the focal length so that the lens can go from wide-angle to telephoto.

The advantage of prime lenses is that they're sometimes sharper than the same focal length in a zoom lens. The advantage of a zoom lens is that a single lens can provide the focal lengths of a bunch of prime lenses. As you'll see, choice of focal length is one of your most important decisions when composing a shot.

Twenty years ago, it was safe to say that zoom lenses were of markedly inferior quality to prime lenses. Nowadays, the difference is not nearly so great, and a good zoom lens can yield excellent image quality, especially when paired with a camera as good as the T1i.

Lens Controls

On most zoom lenses you'll find three controls: a *zoom ring*, which lets you zoom in and out (which is the same thing as choosing a different focal length); a small switch for changing between autofocus and manual focus; and a *focus ring*, which lets you manually focus the lens.

On a prime lens you'll have only a focus ring and an AF switch, and possibly an image stabilization control. We'll be covering all of these controls later in this book.

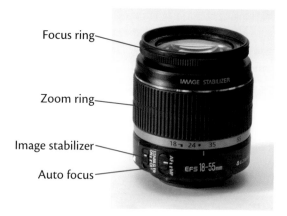

Focus ring

Zoom ring

Image stabilizer

Auto focus

Here you can see the zoom ring (inner), focus ring (outer), and focus switch.

Lens Care

Obviously, with a big expensive piece of glass like a camera lens, dropping it is not a good idea. Your other concern with a lens, though, is keeping it clean and scratch-free. In the previous section, I mentioned the possibility of dust getting in the mirror chamber of the camera. If the dust alights on the sensor, then you'll see visible smudges and smears in your image. Most sensor dust is actually delivered to the inside of the camera by the end of the lens, so one of the best things you can do for your camera *and* lens is to keep the lens clean.

> **WARNING:** I Repeat...
>
> When you remove a lens, put the end cap on immediately!

Don't put a lens in a pocket or bag without an end cap. The end of the lens will trap a lot of dirt, and when you next mount the lens on the camera, you'll transfer a lot of this dirt and debris to the inside of your camera. To keep the ends of your lens clean, use a blower brush to blow any visible dust off of the glass at either end. You can get a blower brush at any camera store.

If there's something on either end of the lens that you can't get off with a blower brush, then you can resort to a lens cleaning cloth of some kind, which you can find at any camera or eyeglasses store. Don't ever try to clean your lens with your shirt or a piece of "found" cloth. While the cloth may look clean, you never know if there's some small abrasive particle that could scratch your lens.

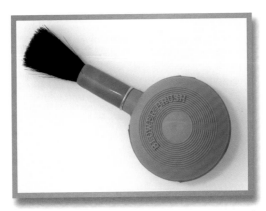

Use a blower brush for cleaning dust off the ends of your lenses.

One of the best things you can do to ensure the long-term health of a lens is to put a protective filter on the end. A skylight or UV filter will not alter the light that passes through the lens, but will provide a significant amount of protection. If the filter gets scratched, you can simply replace it. Even in the event of a drop, a filter can absorb a lot of the impact that would normally smash up the front of the lens.

When shopping for a filter, spend a little more money and buy a *multicoated* filter. Multicoated filters have special chemicals on them that reduce flare and reflections and other image-damaging phenomena. If you've spent a lot of money on a lens, don't hobble it with a cheap, low-quality filter.

Sensor Cleaning

Because you can remove the lens on the T1i, the sensor chamber is exposed to the outside world in a way that it never is on a point-and-shoot camera. This means it's possible for dust and other fine debris to get on the image sensor. And, because you don't ever remove the sensor and replace it with another one—as you do with the film in a film camera—once there's dust on the sensor, it's there to stay unless you take action.

Pixels on your sensor are very, very tiny. Remember, 15 *million* of them are crammed into a space that's smaller than a piece of 35mm film. Because they're so small, it doesn't take a very large piece of dust to obscure thousands of them. Sensor dust will appear in your images as dark spots or smudges.

Fortunately, the T1i has a built-in sensor cleaning mechanism that can greatly reduce the chance of sensor dust problems.

Sensor dust will appear in your image as smudges, smears, or specs—as if there were something on your lens.

Sitting in front of the image sensor is a clear filter. So, "sensor dust" is actually dust that's accumulated on this filter. By default, any time you turn the camera on or off, it vibrates this filter to shake any dust off. A piece of sticky material just below the filter traps the dust so that it doesn't float around the sensor chamber.

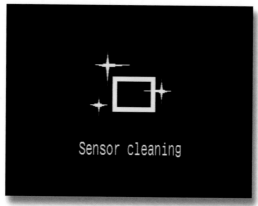

When you turn off the T1i, it automatically engages its sensor-cleaning mechanism.

Although the built-in sensor cleaning is very good, you should still take precautions to keep your sensor clean. Try to avoid changing lenses in windy locations, especially if there's sand or dirt nearby. Keep the camera end of your lenses clean—most sensor dust is delivered to the sensor by the camera lens. When you change lenses, have both lenses in hand *before* you start the change so that you can swap them as quickly as possible.

If you get some dust on the sensor that the built-in cleaning can't handle, then you can take your T1i to a Canon service center for cleaning, or attempt it yourself using special cleaning products, such as those made by VisibleDust. The

VisibleDust website, at *www.visibledust.com*, includes a full selection of sensor cleaning products and accessories.

> **WARNING:** Sensor Cleaning
>
> *Never* spray compressed air into the sensor chamber! Compressed air uses a liquid propellant that can sometimes come out of the nozzle. If this gets on your sensor, you'll have a much *worse* sensor problem. Use only cleaning materials designed for sensor cleaning, or have your camera professionally cleaned.

More Full Auto Practice

In this chapter, we've covered a lot of technical and practical details that are essential to understand if you want to be able to use your camera quickly and effectively. Often, quick use of the camera is what makes the difference between capturing a "decisive moment" and getting a boring shot.

In the next chapter, we're going to start getting more technical about basic photographic theory, but before we go there, you might want to take some time to do a little more practice in Full Auto mode. Shooting in Full Auto does not mean you're a photo wimp. The Rebel T1i in Full Auto mode is a very powerful instrument, and having the camera decide technical details for you can free you up to focus on composition and content. We'll be discussing composition in more detail in Chapter 8, but here are some exercises to try right now, before moving on to the next chapter.

Work with Fixed Focal Length

Zoom lenses can make you lazy. They tend to encourage you to stay in one place and compose from there. As we'll see later, there can be a great difference in images shot from different locations. But zoom lenses also keep you from having to visualize a scene for a particular framing. Here are three quick exercises that will get you seeing and thinking in a different way:

Full wide Zoom your lens out to full wide and *leave it there!* Spend a few hours shooting with it at full wide. Don't zoom the lens. Instead, reposition yourself if you need to frame the shot differently. Be aware that you may not be able to visualize or recognize potential scenes when limited to this one focal length. So, if you think you see something even remotely interesting, look at it through the camera. You don't have to shoot it, but often when you look through the camera, you'll see a potential shot that you didn't recognize when you were looking with the naked eye.

Full tele Now do the same thing as the previous exercise, but this time zoom your lens to its longest focal length. In other words, zoom in all the way. Spend some time shooting as before. No zooming!

30mm On the Rebel T1i, a 30mm lens has the same field of view as a 50mm lens on a 35mm camera. This also happens to be roughly the same field of view as your eye. Consequently, a 50mm equivalent lens is considered a "normal" lens. Some of the most famous, celebrated photos of all time have been shot with a 50mm lens. The great French photographer Henri Cartier-Bresson worked exclusively with a 50. If it's good enough for him, the rest of us should be able to manage.

Set your camera on 30mm and spend a few hours shooting. Again, don't zoom! Some Canon lenses show a dot on the zoom ring to indicate where normal is.

Obviously, with prime lenses—that is, lenses that don't zoom—you get this type of shooting experience all the time. These exercises are a way for you to learn some of the advantages (and disadvantages) of shooting with a fixed focal length lens.

CHAPTER 3

Playing Back Images

REVIEWING AND ANALYZING IMAGES
ON YOUR REBEL T1I

One of the great advantages of a digital camera is the ability to see your images right away. While the compositional advantage of instant review is obvious, you can also perform many types of analysis using your camera's LCD screen. However, it's important to understand what the screen does and does not tell you about your shots. In this chapter, we'll look at all of the Rebel T1i's playback features and learn how they can help you take better pictures and improve your chances of getting the shots you need.

Image Review

By default, any time you take a picture with the T1i, it automatically shows the image on the camera's LCD screen. Also by default, this image review lasts two seconds, which is usually enough time to tell whether you've composed properly or not.

If you want to delete the image while it's being shown during image review, follow these steps:

1. Press the Erase button, located just below the screen.

2. The camera will ask you to confirm the delete. Select Delete by pressing the right arrow button on the back of the camera.

3. With Erase highlighted, press the Set button to delete the image.

You can easily change the length of the image review time:

1. Press the Menu button.

2. Navigate to the first shooting menu (if it's not already active).

3. Press the down arrow key to select "Review time".

4. Press Set.

5. Select a new time and press Set again.

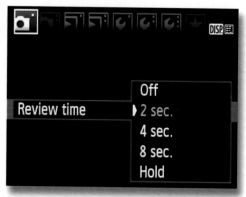

By changing the "Review time" setting, you can control how long the image is displayed after you take a shot.

6. Press the Menu button, or half-press the shutter button to dismiss the menu.

You can choose between Off, 2, 4, or 8 seconds, or Hold. When you choose Hold, the image will stay on the camera's screen until you use any control on the camera. For shots where you need to carefully assess a lighting setup or composition, Hold can be very handy. However, lengthy LCD usage will drain your battery faster, so it's best to use this feature only when you need it.

You can also turn the image review off completely. If you're in a situation where you don't need or have time to use the image review—a fast-moving sporting event, for example—then you might as well turn image review off to conserve the battery.

Some additional features are available during image review. We'll look at these when we explore the DISP button later in this chapter.

Image Playback

While the image review is a great way to quickly assess a shot you've just taken, playback mode is what you'll want to use when you're ready to review a whole batch of shots:

1. To enter playback mode, press the Play button.

   The last image you shot will be shown on the screen. By default, the T1i will superimpose some data about the image.

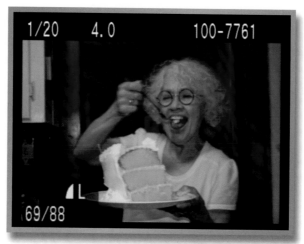

The default image review display.

At the top of the screen, it will show shutter speed, aperture, and exposure compensation, along with the filename and the folder name. Like your computer, the Rebel T1i creates folders on its media card, each with a separate number, and stores the images you shoot in those folders. You'll learn more about folder and filename options later.

2. To scroll through the images stored on the card, press the left and right arrow keys.

   Note that the images "wrap around." If you go past the last image, the camera will show you the first, and vice versa.

Navigating Images with the Main Dial

When you're in playback mode, turn the Main dial. By default, the camera will jump forward or backward 10 images at a time. A scroll bar will appear to show you where you are within the current selection.

You can change how many intervals the Main dial jumps by pressing the up arrow key. The jump interval indicator next to the scroll bar will become editable. Use the up and down arrow keys to change the interval to 1, 10, or 100 images, or to Date, Movies, or Stills. When set to Date, the Main dial will jump to the next image shot on a different day. If you set to Movies, the camera will jump to the next movie file. Similarly, if you select Stills, the camera will jump to the next still image. This provides a simple way to filter out either movies or stills, if you want to view the other.

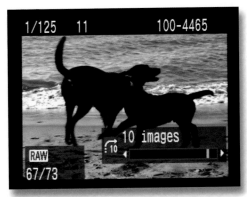

By default, the camera jumps forward or backward by 10 images when you turn the Main dial in playback mode.

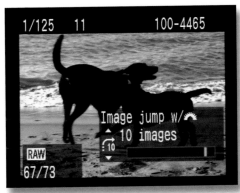

You can change the interval by which the Main dial will jump images.

The camera will remember the last Jump setting that you used. You can also change the Jump interval by going to the "Image Jump With" item in the second Playback menu.

Playback Zoom

When reviewing an image, you can zoom in to view fine details and assess focus. To zoom into an image during image playback, press the Zoom In button. The T1i can zoom in up to 10 times. As you zoom in, notice the navigation panel that appears superimposed over your image.

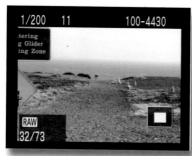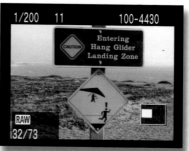

Using the zoom buttons, you can get a closer view of your image and pan around to examine details.

This shows a relative illustration of which part of the image you're viewing. The white box shows you which part of your image is currently being displayed.

- To scroll around an image that you've zoomed into, use the four arrow keys.

- To change to another image but maintain your current zoom level, use the Main dial. This is a great way of comparing focus between two images.

- To zoom out of an image, use the Zoom Out button.

> **WARNING:** Don't Judge Sharpness on the T1i LCD
>
> When you've zoomed into an image to check focus, be aware that the LCD screen on the T1i is a little soft. So, you can't always use the screen as a measure of actual sharpness. If your image looks wildly out of focus, then it probably is, but if it looks a little soft, there's a good chance that it's actually OK.

You can easily perform a quick experiment to learn more about how sharpness on the T1i's LCD screen relates to the sharpness in your final image:

1. Shoot an image with some fine detail and then copy the image to your computer (see Chapter 4 for details on image transfer). Don't delete the image after transfer.

2. Put the card back in your camera and compare what you see on the camera's screen to what you see on your computer. This should give you a better idea of what on-camera sharpness really means.

Exiting Playback

The easiest way to exit playback mode is to give the shutter button a half-press, just as if you were autofocusing. You can also exit playback by pressing the Play button.

CHANGING THE BRIGHTNESS OF THE LCD SCREEN

If you're in bright sunlight, it may be hard to see the camera's LCD screen clearly when viewing images. You can change the brightness of the screen by using the LCD brightness command in tool menu 2.

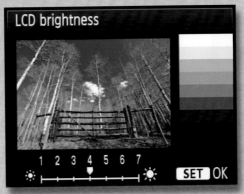

The LCD brightness command gives you seven levels of brightness to choose from. Using the LCD brightness command is very straightforward, but if you need help, refer to page 131 of the T1i user manual.

If you're shooting in a dark location, you might want to turn the brightness of the screen *down*, since a very bright screen can be hard on your eyes if they're already adjusted to low light.

Viewing Image Thumbnails

In addition to zooming *in* to an image to view fine detail, you can also zoom *out* from an image to view more than one image on the screen at a time. Canon calls this *index display*, but I prefer to refer to it as *thumbnail view*. Whatever you choose to call it, viewing multiple images at once makes it easier to navigate quickly to a specific image on the card.

To zoom out to a thumbnail display of all the images on the card, follow these steps:

- Press the Zoom Out button.

- Note that if you were zoomed into an image, you'll have to zoom back out first so that the image fills the entire screen. An additional press of the Zoom Out button will take you to thumbnail view.

- A single press of the Zoom Out button will take you to a four-up view of thumbnails. An additional press will take you to a nine-up view.

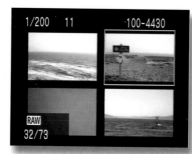 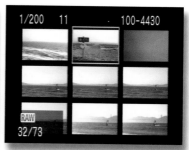

Using the Zoom Out button in playback mode, you can change the number of thumbnails that are displayed on the camera's LCD screen.

- When viewing thumbnails, you can navigate from one image to another using the four arrow buttons, or you can use the Main dial to jump one screenful at a time. As each image is highlighted, the camera's data overlay is updated to show the data for that image.

- To zoom into the selected image, press the Zoom In button.

Using these two simple controls, Zoom In and Zoom Out, you can easily move from up-close views of your images to thumbnail views that provide speedier navigation.

TIP: Persistent Playback Display

The T1i remembers the last view you used in playback mode. So, if you were viewing individual images, the next time you enter playback mode, the camera will show you individual images. If you were viewing thumbnails, then you will see a thumbnail view the next time you enter playback mode.

Viewing Image Info

Like most digital cameras, the T1i automatically stores a fair amount of information with every image you shoot. This information, commonly referred to as *metadata*, is embedded in the image file, so it travels with the image as you copy and move files around.

In addition to the date and time you take an image, the T1i stores all essential exposure information—aperture, shutter speed, ISO, white balance setting, exposure compensation, and much more. Because this metadata conforms to an accepted standard called EXIF, most any image editor can read the data. Having access to your shooting parameters while editing can make certain corrections much easier and help you learn what you did right or wrong while shooting.

You can also view EXIF metadata on the camera itself, and you've already seen a small example of it when viewing your images. The shutter speed and aperture displays that have appeared in your image playback are two bits of EXIF metadata.

To change the image metadata that's displayed, follow these steps:

1. Go into playback mode by pressing the Play button. The last image display mode you used will still be active. If you're viewing a thumbnail display, zoom in to view a single image.

2. Click the DISP button to change to a different info display. The T1i provides four different info displays.

- You've seen the first one already, which is a large image with basic info.

- The second display shows the image as a small thumbnail but provides a larger assortment of exposure parameters.

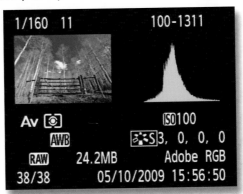

The camera can display a huge amount of information about each of your shots.

The second info display also contains a histogram display, and as you'll learn, these histogram displays can be essential shooting tools that can help you choose an exposure. Many of these other items are self-explanatory; the rest you'll learn about in other parts of this book.

- The third display shows a few exposure parameters and a *three-channel histogram*, which can give you a little more insight into overexposure and white balance problems.

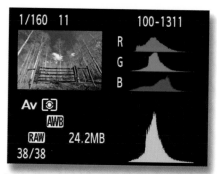

The three-channel histogram can help identify white balance issues and certain types of overexposure problems.

- Finally, the fourth display gives you the clearest view of your image. It shows shutter speed, aperture, exposure compensation, folder, and image number, but it doesn't superimpose anything over the thumbnail.

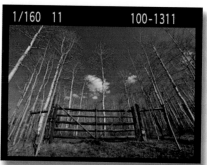

Use the fourth playback screen to get the cleanest view of your image.

The metadata that the T1i displays can be an invaluable aid in difficult shooting situations. However, you don't have to look at it all the time. When you're out in the field shooting, you want the bulk of your attention focused on shooting, not on reviewing your images. In later chapters we'll revisit these modes, and you'll gain a better understanding of what they're for and when to use them.

> **T I P :** Image Info in Image Review
>
> The T1i always remembers the last info display you used and presents that display next time you go into playback mode. However, it also uses that screen during the image review that happens after you shoot. Also, note that you can change the info display during image review, just as you do in playback mode.

Image Rotation

Your camera contains an orientation sensor that it uses to determine whether you're shooting in portrait or landscape orientation (that is, vertically or horizontally). The orientation you use is automatically stored in the metadata of each image. Your image editor can most likely read this data and will automatically rotate the image appropriately.

You can also tell the camera to automatically rotate the images so that they always display at the largest size possible. By default, this feature is turned on, but if you want to turn it off (perhaps because you're working with the camera mounted on a tripod or because you have the camera connected to a TV), then go to the tools menu 1 and select "Auto rotate".

You'll see three options in the Auto rotate menu:

- The first option turns Auto rotate on for both camera display and TV display.

- The second option turns Auto rotate on for only the camera. This means images will be rotated to display as large as possible on the camera's LCD, but will still display in portrait mode on a TV and in your computer.

- Off deactivates all Auto rotate options.

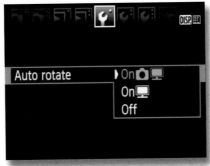

You control whether the camera will automatically rotate images.

OPTIONS

DISPLAYING YOUR IMAGES ON A TV

Viewing your image on a TV is a great way of showing your images to other people as a slideshow, but it can also be handy for shooting in a studio. If you're working with a model or shooting product shots, put your camera on a tripod and connect it to a TV while you're shooting. The same image review that displays on your camera's LCD screen will be shown on the attached TV. Your model, client, makeup crew, or anyone else in the room can see the shots right away and adjust their work accordingly.

The T1i includes a mini version of an HDMI connector, the type of connector that you'll find on most HDTVs, and connecting the T1i to an HD screen yields very beautiful images. However, your HDTV probably includes a full-size HDMI connector, so you'll need an adapter cable. Canon sells an HTC-100 HDMI cable, but you can probably also find third-party cables at an electronics store.

If you want to connect the T1i to a standard definition TV that has an S-Video input, you can use the included video cable. See page 156 of the T1i manual for details on connecting the camera to a TV. Note that though you may find another S-Video cable that appears to have the same connectors as the one included with your camera, it may not display your images properly when connected to a TV. For best results, use the included cable.

Note that the camera's Video System setting must be set to match the TV you're connecting to. In other words, if you're connecting to an NTSC TV (the type found in North America), you must be sure the camera's Video System is set to NTSC. You'll find the Video System setting in the second Tools menu.

Manual Image Rotation

Sometimes autorotation gets confused and images don't get properly rotated. This can be because you were holding the camera at an odd angle or possibly because you changed orientation and shot very quickly. Whatever the reason, if you need to manually rotate an image, you can do so using the Rotate menu command.

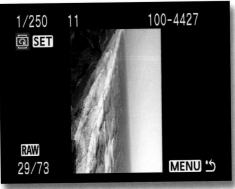

Sometimes you need to rotate an image manually.

To manually rotate an image, follow these steps:

1. Press Menu and go to the Playback page.

2. Choose the Rotate option.

3. Navigate to the image you want to rotate.

4. Press the Set button to rotate the image 90° clockwise. Each press will rotate the image 90°.

You can use the Main dial or the left and right arrow buttons to navigate to other images and rotate them. When you're done rotating, press the shutter button halfway to exit playback mode. Your image editor may or may not show these images with your chosen rotation. Also, note that rotating the image this way will not make it always display "full-screen" on your camera. For that, you need to change the Auto Rotate setting, as shown in the last section.

Slideshows in the Field

The T1i can automatically play a slideshow of the images on its card.

To start a slideshow, follow these steps:

1. Go to the second Playback menu.

2. Choose Slide Show. You'll be presented with the Slide Show menu.

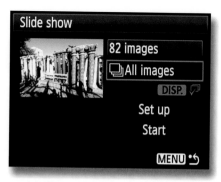

The Slide Show menu lets you configure the Rebel's slideshow playback.

3. By default, the slideshow will show all of the images on the camera's card. Use the arrow keys to highlight All Images, and then press Set to cycle through additional options. You can choose to show only stills or movies, or select a date to show only images shot on that date.

4. Select the Set Up button and click Set to view the Set Up menu, which allows you to change the duration of each slide, as well as whether the slideshow repeats.

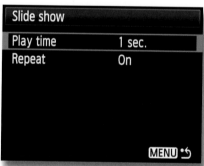

You can specify a duration for each slide, and set the slideshow to repeat.

5. Press Menu to return to the main Slide Show menu. Highlight Start and press Set to start the slideshow. The Disp button will cycle through the various display modes (histogram, three-channel histogram, etc.), just as it does when you're viewing an individual image. While the slideshow is playing, you can use Set to start and stop the show, and you can cancel the show at any time by pressing Menu.

Obviously, if you have connected the T1i to a video monitor, then the slideshow will play on that screen. Otherwise, it will play on the camera's LCD screen.

Erasing Images

You can erase images from the T1i's card using some simple menu commands. Erasing images gives you a way to free up space on your card, if you find that you need more room for shooting. Deleting extraneous shots can also help speed up your postproduction workflow. If you *know* a shot was bad—your finger was in front of the lens, you accidentally took a shot of the lens cap, your model sneezed right when you pressed the shutter button—it's not a bad idea to just delete the image so that you don't have it cluttering up your postproduction sorting and editing. Obviously, if you're in a situation that demands speedy shooting, you shouldn't waste time sorting and deleting images, but if you have the time, excising those images that aren't keepers can speed up the later parts of your photographic process.

Deleting an Image During Image Review

If your camera is set to show an image review (a quick view of your image immediately after you shoot), you can delete the image when it appears on your screen.

To delete an image during image review, follow these steps:

1. When the image appears onscreen, press the Delete button.

2. Use the right arrow button to select Erase.

3. Press the Set button to erase the image.

Deleting an Image During Image Playback

When in playback mode, you can delete an image simply by pressing the Delete button, just as you do during image review. As in image review, the camera will give you one chance to cancel the operation. If you choose Erase, it will delete the image.

If you want to erase lots of images, follow these steps:

1. Choose "Erase images" from the Playback menu.

2. From the Erase images menu, choose "Select and Erase images".

3. Navigate to an image you want to erase and press the up or down button. A checkmark will be displayed in the upper-left corner of the image. If you want to uncheck the box, press either button again.

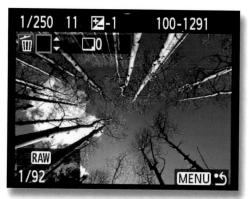

Navigate to an image you want to erase.

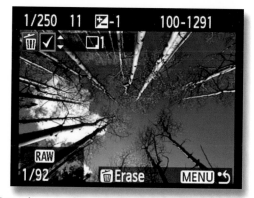

Press the up or down button to turn the checkmark on.

4. Navigate to any other images you want to erase, and press the up or down button on each.

5. When you've selected all of the images you want to erase, press the Delete button.

The camera will give you a chance to cancel. Select and press OK to delete the checked images.

Deleting All of the Images on the Card

Normally, you'll erase a card only *after* you've transferred its contents to your computer. However, sometimes you might need to erase an entire card in the field. Perhaps you realize you've been shooting for the last hour with manual settings that have grossly overexposed all your images. Or maybe you forgot to erase the card when you last transferred images to it and it's full of old pictures.

In the Erase images menu that you saw in the previous section, there was an option to called Erase All Images. Although this works, it's not the best way to erase the card. A much better option is to choose Format from the tools menu 1. If you use Erase All, there's a chance that the card will not be readable in your computer. Format performs a "cleaner" erasure of your card, one that is more likely to be compatible with your computer's operating system.

> **TIP:** If Your Computer Can't Read the Card
>
> Erase All Images can sometimes result in directory problems on the card that can confuse some operating systems. If you find that you're consistently having trouble reading a card in your computer, even after formatting, then you might want to consider doing a low-level format. Choose the Format command as normal, and then press the Erase button to check the Low Level Format checkbox. Select OK to start the low-level format.

Protecting Images

If you've shot a once-in-a-lifetime, keeper image that you absolutely *don't* want to lose, then you might consider protecting the image. This locks the file on the card so that it can't be deleted. If you're on a long trip and won't have the time or opportunity to clear off your media cards, protecting images provides a way of guaranteeing that an image won't be deleted by most normal erase options.

To protect images, follow these steps:

1. In the Playback menu, choose Protect Images.

2. Navigate to the image you want to protect and press Set. A key icon will appear on the image.

3. Navigate to the next image you want to protect and press Set again.

To stop protecting images, press the Menu button.

A protected image cannot be deleted using the Delete button or using the Erase All Images command. However, formatting the card *will* erase protected images. Now if you choose Erase All Images, only unprotected images will be deleted. Your protected images will remain untouched. In addition to keeping you from accidentally deleting images, protecting images provides an easy way to bulk delete some of the images on your card.

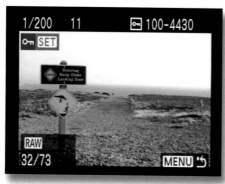

You can protect a critical image from most delete operations.

OOPS!

RECOVERING DELETED IMAGES

There will probably come a day when you will accidentally delete an image, or even accidentally format your camera's media card. You might be able to recover deleted images from your camera's media card.

The reason it's possible to recover files that have been erased is that when you delete a file, the camera doesn't actually erase the image data. Instead, it removes that image's entry from the directory of contents on the card and marks that image's space as available. Even if you have already shot more images, the image data for a deleted image probably hasn't been overwritten. Special recovery software can construct a new directory to your deleted files. When you realize you've deleted an image that you want to recover, *immediately* stop shooting with that card. Take it out of the camera and use a different card until you get back to your computer.

Normal file recovery software (the type you use with your computer) won't work for your camera's media cards. My favorite media card recovery software is PhotoRescue from Data Rescue. You can download a fully functional version of PhotoRescue for free from *www.datarescue.com/photorescue*. The free download lets you analyze your card and shows you which pictures, if any, it thinks it can recover. If you see images you want to recover, you can then pay the $29 purchase price to unlock the software and perform the recovery. What's great about PhotoRescue is that you don't have to spend anything to determine whether you can recover your lost images.

CHAPTER 4

Image Transfer

COPYING IMAGES TO YOUR COMPUTER

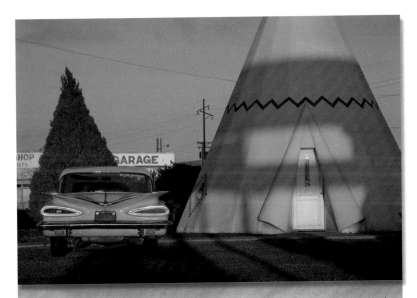

In the old days, you pulled the film out of your camera and dunked it in toxic chemicals, or hired someone else to do that for you. With a digital camera, there's no need for chemistry or lightproof rooms. Instead, you'll transfer your images to your computer where you can edit and correct them. There are several ways to perform this transfer. In this chapter, we'll take a look at your transfer options and explore Canon's bundled software. Before we get started, let's consider your camera's media card.

Media Cards

Film is an amazing invention because it's a single material that can both capture an image *and* store it. With a digital camera, the image sensor does the capture, but it doesn't have any capability to store an image. For that, a digital camera employs a memory card of some kind . As you've already learned, the T1i uses Secure Digital (SD) cards (or SDHC cards, a faster, higher-capacity version of SD).

Flash memory cards are similar to the RAM that's in your computer, but with one important difference: they don't require power to remember what's stored on them. So, after you turn the camera off, the images remain on the card, even if you remove it. Consequently, it's perfectly safe to take out a full card and replace it with another.

Your camera treats the card just the way your computer treats your hard drive. The camera creates folders on the card, and stores files in those folders, each with a different name.

Because cards are so small, and because they can pack *huge* capacities, it's possible to shoot a tremendous number of images with just one or two cards. In fact, because the T1i's battery is good for "only" about 500 shots, if you're carrying a couple of high-capacity cards, you'll probably run out of battery before you run out of storage.

One Big Card? Or Lots of Small Ones?

With the range of capacities available, there are several ways of carrying storage. You can get a few high-capacity cards or more lower-capacity cards. The advantage of a high-capacity card is that your shooting won't be interrupted with a card change. The risk, though, is that if something happens to the card, all of your images will be lost.

Though it's rare, a Secure Digital card *can* be corrupted. Sometimes static electricity can do it, and sometimes a glitch in your computer or in your camera can mess up a card. While the card probably won't be permanently damaged, its contents can be rendered unusable. So, you might want to consider using more lower-capacity cards so that if one goes bad you won't lose as many images.

For maximum flexibility, you might want a combination: a big card that you can use when you're shooting events—such as a performance or sporting event—and don't want to miss shots because of a card change, and smaller cards that you use for everyday shooting. You may have to change them more often, but your images will be safer in the event of a card failure.

Card Management

When you're in the field, you'll need to keep track of which cards you've used and which are available for shooting. If you're shooting on-the-go, you don't want to have to worry about whether the card you're about to use already has images on it. There are a few ways to ease your card management hassles when shooting.

First, after you transfer your images to your computer, erase the card. We'll look at how to do this later in this chapter. After you've transferred images, if you just throw the cards back in your camera bag with the idea of erasing them when you're ready to use them, you can easily end up confused as to whether the card has already been transferred. If you become uncertain, you might be less willing to use the card, and then you can end up short on storage. Also, if you erase beforehand, when you put the card in the camera, it's ready to use right away.

If you have a camera bag with a lot of pouches and compartments, consider using one pouch for unused cards and another for used cards. This makes it simple to keep track of which media is ready for use.

I carry my cards in a small holder. When I fill up a card, I place it back in the holder, face-down. That way, I can easily see how many cards are remaining, and be certain that I'm grabbing a card that's ready for use. I use a holder made by LowePro (*www.lowepro.com*).

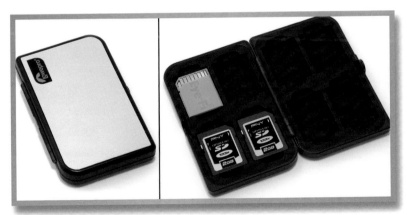

A card holder can make it much easier to keep your cards managed while shooting. Face-down cards are full, face-up cards are ready for use.

At some point, though, your cards will be full, and you'll be ready to transfer your images to your computer.

Transferring from Your Camera

Every image you shoot is stored on your camera's media card as an individual file. The file is a document, just like one you might create on your computer. Before you can do any editing of your images using your computer, you have to copy those image documents from your camera's media card onto your computer's hard drive.

There are two ways to transfer images from your camera. Either plug the camera directly into your computer, or remove its media card and place it in a media reader that is connected to your computer.

The advantage of a card reader is that it doesn't consume any of your camera's battery power. Also, most card readers support lots of different formats, so if you have more than one camera (say, the T1i and a small point-and-shoot) that use different formats, then you only need to carry one card reader and a cable.

Depending on the type you get, a card reader might provide faster transfer than the T1i. You should be able to find card readers that connect to your computer's USB-2 or FireWire port.

If you have a laptop with a PC Card slot or a CardBus 34 slot, then you can get card readers that will fit in those slots. These are typically the fastest readers of all, but they rarely support multiple formats.

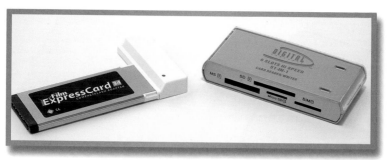

On the left is a CardBus card reader that can plug directly into a cardbus slot on a laptop. On the right is a card reader that plugs into a USB-2 slot. Note the huge number of card formats that it supports.

REMINDER: Don't Forget SDHC

If you're shopping for an SD card reader, be sure to get one that also supports SDHC. You might end up buying SDHC cards at some point, so you might as well have a reader that can handle them in addition to regular SD.

The T1i also ships with a USB cable that you can plug directly into your computer. This allows you to use your camera as a card reader, saving you the hassle of keeping track of an extra piece of gear. However, if you have an especially speedy reader, transferring from the camera might be slower and, as mentioned before, camera transfer will use up battery power. (Note that transferring via USB cable will not work if the camera is in Movie mode. Any other mode is fine.)

QUESTION: What If a Card Won't Read in My Card Reader?

Sometimes you might find that a card that has always worked fine in your card reader suddenly won't read. If this happens, put the card back in the camera and see if you can view images on the camera's screen. If you can, then you know that the camera can read the card just fine. Plug the camera into your computer and try transferring the images that way. It will usually work. When you're done, perform a low-level format (as explained in Chapter 3). This will usually get the card working with your card reader again.

What happens on your computer when you plug in a card reader or camera will vary depending on the operating system that you're using. In the next two sections, we'll go over the separate options available for Windows and Mac users.

Installing the Canon Software

Even if you plan on using some other software for editing, it's worth taking a look at the bundled Canon software. Although ultimately you may not use it in your workflow, it's worth knowing what it's capable of, and we'll be using it for some of the examples in this book, so it will help you to follow along.

The Canon EOS Digital Solutions CD that's included in the T1i box is a hybrid disk that works with either Mac or Windows. To install the software, insert the CD in your computer and run the installer. The disc puts a number of applications on your computer, with some slight variations between Mac and Windows. We'll look at how you might use this software in the following sections.

Transferring Images to a Windows Computer

If you're using Microsoft Windows XP or Vista, you'll find that Windows will take care of a lot of image transfer hassles for you. If you want to customize your transfer experience, you can easily do that to build the type of workflow that you like.

When you plug a card reader or camera into Vista or XP for the first time, Windows might make some kind of mention of installing a new driver.

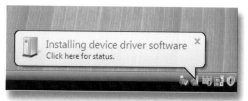

Windows might tell you it's installing a new driver.

Follow any necessary on-screen instructions to get the camera or card reader working. Once the card reader or camera is configured, Windows will show you a simple window that lets you specify what you want done with the images on the card.

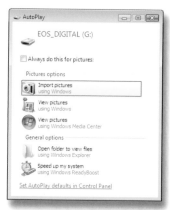

Windows lets you choose what you want to have happen when you plug in a card reader or camera.

Import Pictures lets you copy the images on your card to a specific directory on your hard drive. By default, Import Pictures copies images into your Pictures directory. When you first choose Import Pictures, Windows will show you a simple dialog box, which gives you an Import button and an option to add a text tag to your images. Tags make it easier to sort and filter your images later.

If you click the Options button, you'll see a more advanced dialog box that offers additional options:

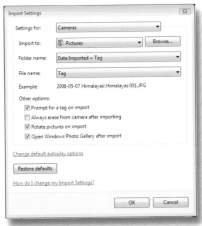

Using these controls you can specify which directory you want the pictures imported into, and define naming conventions.

Once your images have been imported, Windows will show them to you in Windows Photo Gallery.

View Pictures using Windows will open the Windows Photo Gallery, which lets you thumb through large views of your images. Using the menu items at the top, you can choose to import the images, print, them, or even perform simple image edits.

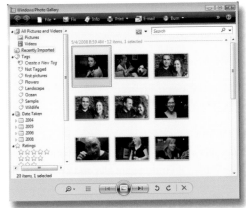

The Windows Photo Gallery lets you browse your images as thumbnails, making it easier to sort, rate, and organize.

View Pictures using Windows Media Center lets you view the images on the card using the Windows Media Center, which offers a full-screen interface, with easy navigation to other images on your system.

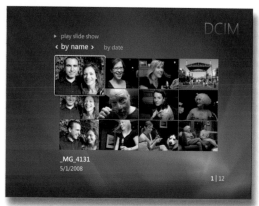

Windows Media Center provides a full-screen environment that lets you view images on your computer, present slide shows, and more.

Finally, notice the "Always do this for pictures" checkbox at the top of the dialog box. This allows you to specify default behavior for a card insertion.

> **TIP:** Changing Your Media Card Preferences
>
> If you check the "Always do this for pictures" checkbox and configure an option, and then decide later that you'd like something else to happen when you insert a card, you can change Windows' behavior using a Control Panel. From the Start Menu, choose Control Panel, and then select Hardware and Sound. On the following screen, find the AutoPlay section, and click "Change default settings for media or devices". Here you can edit the Pictures category to select a different option, or choose "Ask me every time" to get Windows to present you with a dialog box of choices.

The right option for you depends largely on the rest of your workflow. If you think you can manage your entire postproduction workflow in Windows Gallery or Windows Media Center, then these are all good options. If you plan on using some different image editing software, you can still use the Import Pictures command to copy your images to a directory.

Alternately, you might want to use the "Open folder to view files using Windows Explorer" option, which gives you the chance to manually copy the files using

Windows Explorer. Depending on what software you have installed, the menu might contain other options, such as Adobe Bridge. Once you've copied the files, you can work with them using your choice of programs. I'll outline some other options next.

Using Canon ZoomBrowser EX

If you installed the Canon Digital Solutions Disk, then you should have a shortcut to Canon ZoomBrowser EX sitting on your desktop. ZoomBrowser also provides you with import capabilities, as well as simple browsing, editing, searching, and sorting.

It's worth playing around with ZoomBrowser to see if you like it. If you do, you might want to make it the default application that gets launched whenever you insert a media card. You can do this using the same method described in the previous tip, choosing ZoomBrowser EX from the Pictures menu instead.

Using Adobe Photoshop Elements for Windows

If you've installed Adobe Photoshop Elements 6 or later, when you attach a media card reader or camera to your computer, the Elements 6.0 Photo Downloader will launch automatically. The Photo Downloader lets you choose a location to store your files, and can create subfolders within that location based on the date and timestamp on each image. Photo Downloader can also rename your images from the nonsensical camera names to something more meaningful.

If you click the Advanced Dialog button at the bottom of the screen, you'll get an interface that lets you select which images you want to download and offers some more advanced options, such as the ability to add metadata to each image. Metadata are notes and tags—such as your name, copyright info, or organizational keywords—that get added to the image.

Photoshop Elements is a great image editor with all of the features you'll need for almost any image editing task, so if you plan on using Elements for your image editing, you might want to explore Photo Downloader for your image transfers, simply because of its Elements integration.

Using Adobe Photoshop

The full version of Photoshop provides all of the features of Photoshop Elements, along with some more high-end features that you may or may not need. If you think you might need the ability to prepare images for offset printing, or if you routinely work with high-end 3D imaging, scientific, or video/film production software, then Photoshop will be a welcome addition to your toolbox. Otherwise, it's probably overkill for your photo editing needs, and the money you'd spend on the full-blown version of Photoshop would easily pay for Elements *and* a new lens for your Rebel.

If you do install Photoshop CS4, you'll also get Adobe Bridge, an excellent image browser that has its own image transfer features.

Transferring Images to a Macintosh Computer

Whether you use a card reader or plug directly into your camera, transferring images to your Mac is very simple, and you have a number of options for determining what happens when you attach the camera or card reader.

Depending on what kind of Mac you have and when you bought it, you might have a copy of iPhoto, Apple's image organizing and editing program. iPhoto is very good, and can handle the transfer of images from your media card, as well as help you with the rest of your photographic workflow, from organizing to editing to output.

iPhoto is part of Apple's iLife suite, and it comes bundled on many new Macs. If your Mac doesn't have it, you can buy the latest version from any vendor that sells Apple products.

Whether or not you have iPhoto, every Mac ships with a copy of Image Capture, a small utility that helps manage the transfer of images into your computer. Image Capture has no editing or organization features; its sole purpose is to get images copied onto your hard drive. Once they're there, you can decide what to do with them.

If you installed the Canon EOS Digital Solutions disk, then you'll have some additional software on your Mac, which we'll take a look at later in this chapter. You might also have other editing software that you want to use, such as Adobe Photoshop or Photoshop Elements. These programs can also manage the transfer of images from your computer.

Configuring Your Mac for Image Transfer

You can tell your Mac what you want to have happen when you plug in a camera or media card reader. This makes it simple to choose what software you want to use to transfer your images.

By default, when you plug a camera or card reader into your Mac, Image Capture will open automatically, and will present a window for managing the transfer of images.

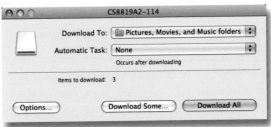

Image Capture is included on all Macs and provides a simple way to manage the transfer of images from a camera or media card reader.

Image Capture lets you choose where you want your images downloaded and what to do after the images have copied, and if you press the Download Some button, you can even select specific images to copy.

Image Capture also lets you specify what you want your Mac to do when you plug in a card reader or camera. If you go to the Image Capture menu and choose Preferences, you'll see a pop-up menu that lets you select which application you want to have launched whenever a camera or media card reader is plugged into your Mac.

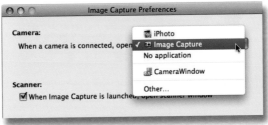

Using the preferences in Image Capture, you can control what should happen when a camera or media card reader is connected to your Mac.

By default, the menu will list iPhoto (if you have it), Image Capture, and possibly other applications if you have them installed. If you have a program installed that you'd like to use but don't see it listed, choose Other.... Image Capture will present you with a dialog box that allows you to pick the program you'd like to use.

Finally, if you'd like complete manual control, you can choose No Application.

You can change this menu at any time if you later want to change your image transfer preference. We'll go over a few image transfer options next.

Transferring Images Using Canon ImageBrowser

After installing the EOS Digital Solution Disk that shipped with your T1i, your Mac's default behavior will be to launch Canon's EOS Utility any time you plug in a camera or card reader. EOS Utility will let you copy images from your card to a specified folder, just like you can do by hand in the Finder. However, it offers you the ability to see preview thumbnails of your images, and to select only the files that you want to copy. It also lets you print your images, either as individual prints or as contact sheets. (Note that the EOS Digital Solution Disk may config-ure your Mac to launch CameraWindow, which in turn will take care of launching EOS Utility.)

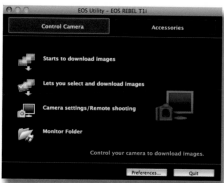

After you install the EOS Digital Solutions disk, this window will appear any time you attach a camera or card reader.

Before you use EOS Utility, you need to configure its preferences to determine where it will store your files. From Image Browser's main dialog box, click the Preferences button. (Note that this is different from the dialog box that is shown when you choose Preferences from the EOS Utility menu.)

Change the pop-up menu to Destination Folder. The Destination Folder field shows the default location where Image Browser will store your images, in most cases the *Pictures* folder. EOS Utility will automatically create subfolders within the destination folder that you specify. By default, it creates folders that group your images together by shooting date, but you can change this by opening the

Shooting Date pop-up menu, and further refine it by clicking the Customize button next to the menu.

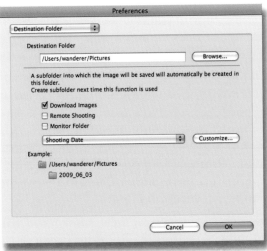

You can specify where you want Image Browser to store your images, as well as configure naming options and other settings.

When you're done configuring preferences, click the OK button.

If you choose to download only selected images, EOS Utility will show you a screen with thumbnails of each of your images. Click the checkbox on any image that you want to download, and then click the Download button.

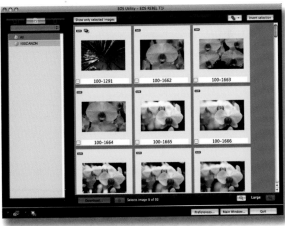

You can select individual images to download by clicking the checkbox beneath each image.

Transferring Images Manually Using Windows or the Mac

If you want complete manual control of your image transfers, configure your computer to do nothing when a camera or card reader is plugged in. This will simply mount the camera or card reader on your desktop, just as if it were a hard drive, leaving you free to copy files as you please.

The advantage of taking a manual approach is that you can completely control where files are placed, and create a folder structure on your drive that makes the most sense to you. The downside to importing using this approach is that, depending on which version of your operating system you're using, you won't necessarily be able to see thumbnail previews of your images before you transfer, which means you won't be able to pick and choose which images to copy. Obviously, you can always sort through them later.

To transfer images manually, simply plug in the camera or card reader. When the camera or card reader icon appears on your desktop, open it up. You should see a folder inside called *DCIM*. There might be some other folders, but *DCIM* is the only one you need to worry about. It is the standard location that camera vendors have agreed upon for storing images.

Inside the *DCIM* folder you will find additional folders, usually named with some combination of numbers and "Canon" (i.e. "100CANON"). Depending on how many images you've shot, there may be more. Open each folder and copy its contents to your desired location.

Using the Camera to Select Images for Transfer

When you plug the T1i into your computer, the Direct Transfer screen will appear. From this menu, you can choose to automatically transfer all images or only new images since the last transfer, or you can select specific images and transfer those. The Wallpaper setting lets you select a JPEG image that will automatically be transferred to your computer and set as the background image (this works for both Windows and Mac users).

While reviewing images in your camera, you can specify which images you want to transfer to your computer. Of course, you could also just delete the images that you don't want, which would free up more storage on your card. However, if you've shot a bunch of images and need to quickly process and deliver just a few, then marking only those images for transfer will let you quickly get those images to your computer for processing. You can transfer the rest later.

Of course, you can also select images for transfer using your transfer software, but marking images in the camera can be convenient, both because it's something you can do in the field when you have spare time, and because you can mark a "keeper" image as soon as you shoot it.

To mark an image for transfer, view the image on the T1i's screen, then hit the Menu button. Choose "Transfer order" from the first Playback menu. On the resulting menu, choose Sel. Image. Use the left and right arrow keys to navigate through your images, and press the up arrow key to tag any image that you want to include in the transfer order. When you're finished, click the Menu button to exit the "Transfer order" menu.

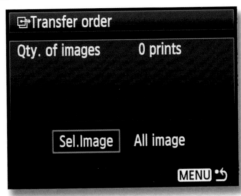

You can control which images will be transferred to your computer.

The Direct Transfer menu and the EOS Utility let you choose to download only images that have been marked in the camera, providing you with a one-button method for getting your designated order into your computer.

REMINDER: Using Photo Management Software

If you're using Apple's iPhoto or Aperture, or Adobe's Lightroom (on either a Windows or Mac machine), then those programs can take care of image transfer for you. As with any other application, you'll need to specify that you want those applications to take over image downloading. Consult the documentation for all three programs for more information, and be aware that these applications all copy your images into their own library systems, so you don't need to worry about where the images should be stored. Each program will take care of putting the files in a location that's right for them.

Organizing Your Images

No matter which method you use to transfer images to your computer, if you're managing your image organization yourself (as opposed to having a program such as iPhoto, Aperture, or Lightroom do it for you), you will want to think about how to organize your files.

You'll be best-served in your organizational chores by making good use of folders. How to organize these folders is entirely a matter of personal preference; just find a scheme that makes sense to you. You can create folders by subject—*Arizona Vacation, Winter holidays, Family reunion*—or by date. You'll probably find that some combination of both works best, especially if you find yourself shooting a lot of similar events. As you accumulate more vacation folders, for example, you can group these together into other folders. With well-named folders, you can easily rearrange your taxonomy later, creating new branches of your naming "tree" and then rearranging photos as needed.

What you probably won't need to do is rename files. Yes, the images that come out of your camera have pretty meaningless names, but with a browser program such as the one that came with your camera, or programs such as Adobe Bridge or Camera Bits Photo Mechanic, you can search and sort your images by viewing thumbnails, rather than by digging through lists of arcane filenames.

If you do feel compelled to rename your images, renaming by hand is probably not the way to go, unless you're talking about only a handful of images. Programs such as Bridge, Photo Mechanic, and most image browsers provide tools for automatically renaming batches of files.

After You've Transferred Your Images

Once you've transferred your images, you'll be ready to start the rest of your post-production workflow—correcting, editing, adjusting, and outputting your images. We'll discuss some of these concerns in Chapter 13. For now, though, we're going to return to shooting. With these first four chapters, you should know how to shoot in Full Auto mode and how to transfer your results to your computer. This means you can continue to practice while we cover some new topics.

Although modern image editing software can do some amazing things, how much editing you can do is limited by the quality of your original shot. So, next we're going to delve more deeply into some photographic theory, and you'll learn to use the more advanced features on the Rebel T1i. This will allow you to shoot images that can withstand a much higher level of editing and adjustment.

FOOD FOR THOUGHT

FILE NUMBERING OPTIONS

As you may have already noticed, image files that come out of the Rebel T1i have meaningless names. The T1i usually labels its images _IMG_, then a sequential number, and then a file extension, either JPG or CR2.

By default, every time you start shooting, the camera picks up with the next number in the series, even if you change media cards. If you'd rather, you can configure the camera so that it starts with new numbers every time you change the card. With this scheme, though, you have to be careful when transferring new images into a folder that contains previously transferred images, as many images will have the same name.

So, if you think you'll always be putting new images in their own folders, then having the numbers reset might be a good choice, as each folder will have its own numbering scheme that starts at 1. If you want to be able to throw new images into existing folders that already have images, you'll probably want to stick with continuous numbering, so that you don't have to worry about new files overwriting old.

To change the file numbering preference, go to the first Tools menu and choose "File numbering". You'll find three options: Continuous, which is the default behavior; "Auto reset", which resets the numbers every time you change cards; and "Manual reset", which creates a new folder on the camera's media card and resets the file numbering scheme.

Manual reset can be a handy way to keep images organized into different folders on the camera's media card. For instance, each morning of a trip, you can reset to create a new folder. Or, every time you change locations, you could reset to create a new folder. When you get home, you'll have separate folders with specific images in them. Copy these to your hard drive, and your images will already be sorted into an appropriate folder structure. Once you've identified the subject or date of each folder, you can rename that folder accordingly.

CHAPTER 5

Photography 101

THE FUNDAMENTAL THEORY OF EXPOSURE

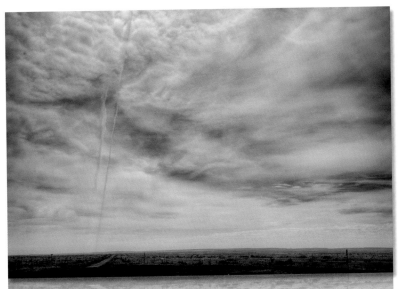

In this chapter, we'll take a break from cameras and computers and focus on basic photo theory. In the old days of manual cameras, you couldn't learn to shoot without certain fundamental knowledge. With today's automatic cameras it's possible to take great photos without having the slightest notion of how different parameters affect your image. However, you'll most likely find that shooters who do understand the basics have a broader creative palette to work with and can push their photography further. We'll be using the concepts covered in this chapter through the rest of the book.

The Rebel T1i Sensor

In Chapter 2 we took a quick look at the anatomy of your Rebel T1i, and you learned something about the architecture of an SLR camera. In that discussion I mentioned the image sensor in your camera. As you already know, in a digital camera, the image sensor takes the place of a piece of film and is the mechanism by which the camera can "see" an image.

The image sensor is a chip that is mounted parallel to the back of the camera so that the light focused by the lens hits it head-on. In the Rebel T1i, the image sensor is the same size as a piece of APS film.

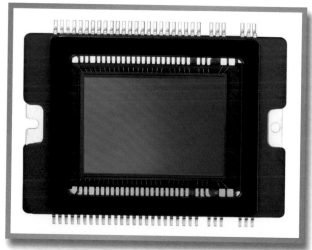

The image sensor in your Rebel T1i is a large silicon chip with an imaging area that's the same size as a piece of APS film. It is this area that is sensitive to light.

The Rebel T1i image sensor is based on a technology called *complementary metal-oxide semiconductor,* or CMOS. All Canon SLRs use CMOS image sensors, while many other SLRs and most point-and-shoots use Charge Coupled Device, or CCD, image sensors. You will often see people praise the merits of one sensor over another, and although these can be interesting engineering discussions, as a photographer the only thing you need to worry about is final image quality. If your image sensor delivers excellent images in a range of lighting situations—which the Rebel T1i does—then the relative merits of sensor technology are fairly moot.

Whether CMOS or CCD, most image sensors employ the same basic design. A rectangular area on the sensor is sensitive to light. This area is divided into a grid, with one cell for each pixel that the sensor can capture. So, the Rebel T1i's 15-megapixel sensor is divided into a grid with 15 million cells (for those of you who are sticklers for accuracy, it's actually closer to 15.1 million cells), and on each cell is a tiny electronic circuit called a *photo diode.*

When you turn your camera on, the image sensor is given a charge, so that each photo diode has a certain voltage stored in it. When you press the shutter button, the sensor is exposed to light. When a photo diode is struck by light, it *releases* some of its voltage, and the more light that it receives, the more voltage it releases. After the shutter closes, the camera measures the voltage at each cell, to determine how much signal struck each cell.

Since the camera knows how bright each pixel should be, and since it has so many pixels on its sensor, the image sensor can build up a very detailed image. Obviously, all of this happens in a fraction of a second, and in practice you don't have to worry about what the image sensor is doing at the individual pixel level. However, you do have to think about the amount of light that you expose the sensor to, because if there's too much or too little, your shot will be ruined. What's more, you can change the method by which the sensor is exposed and achieve very different results.

FOOD FOR THOUGHT

WHERE COLOR COMES FROM

If you haven't noticed already, the process I just described does not actually describe anything about the color of an individual pixel. In other words, the only thing the image sensor can determine from the photoelectric effect is how *much* light struck an individual pixel. It can't actually tell anything about the *color* of the light that struck each pixel. A digital image sensor is inherently a *luminance* or *brightness* sensor. In other words, it sees in black and white.

To achieve a color image, each pixel on the sensor is covered with a colored filter. On the Rebel T1i, the filters are either red, green, or blue. As you may already know, red, green, and blue are the primary colors of light. Those three colors can be mixed together to form every other color.

The filters allow the image sensor to know how much of a particular color struck each pixel at the time of exposure. Using complex algorithms, the camera is able to analyze all of this information to interpolate the color of each individual pixel. This interpolation process is called *demosaicing*, because the mosaic of primary colors on the image sensor gets converted back into a full-color image. If this sounds difficult and complicated, that's because it is, and demosaicing algorithms are some of the most important trade secrets in the camera industry.

Over- and Underexposure

At its most basic level, exposure is pretty easy to understand. If you turn out the light in your room at midnight, your eye won't be able to gather enough light for you to be able to see anything. In other words, your room is underexposed.

Conversely, if someone shines a bright light in your eyes, you may not be able to see because the sensors in your eyes will get overdriven. In other words, your field of view will be overexposed.

The image sensor in your camera (or a piece of film in a film camera) works the same way. If you underexpose a scene—either because there's simply not enough light or because you use bad exposure settings—then the scene will be too dark. If you overexpose a scene, then the image will be too bright.

Even within an individual shot, some areas can be overexposed, and some areas can be underexposed.

So, one of your primary concerns as a photographer is to make sure that you're choosing settings that expose the camera's sensor to an amount of light that will render a scene that is neither too bright nor too dark.

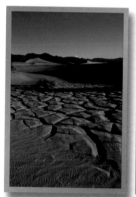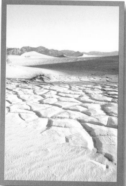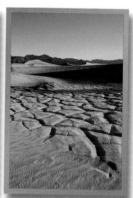

The left image is underexposed: it's too dark overall, and shadow areas have plunged into complete black. The center image is overexposed: it's too bright, and highlight areas have blown out to complete white. The right image is properly exposed, revealing good detail from shadows to highlights.

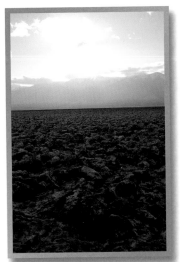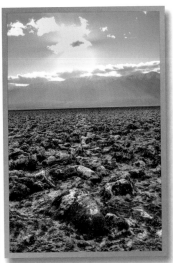

This image has highlights that are overexposed and shadows that are underexposed. There's no way to capture the full range within the camera, but if you expose properly, you can restore highlight and shadow detail later using an image editor.

Exposure Mechanisms

Your camera gives you two mechanisms for controlling the amount of light that hits the image sensor. Using these mechanisms, you can ensure that you don't end up with images that are too bright or too dark.

In Chapter 2, you learned about the shutter, a curtain that opens and closes in front of the sensor to expose it to the light that is focused through the lens. By using a faster shutter speed, the shutter will open for less time and thus expose the sensor to less light.

The second mechanism that the camera uses to control light is the iris, or aperture. This concept should be somewhat familiar because your eyes have irises in them, and if you've ever walked out of a dark movie theater in the middle of the afternoon, you know what it's like to wait for your pupils to close down so that your field of view ceases to be overexposed.

The iris in your camera is built from a series of interlocking leaves that, when rotated, create an expanding or shrinking opening, or aperture. The wider the aperture, the more light that gets let through to the sensor.

The aperture is positioned at the very end of the lens, just before the mount that attaches the lens to the camera body. As mentioned in Chapter 2, the shutter is positioned just in front of the image sensor.

> **DEFINITION:** It's Curtains!
>
> The shutter in your camera is composed of two curtains that pass in front of the lens. As the first one passes, the sensor is exposed. The second one then passes to close off the sensor. At a high shutter speed, there's a good chance that there will be very little time between when the two curtains start moving. This means that the actual opening created by the shutter is just a thin slit that passes in front of the sensor.

ISO: The Third Exposure Parameter

In a digital camera, you have one additional parameter that you can change to control exposure.

As you just learned, your image sensor measures voltages on the sensor's surface to determine how much light struck each pixel. These voltages must be amplified before they can be measured. If you amplify the voltages more, then the sensor will effectively be more light-sensitive because dimmer light levels will be boosted.

ISO is a standard for measuring the sensitivity of film. Digital vendors have adopted the standard for specifying the sensitivity of a digital image sensor. When you increase the ISO setting on the Rebel T1i, you're essentially making the sensor more light-sensitive. As the sensor becomes more sensitive, it will require shorter exposures to be able to "see" a scene. We'll discuss ISO in more detail later.

Shutter Speed

As you've learned, the shutter sits just in front of the image sensor and opens and closes to expose the sensor to light. The shutter speed that you (or the camera) chooses determines how long the shutter will stay open.

Shutter speeds are measured in seconds, and a longer shutter speed exposes the sensor to light for a longer period of time than a shorter shutter speed. The T1i has a shutter speed range of 1/4,000th of a second on the fast end to 30 seconds on the slow end. The T1i also provides a Bulb mode, which lets you keep the shutter open indefinitely.

DEFINITION: Stops

To a photographer, a *stop* is a measure of light. More specifically, a stop represents a doubling of light. So, any time there's a doubling of light—whether we're talking about the light in a scene or the light hitting your sensor—we say that the amount of light has increased by one stop. Conversely, a halving of light means that the light has decreased by one stop. We will be using this term extensively throughout the rest of the book. Experienced photographers are often able to recognize one or two stops of light by eye. While that can take years of practice, it's not a necessary skill to use your camera well. However, you will need to understand the term and how it applies to the different exposure settings.

In the Full Auto shooting that you've been doing, the camera has been calculating an appropriate shutter speed for you automatically, and you can see its decision in the camera viewfinder status display.

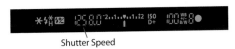

Shutter Speed

Here, the camera is indicating that it has chosen a shutter speed of 1/125th of a second.

On the status display shown on the back of the camera, shutter speed is the number in the upper-left corner.

Shutter Speed

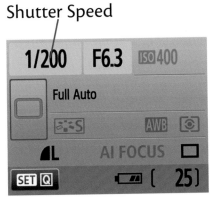

Shutter speed is also shown on the rear LCD screen.

In later chapters, you'll learn how to control shutter speed manually.

Aperture

Like shutter speed, the size of the aperture (which we discussed earlier) can be controlled automatically by the camera or manually by you. Aperture size is measured in f-stops, and an f-stop number is often fractional, so you'll see f-stops with values such as f5.6, f8, or f11.

QUESTION: What Do Those Numbers Mean?

An *f-stop* is a measure of the ratio of the focal length of the lens to the size of the aperture. Many of the numbers are fractional because you're dealing with the area of a circle, and the math quickly gets complex. Don't worry about trying to understand that ratio; you don't have to understand the math to effectively use f-stop values.

Unfortunately, f-stops can be a little unintuitive because the way they're measured can seem backward. A larger f-stop number—say, 16—indicates a smaller opening.

Let's try a little experiment that will make all of this a little clearer.

1. Take your Rebel T1i and set the Mode switch to M, for manual. We'll be looking at Manual mode in detail in Chapter 9, but for now we're going to use it so that you can see your lens's actual aperture.

2. Turn the Main dial to the left until the Shutter Speed readout on the rear LCD says BULB.

3. Now press and hold the Exposure Compensation button (⊠)on the back of the camera while you turn the Main dial. This allows you to change the aperture. Turn the wheel until the Aperture readout says F16. The status display should look something like this:

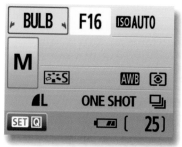

When shutter speed is set to BULB, the shutter will stay open for as long as you hold down the shutter button.

4. With the shutter speed set to BULB, the shutter will stay open for as long as you hold down the shutter button.

5. Set the camera lens to manual focus by changing the focus switch on the lens from AF to MF.

6. Orient the camera so that you can see the front of the lens, and watch what happens when you press and hold the shutter button. You should see the iris close.

f16 Aperture

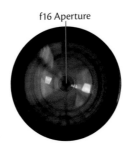

If you look closely at your lens while the shutter button is down in Bulb mode, you can see the aperture close down to your current aperture setting.

7. Take a closer look, and you'll be able to see the interlocking metal leaves that make up the iris.

8. Now release the shutter button, and the iris will open again.

It's pretty easy to see that when the aperture is smaller, it blocks (or stops) a lot of light. For this reason, when the shutter button is not pressed, the aperture opens as wide as it can go to ensure that as much light as possible makes it to the viewfinder so that you can more easily see and frame your shot. When you press the shutter button, the camera closes the aperture down to your chosen aperture setting, opens the shutter to make the exposure, closes the shutter, and then opens the aperture back up all the way so that you have a clear view out the viewfinder.

Now press and hold the Exposure Compensation button and dial the aperture to f8. Again, look at the front of the camera and press and hold the shutter button. The iris will close, but it should be obvious that it's not closing as far as it did when the aperture was set to 16.

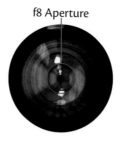

f8 Aperture

At f8, the aperture will be slightly larger than at f16.

Dial up some other apertures and take a look at them. When you're finished, be sure to set your lens back to autofocus by moving the focus switch to AF, and set the Mode dial back to Program.

What you should have seen is that when you choose a higher f-stop number, you're electing to stop more light with the aperture. That is, you're selecting a smaller opening.

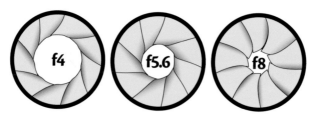

As aperture size increases, less light strikes the sensor.

In this book, we'll use a few aperture-related terms that you'll regularly hear photographers employ. When we speak of stopping down a lens, we mean choosing a smaller aperture (larger f-number). Opening up the lens means choosing a larger aperture (smaller f-number). Shooting full wide means choosing the largest possible aperture (the one with the smallest number).

This last term can be a little tricky because, on a zoom lens, the largest possible aperture can vary depending on your current focal length. For example, if you're using the 18–55mm lens that Canon bundles with the T1i, then you have a large aperture of f3.5 when shooting with the lens at full wide but a large aperture of f5.6 when shooting with the camera at full telephoto. In other words, the aperture can't open as wide when you zoom the lens in all the way. This is simply because of the nature of engineering a lens. (If you look at the front of the lens, you'll see that it says "1:3.5-5.6." This tells you the aperture range, from full wide to full telephoto.)

Why There Are Two Ways to Control Light

So, you can limit the amount of light that hits the sensor by changing the amount of time that the shutter is open, and you can limit the amount of light that hits the sensor by changing the size of the aperture in the lens. But why do you need two mechanisms for controlling light? If your concern is just to ensure that the image is neither too bright nor too dark, wouldn't one mechanism be enough?

If brightness were your only concern, then yes, one mechanism would be enough, but because of the way the physics of light works, there can be a big difference in your final image depending on whether you try to control exposure using shutter speed or aperture. In fact, after compositional choices, the bulk of your creative power as a photographer comes from how you choose to manipulate these two controls.

How Shutter Speed Choice Affects Your Image

This next bit should be pretty intuitive. As you choose a faster shutter speed, you will have more ability to freeze motion in a scene. That is, when the shutter is open for a very short time, a moving subject will be frozen. When the shutter is open for a longer time, a moving subject will be blurry and smeared.

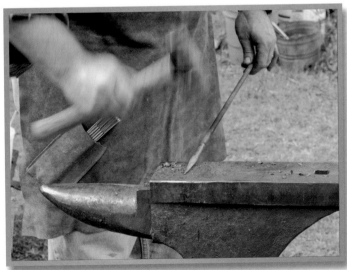

With a slower shutter speed, you can blur your subject to create a more dynamic image.

You may think that blurry and smeared is inherently bad and that you would always want your images sharp and clear. But consider the following two images:

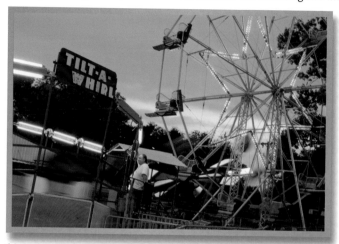

In this image, the slower shutter speed lets us see the movement of the rides.

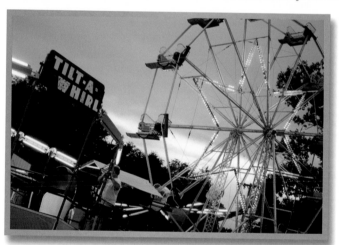

In this image above, the faster speed makes the rides look like they're sitting still.

If we shoot this scene with a fast shutter speed so that it is completely frozen, then we no longer see this as a moving Ferris wheel. In fact, it looks stopped. Blurred motion is often a way to introduce a dynamic feel to your images. When shooting a dynamic scene, you'll want to think about what best conveys the sense of dynamism that you feel there. Is it a perfectly frozen, fast shutter speed choice? Or a blurred, slow shutter speed choice?

There's another concern with shutter speed, which is the fact that your hands and body aren't always steady. You don't want to choose a shutter speed that's so slow that the natural shakiness of your hands will cause the image to be soft or blurry. In Chapter 6, we'll discuss how to calculate the slowest possible shutter speed for handholding in any given situation.

How Aperture Choice Affects Your Image

As you saw when you looked at the front of your lens with the shutter button held down, when you choose a higher f-number, the aperture in your lens is closed off more and blocks more light. Obviously, this will make your final exposure darker. But changing aperture has another effect on your image.

As you go to a smaller aperture, the depth of field in your image gets deeper. Depth of field is simply a measure of how much of your image is in focus.

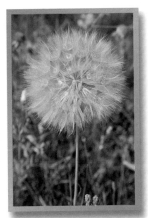 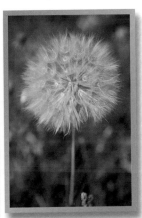

The image on the left has a deep depth of field, whereas the image on the right has a very shallow depth of field.

Here, the figure on the right has a very shallow depth of field. Notice that the background is out of focus, and even some parts on the front and back of the dandelion are slightly out of focus. The image on the left has very deep depth of field, with everything in the image in focus.

Depth of field is measured around your point of focus. So, if you've chosen an aperture that gives you, say, 10 feet of depth of field, then an area 10-feet deep will be in focus centered around the distance you focused at. What's more, if you're shooting something very far away, about a third of that depth will be in front of the point of focus, and the other two-thirds will be behind. For most shots, though, your depth of field will be evenly centered around your point of focus.

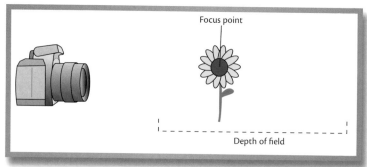

When shooting things far away, about a third of the depth of field in your scene will be in front of your subject, with the remaining two-thirds falling behind your subject.

Isn't it usually best to have everything in your image in focus? Not necessarily. Sometimes, having a sharply focused background can distract the viewer from your foreground subject. Portraits are the most common example of a shallow depth of field application. If you choose a larger aperture for a portrait, you'll create a softer background that will bring more attention to the subject of your portrait.

Just as you'll make shutter speed choices to control motion stopping, sometimes you'll need to consider how depth of field can be used to better express the subject or scene you're shooting. For instance, in the dandelion example, if you knew you wanted to shoot it with shallow depth of field, you would opt for a wider aperture, which means a smaller number. With the T1i's kit lens, then, you would try to get an aperture value that's as low as possible.

The widest possible aperture on the T1i's kit lens varies depending on your focal length. When you're zoomed out all the way, the lens can open up to 3.5. When you're zoomed in all the way, it can only open to 5.6. So your widest aperture will vary depending on how far you're zoomed in.

If you're trying to go for really deep depth of field, be aware that every lens has an aperture "sweet spot." On most lenses, if you stop down too far, you might suffer a sharpness penalty. Depending on how big you intend to print your final image, this penalty may be irrelevant. In general, most lenses start suffering a noticeable sharpness penalty if you choose an aperture greater than 11. However, sharpness is subjective, so you might want to do some experimenting with your lenses, to determine which apertures you find acceptably sharp.

> **TIP:** The Other Depth of Field Factor
>
> Aperture is not the only factor that controls how deep or shallow your depth of field is. Just as important (if not more, in many cases) is the effect size of the objects in the background of your image. If you're using a very wide aperture, but the background in your image is very small and far away, then your shallow depth of field will not be noticeable. Therefore, the way you compose your image has a lot to do with whether or not you will see shallow depth of field. We'll learn more about this in Chapter 8.

Shutter Speed/Aperture Balance

So, you can control how sharp or blurry a subject is by choosing a slower or faster shutter speed, and you can control how deep the focus is by choosing a larger or smaller aperture.

However, each of these choices will also render your scene brighter or darker. For example, if you decide you want to use a very fast shutter speed to stop a fast-moving object, then your scene might end up underexposed. The faster speed will allow less light to hit the image sensor, and your final image might end up dark.

You can compensate for a faster shutter speed, though, by using a wider aperture. A wider aperture will allow more light to pass through the lens and will restore a good level of brightness to your scene. Of course, a wider aperture might mean less depth of field. So, if you want to stop motion and have a deep depth of field and a scene that is properly bright, you might have a problem. Balancing all of these factors is one of the tricky things about photography. To better understand this balance, you need to learn a new term.

Reciprocity

Let's go back to the subject of stops for a moment. As discussed earlier, a stop is a measure of light. When you double the amount of light that hits the sensor, we say that you have increased the amount of light exposure by one stop. Conversely, if you halve the light, you decrease the exposure by one stop.

Consider these shutter speeds:

1/60 1/125 1/250 1/500 1/1000 1/2000 1/4000

Each one is double the previous shutter speed. In other words, there is a one-stop difference in the amount of light exposure generated by each of these speeds.

Now consider these apertures:

f4 f5.6 f8 f11 f16 f32

This one is not so obvious, because most of us aren't immediately familiar with calculations of circular area. But trust me when I say that each one of these apertures represents an opening that's twice as big as the previous aperture. In other words, there's a difference of one stop of light exposure between each of these apertures.

When it comes time to balance motion-stopping power with depth of field with overall illumination, you can take advantage of the fact that both shutter speed and aperture can be adjusted by the same amount in opposite directions. In other words, the two values have a reciprocal relationship.

For example, let's say your light meter recommends an exposure of 1/500th of a second at f8. It doesn't know how much motion stopping you might want, or how much depth of field, so it's simply trying to recommend a shutter speed and aperture that will give you a good level of illumination. But if you decide that you want more motion-stopping power and so increase shutter speed from 1/500 to 1/1000 (one stop), you'll run the risk of darkening your image. But, you can open your aperture from f8 to f5.6 (one stop) to compensate for that one stop of darkening that you introduced with the shutter speed change.

Because of this reciprocal relationship, many different shutter speed/aperture combinations yield the same overall exposure. That is, many combinations produce an image of equal brightness. However, some of those combinations might produce an image with more depth of field than others, or some might produce an image that has blurrier motion than others.

For the moment, don't worry about how you manage all of this on your camera. In this chapter, the goal is to understand the concepts. We'll get to the application and the actual controls in the next chapter.

TIP: Reading Shutter Speed

On the status display on the back of the camera, the T1i displays shutter speed as a full fraction. So, you might see 1/60. In the viewfinder status display, the T1i displays only the denominator—60, in this case. When you get to shutter speeds that are longer than a second, the T1i will use a quote mark to denote seconds. So, 1 1/3" denotes one-and-one-third seconds, and 2" would be two seconds.

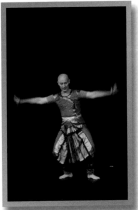 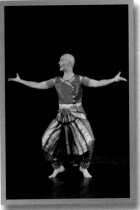

These two images have reciprocal exposures. That is, they have the same overall illumination, but the left one was shot with a combination that had a slower shutter speed than the right image.

Bringing ISO into Your Exposure Calculations

Earlier in this chapter, you learned about ISO. The Rebel T1i offers these ISO settings:

100 200 400 800 1600 3200

You can probably already see where this is going. Each ISO setting is double the previous, meaning there's a one-stop difference between each ISO. So, if you end up in a situation where your shutter speed and aperture choices have left your scene underexposed by a stop, you can increase your ISO setting by one stop to compensate.

Fractional Stops

In the days of manual cameras, shutter speed and aperture controls used the progression of settings that we've looked at here, with one stop of exposure difference between each setting (however, they provided a wider range than what I've shown).

However, it's possible to adjust shutter speed and aperture by intervals that are smaller than a whole stop, and by default the T1i will use values that are fractions of stops. So, as you adjust the shutter speed control on the T1i, you might see a progression that goes like this:

1/15 1/20 1/25 **1/30** 1/40 1/50 **1/60** 1/80 1/100 **1/125** 1/160 1/200

I've put the traditional one-stop increments in bold. The other values are increases of a third of a stop. All the same reciprocal rules apply when dealing with fractional stops. These fractional stops simply give you a more granular, finer-level of aperture control. As you'll see later, it's possible to change the interval to 1/2 or even 1/3 stop changes.

FOOD FOR THOUGHT

IMAGE ANATOMY

You need to learn an additional bit of theory if you want to get the most out of your image-editing software. Just as good film shooters needed to have a certain understanding of film and paper chemistry, as a digital shooter you need to know something about how a digital image is constructed.

Pixel is a pretty common term these days, and I've been using it off and on already, but just in case there's any confusion about it, here's a definition: pixel stands for *picture element* and is used to refer to any individual unit of information in a *raster* image. A *raster* image is simply an image that's made up of colored dots. So, the image on your computer screen is a raster image made up of pixels.

Similarly, your digital camera produces a raster image of different-colored pixels.

A pixel's color is simply a numerical value, with a different number representing each color that the pixel can be. The range of color that any individual pixel can be is limited only by the amount of memory that your imaging device devotes to that pixel. For example, your computer monitor probably uses 24 bits of data for each pixel. With 24 bits you can count from 0 to roughly 16 million, which means that any pixel on your screen can be one of roughly 16 million colors. Your Rebel T1i uses 14-bit pixels, which means it can record a huge variation of color.

When you were a kid, you probably learned about the color wheel and learned you can mix the primary colors of ink together to create other colors. You probably also learned that as you mix colors together, they get darker until they eventually turn black.

Light works mostly the same way. The primary colors of light—red, green, and blue—can be mixed together to form every other color of light. But, as you mix the primaries of light, they get brighter until they eventually turn white.

A digital image is actually composed of three separate *channels*. One contains all of the red information in the image, the second contains all of the blue, and the third contains all of the green.

We'll be referring to this three-channel color process at various places in this book.

FOOD FOR THOUGHT

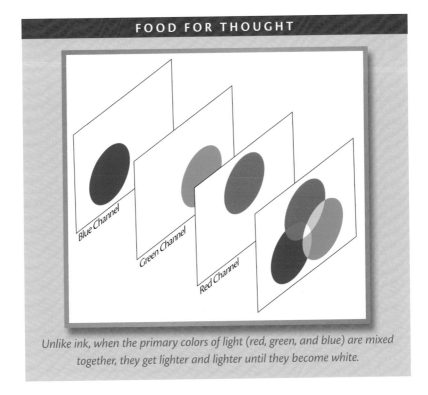

Unlike ink, when the primary colors of light (red, green, and blue) are mixed together, they get lighter and lighter until they become white.

Thinking Again About Full Auto Mode

Now that we've identified all the mechanisms that go into making an exposure, let's look again at the Full Auto mode that you've been shooting with. As you learned in Chapter 1, when you press the T1i shutter button halfway down, the camera focuses and calculates an exposure. That exposure is a shutter speed setting, aperture setting, and ISO choice. The camera has determined that these settings will yield an image that is neither too bright nor too dark.

When the camera has calculated these values and autofocused, it displays its choices in both the viewfinder and rear LCD status displays. These numbers should make a little more sense to you now.

As you just learned, many combinations of shutter speed and aperture settings yield the same overall exposure. So how does the camera choose? Its algorithms are designed to take the "safest" possible combination, that is, a shutter speed and aperture that will yield a good overall exposure, without risking handheld shake from a slow shutter speed or image softness from an extreme aperture.

Summing Up

I've thrown a lot of theory at you in this chapter, and it's worth spending a little time studying it. However, the rest of this book will reinforce these theories with actual practice.

To sum up, it takes a certain amount of light to yield an image that is neither too bright nor too dark. Your camera offers two ways to control this light: shutter speed and aperture. Shutter speed allows you to control how still or blurry a subject is, and aperture lets you control how deep the depth of field in your image is. In addition, ISO lets you control how light-sensitive the sensor is.

All these controls are measured in stops, with a change of one stop representing a doubling or halving of light. These three parameters have a reciprocal relationship, which means that if you change one, you can alter one of the others to make up for that change and ensure that your overall exposure remains the same.

CHAPTER 6

Program Mode

TAKING CONTROL AND UNDERSTANDING
MORE ABOUT EXPOSURE

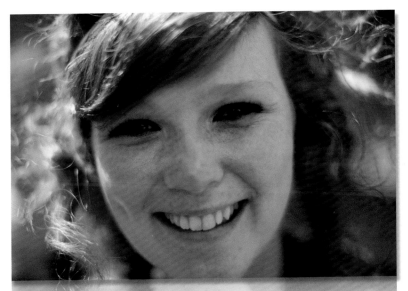

So far, you've been using your camera in its fully automatic mode. In Full Auto mode, the camera makes all critical decisions for you. Program mode, on the other hand, provides a great balance of automatic and manual modes, letting you continue to shoot snapshot-style but with additional manual control when you need it. Because of this and because of the ease with which the T1i lets you take manual control when you need it, you'll probably use Program mode more than any other mode on the camera.

However, no algorithm can know what's right for every situation or know what your particular taste is. Some photographic situations require more complicated decision making than the camera can perform, and some pictures that you see in your head simply can't be captured by the camera. They require additional image editing. For all these situations, you'll need to take some additional control. In this chapter, we'll explore all of the manual overrides available in Program mode, as well as some of the other creative choices you make when shooting.

Switching to Program Mode

In Chapter 1, I showed you the Mode dial, the dial on the right side of the top of the camera that you use to select a shooting mode. Each mode specifies a different set of parameters that the camera will handle automatically. For this chapter, change the shooting mode to P, Program mode.

Program mode is a lot like Full Auto mode in that your camera will automatically determine shutter speed and aperture for you, and can be set to automatically calculate white balance and ISO.

However, Program mode does *not* automatically pop up the flash if the camera determines that your scene is too dark, and it *does* offer you some important manual overrides, including white balance, image format, ISO, and more. Here's a table that shows the basic feature comparison between the two modes.

Feature	Program mode	Full Auto mode
Program Shift	✓	
Manual ISO selection	✓	
Manual white balance selection	✓	
Exposure compensation	✓	
Autofocus mode selection	✓	
Picture Styles	✓	
Drive Mode	✓	Limited
Focus point selection	✓	
Exposure Lock	✓	
Image format	✓	✓
Auto flash activation		✓

What do these manual controls change in terms of shooting? They mean that in Program mode, you're going to have more creative control—the control to stop or blur motion, to change depth of field, to better handle difficult lighting situations, and to choose exposures that change the way light and dark tones are represented in your final image.

Focusing Revisited

With your work shooting in Full Auto mode, you should now be comfortable with the autofocus mechanism of the T1i, and pre-focusing—the process of pressing the shutter button halfway down to autofocus—should be second nature.

While the T1i's autofocus system is very good, no autofocus system can work perfectly in every situation, and there will be times when you'll need to over-ride, or take manual control of, the T1i's focus. Fortunately, the camera provides a number of autofocus control mechanisms.

Understanding Focus Points

The T1i uses a nine-point autofous system. You've already experienced the nine autofocus points in the work you've done in Full Auto mode. So, you know that when you half-press the shutter button to autofocus, the camera assesses your scene and tries to determine what the subject is. It then focuses on that subject.

To let you know what it has focused on, the T1i lights up any of the autofocus points that are on the subject it has chosen. When focusing, it's important to keep an eye on which points light up so that you know exactly where the camera has focused. However, sometimes the camera chooses the wrong subject, especially if you're framing a scene with different subjects at different depths or a subject on the edge of the frame.

In the following example on the next page, the camera chose to focus on the wall behind the woman, leaving her silhouette slightly out of focus. Fortunately, for situations like these, the T1i lets you select exactly which focus point you want to use.

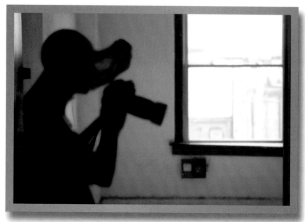

Here, we wanted to focus on the woman in the foreground, but the camera chose the wrong focus points and focused on the wall.

Manually selecting a focus point

To manually choose a focus point, first press the AF Point Selection button.

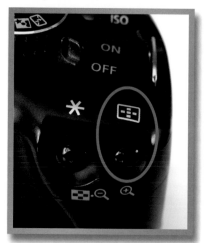

The focus lock button lets you select which focus point you want to use.

The rear LCD screen will display the AF point selection screen. The currently selected focus point will be outlined in white. If you're still using the default, Auto Select, then every focus point will be filled with blue and outlined in white.

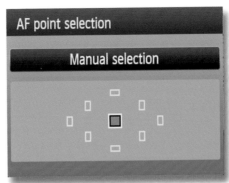

You can use the AF point selection screen to specify which autofocus point you want to use.

Rotate the Main dial to select a different focus point, or use the four-way buttons on the back of the camera. Only one point at a time can be selected.

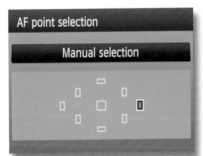
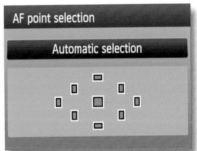

Using the AF point selection screen, you can manually choose a focus point. When all points are selected, the camera will choose a point automatically.

When you've highlighted the point you want, either press the AF Point Selection button again, or half-press the shutter button.

If you want to return to autoselect, continue to rotate the Main dial until all points are selected.

When to manually choose a focus point

As I mentioned earlier, when using autofocus point selection (which is the only option in Full Auto mode and the default in Program mode), you must pay attention to what the camera says it's focusing on. Any time it decides to focus on the wrong subject in a scene, you'll want to manually select a focus point.

USING ONLY THE CENTER FOCUS POINT

Some people like to set the focus point on the center point to gain better control of the camera's autofocus mechanism. The technique works like this: Set the T1i to the center focus point, and from now on you'll know that the camera will *always* focus on the center. If you have a tricky composition, you can place the center focus point on your subject, press the shutter button down halfway to lock focus, and then reframe *while continuing to hold down the shutter button.*

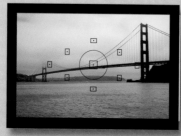 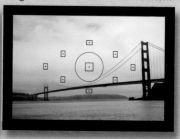

To guarantee that the bridge was in focus, I switched to center-point focusing, focused on the bridge, and, with the button held down, reframed my shot to get the composition I wanted.

As you know, once you've locked focus, the camera will hold it until you release the shutter button or press it the rest of the way to take a picture. So, once you've locked focus, you can reframe as much as you want without losing that focus. When you have the image composed the way you want, press the button the rest of the way to take the picture.

The advantage to this technique is that you don't have to pay attention to where the camera is focusing. Instead, because you've made the decision, you always know what the camera is focusing on. Also, the center focus point calculates focus on both the horizontal and vertical axes; the other points only look horizontally. This means the center point can have an easier time focusing on horizons and other horizontal lines.

One caveat, when using this technique, is that it's best to change the camera's light meter from its default of Evaluative Metering. I'll explain why in the next section.

Certain types of scenes might consistently confuse the camera's ability to automatically select a focus point. Landscape scenes can often yield wrong focus point choices, as can shots of still lifes, such as a picture of a product that you want to post on eBay. Manual focus point selection can quickly solve all of these problems.

You can also select a focus point manually when looking through the viewfinder. When you press the AF Point Selection button, the T1i will light up the current focus point selection, just as it does on the rear LCD. Spinning the Main dial will cycle through all the focus points. Press the AF Point Selection button or half-press the shutter button to accept the selected focus point.

Focus Modes

Canon calls the type of focusing we've been doing so far *one-shot autofocus*. No matter which focus point you're using, you set focus once for your shot and then take the picture.

If you're shooting a moving subject, though, especially one that's moving toward you, then you might have to refocus several times. Remember: when you focus, you're focusing on an object that's at a specified distance. If that object moves closer or farther, then your focus will no longer be accurate. If it moves side to side but stays at the same distance, your focus should be fine.

AI Servo

For moving objects, you have two choices. As the object moves, you can reframe and refocus. To refocus, you'll have to let go of the shutter button and then give it another half-press. If you're using autofocus point selection, then you need to ensure that the camera is focusing in the right place. If you're using a single focus point, you'll need to ensure that it stays on your moving subject as you refocus. Another option is to use AI Servo autofocus. This is a special autofocus mode that automatically tracks a moving subject and keeps it in focus.

To activate AI Servo autofocus, press the right arrow button on the back of the camera, the one with AF next to it. The AF mode menu will appear.

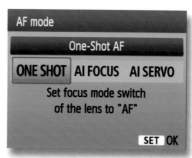

You can change the T1i's autofocus mode using the AF mode menu.

Press the right arrow button twice to select AI Servo (alternately, you can press left once, or you can rotate the Command dial). Press the Set button to execute the change.

To use AI Servo, focus on your subject as you normally would, and then continue to hold the shutter button down halfway. The camera will continuously refocus and adjust its exposure as your subject moves and you reframe.

Because the camera is continuously focusing, it will never beep or show its green ready light, as it does in normal autofocus modes. So, you can simply take the shot whenever you want. If the camera has not managed to lock focus or is currently changing focus, then there might be a slight lag before the shutter is actually tripped. In general, though, you should find that Servo focus does a very good job of keeping your subject in focus in a timely manner.

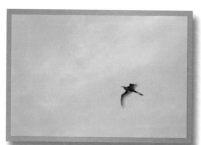 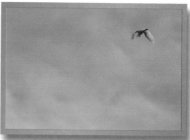

AI Servo focus will keep your image in focus, even as your subject moves and your framing changes.

AI Focus

If you're in a dynamic situation where you sometimes want to shoot with one-shot AF but also need to be able to shoot moving objects, then you might want to use AI Focus mode, which automatically switches between normal one-shot behavior and Servo mode. With AI Focus, your T1i will default to one-shot focusing but automatically engage Servo focusing when your subject moves.

If this mode is truly the best of both worlds, why even have the other modes? Well, sometimes you'll want one-shot focus behavior but will be shooting a scene with moving objects in it. For these instances, you'll want to switch to One-Shot mode. Conversely, there might be other times where you're trying to get a shot of a moving object that occasionally stands still. You don't want the camera switching into One-Shot mode and so might choose to lock it into Servo mode. Practicing with all three modes will help you better understand when to use each one.

> **REMINDER:** It's Always in the Eyes
>
> When shooting people, remember that the most important thing to consider in a portrait is the eyes. As long as the eyes are in focus, it probably won't matter if there's a little softness in the rest of the image. So, if you're using autofocus point selection, make sure the T1i indicates that it has the eyes in focus. Or, switch to center-point autofocus, put the center focus point on the subject's eyes, autofocus, and then reframe. This will ensure that the eyes are sharp.

What to Do When Autofocus Doesn't

The autofocus mechanism in the Rebel T1i is dependent on contrast; the sharp edges in an image are composed of high-contrast lines.

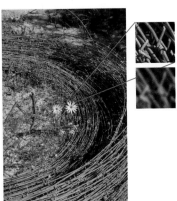

A crop of this image shows how much contrast there is. The lower crop shows an unfocused version of the image. As you can see, there is very little contrast in the image, since it is out of focus.

When you half-press the shutter button on the T1i, it measures the contrast in your scene, and then it zooms in a little and measures the contrast again. If the contrast has increased, it zooms in more until there's no additional contrast improvement. If the camera zooms in and the scene's contrast *decreases*, then it zooms back out. If you see the lens zoom in and out and back in before it beeps to tell you it's found focus, then you've just experienced it searching and zeroing in on the most contrasty focus distance.

However, if you're shooting a scene that *lacks* contrast, then you may have a hard time getting the camera to focus. You'll hear the lens search back and forth, and you'll see the image in the viewfinder alternate between focused and blurry, but you'll never hear the beep of the focus lock. This usually happens for two reasons: either the camera's focus points are all on a contrastless part of the scene, such as the sky, or they're pointed at a textureless object. In these situations, you must use a focus and reframe technique. Reframe your shot so that the camera's focus points are positioned on an object that's at the same distance as your desired focus, and then press the shutter button halfway. After the camera has locked focus, keep holding the button halfway down as you reframe to your desired composition, and then press the button the rest of the way to take the shot.

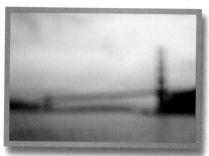

When all the focus points land on contrastless fog, the camera can't set focus.

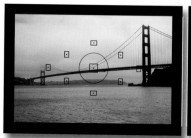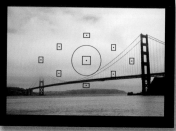

Tilt down so that the camera's focus spots are on the contrasty bridge. Press the shutter button halfway to lock focus; then reframe and take the focused shot.

WARNING: Use Something at the Same Distance to Set Focus

Remember, though, for this to work, you must focus on something that's at the appropriate distance. Don't lock focus on something in the foreground or way in the distance. When you reframe, your camera will be focused at the wrong point.

Low-light autofocus problems

Sometimes your scene lacks contrast because it's too dark. When this happens, the camera may have trouble locking focus. If you hear the camera focus in and out for a while and it still doesn't lock focus, then probably the scene is too dark for the autofocus mechanism to work.

To give the camera some help, pop up the built-in flash. Now when you press the shutter button halfway down, the camera will fire some quick flash bursts to illuminate the scene. This extra light can help it lock focus. If you don't want the flash to fire during the shot, keep the shutter halfway down while you close the flash. Now you'll have a locked focus and can shoot without flash.

TIP: Disabling Flash Firing

If you choose Flash Control from Shooting Menu 1, you can disable flash firing. This will still let the camera use the flash for focus assist, but the camera won't fire the flash when it takes the shot.

Obviously, this focus-assist feature, like the flash, has limited range, so it won't help if you're shooting a landscape shot or something very far away. But if you're taking a portrait or snapshot, it will probably be fine. You might want to warn your subject that the camera is going to shine a light at them, although these days most people are used to weird lights coming out of cameras.

If the focus-assist light doesn't solve your focus problem, try the focus and reframe trick. Very often, you can find a bright highlight or reflection in a dark scene and focus on that, if it's at the right distance.

Manual Focus

While the T1i packs a great autofocus system, don't give short shrift to manual focus. By switching the focus switch on your lens from AF to MF, you get full manual control of focus.

All T1i lenses will have a manual focus ring, though different lenses will put the focus ring on different sides of the zoom ring. Simply turn the ring to focus the lens. On some lenses, you must first switch the lens to manual focus before the manual focus ring will work. On other lenses, manual focus will automatically work as soon as you turn the ring. So, if autofocus focuses and you don't like the results, you can simply turn the focus ring to refocus, and the camera will leave it alone.

Manual focus is great for those times when autofocus isn't working because your scene is too dark or you're shooting a subject that lacks contrast. Manual focus is also great for times when your subject isn't moving or changing. For example, you can autofocus on your subject and then switch to manual and know that your lens is locked on the right focus. With the lens set to manual focus, you'll be able to shoot much faster because you won't ever have to wait for the camera to focus. This is also great for shooting still life and product shots.

When shooting an object that's moving in a predictable fashion, many people think manual focus allows them to track faster than Servo focus. Quickly focusing manually requires practice, though, and the T1i Servo focus is very good, so you should experiment with it before you switch over to manual.

Getting Creative with Program Shift

In the previous chapter, you learned about the effects that different shutter speed and aperture choices have on your final image. You saw that by controlling shutter speed, you can choose how much you want to freeze or blur motion, and that by controlling aperture, you can choose how much you want to blur out the background. You also learned that these parameters have a reciprocal relationship: if you change one, you can change the other to compensate.

The Rebel T1i has a lot of different ways to change shutter speed and aperture, allowing you to take complete creative control of motion stopping and depth of field. If you've taken some shots already in Program mode, then you've seen that it works just like Full Auto mode. When you half-press the shutter, the camera autofocuses and meters. Once it has determined a shutter speed and aperture that's appropriate for the scene, it displays those values on the status display inside the viewfinder and on the back of the camera.

FOOD FOR THOUGHT

PANNING WITH A SLOW SHUTTER SPEED

When you shoot with a slow shutter speed to try to introduce blur into your shot, you have two choices: you can hold the camera still, and let the object move through your scene to create a blurred subject, or you can pan the camera to follow your subject and create a blurred background.

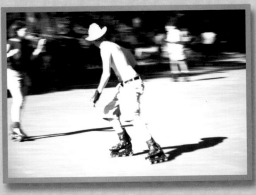

When shooting with a slow shutter speed, you can pan the camera to follow a moving subject, rendering the background a blur.

To create a blurred background, you pan the camera while the shutter is open. It can take some practice to do this well, without too much camera shake, and without blurring your subject too much, but give it a try.

Press the shutter button halfway to meter your scene; then spin the Main dial to dial in a slower shutter speed. Then, press the button all the way to open the shutter, and pan to follow your subject as it passes through your scene.

With a really fast-moving object, you don't need a super-long shutter speed. On a bright day, even a 50th of a second might be enough. Try different shutter speeds and pans until you get the amount of background blur that you like.

As I mentioned in the previous chapter, the camera's built-in meter aims for a shutter speed that is appropriate for handheld shooting and an aperture that's not too extreme. But as you've learned, many different combinations of shutter speed and aperture yield the same exposure. Some of these combinations will have a faster or slower shutter speed and, conversely, a larger or smaller aperture.

In Program mode, you can automatically change from the current exposure to any equivalent, reciprocal exposure by turning the Main dial after the camera has metered.

So, for example, if I press the shutter halfway to meter and the camera yields a reading of 1/125th at f7.1 and I then rotate the Main dial to the right, the meter reading changes to 1/200th at f6.3. Another turn to the right gives me 1/250th at f5, and so on. Each of these exposures is equivalent, but as I spin the dial to the right, my shutter speed is getting faster, which gives me more motion-stopping power. The aperture is also getting wider, which might yield a shallower depth of field.

Here's a real-world example: The following two images have the same exposure, but they achieve it through different exposure settings. In the left image, I metered and then turned the Main dial until the aperture read 5.6, the widest aperture available for the focal length I was using. The wide aperture gave me a shallow depth of field. For the second image, I turned the Main dial until the aperture read 11. This yielded the same overall exposure but gave me a deeper depth of field.

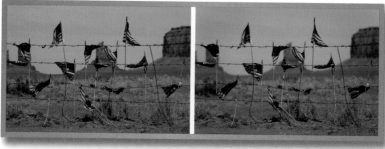

By using Program Shift, I was able to shoot the same scene with different depths of field.

Program Shift is a very powerful function. With it, you have the ability to manually select a shutter speed or aperture while ensuring that your exposure is correct, but you don't have to leave the automatic features of Program mode. This makes it easy to grab a little manual control when you need it.

Handheld Shooting and Shutter Speed

No matter which mechanism you use, once you start fiddling with shutter speed, you have to be very careful about the shutter speed you choose. Pick one too low, and you'll run the risk of getting blurry images due to camera shake. The problem is simply that it's impossible to hold a camera perfectly still. As animals, we don't stand still, we sway—it's a necessary part of balancing on two legs. When you throw in breathing and a beating heart and possible windy conditions, holding a couple of pounds of camera perfectly still becomes impossible.

So, what's the slowest shutter speed that you can use when shooting handheld? That depends on your lens and on the focal length you're shooting at.

With a longer focal length—when an image is greatly magnified and has a very narrow field of view—holding the camera steady is much more difficult, because any tiny movement or vibration is much more noticeable than at wide angles, when you have less magnification and a broader field of view.

The rule of thumb is that the slowest shutter speed you should use is 1/focal length. So, if you're shooting with a 100mm lens, you shouldn't use a shutter speed that's less than 1/100th of a second. But, as you learned in Chapter 4, the effective focal length of any lens that you put on the Rebel T1i is the lens focal length multiplied by 1.6. So, if you set your zoom lens to 100mm, the slowest shutter speed you should use is actually 1/160th of a second, or 100 x 1.6.

So, when using the Program Shift feature (or any other shutter speed control mechanism), keep an eye on the shutter speed, and make sure it doesn't go too low if you're shooting handheld.

Image Stabilization

If you have a lens with image stabilization (or *IS*), then you have some more hand-held shooting latitude. For example, the 18–55mm lens that Canon bundles with the Rebel T1i includes built-in stabilization, as do many other Canon lenses and several third-party lenses.

Image stabilization is a seemingly magical technology. When activated, the stabilization system detects tiny movements of the camera and adjusts its optics on the fly to counteract those movements, resulting in a more stable image. Image stabilization is not a substitute for a tripod—it won't render the camera perfectly still. It also can't smooth out extreme jarrings of the camera. If you're shooting from a Jeep in rough terrain, image stabilization isn't going to render your camera still. But for ordinary vibration and shake caused by handholding, it can mean the difference between getting a usable shot and getting a shot that's soft and blurry.

If you have an IS lens, like the 18–55mm that's bundled with the Rebel, try this: zoom the lens to full telephoto; then switch the Stabilizer switch on the camera to Off.

Keep your finger on the Stabilizer switch while you look through the viewfinder. Pay close attention to one edge of the frame and notice how much it's moving. Now, without moving your eye from the viewfinder, flip the Stabilizer switch to On. You should see that the image stops jittering and the edge of the frame is much steadier. (Obviously, the whole image is steadier; it's just easier to see the motion when you look at the edge of the frame, because you have the frame edge to use as a reference.)

With the image stabilized, you can use longer shutter speeds when shooting handheld. How much longer depends on the quality of the stabilizer in your lens. The 18–55mm bundled with the Rebel T1i has a stabilizer that provides three to four stops of stabilization, depending on who you believe. To be safe, let's assume three.

Remember, a stop is one doubling of exposure. If we're shooting with the 18–55mm at full telephoto, then we're shooting at an equivalent focal length of 88mm. This means that we shouldn't try to handhold with a shutter speed below 1/88th of a second. But, with three stops of stabilization, that works down from 1/88th to 1/44th to 1/22nd. So, in theory, you can shoot with that lens at 1/22nd of a second when shooting at full telephoto. Whether or not you really can depends on how steady you are at holding the camera.

Why would you want to shoot this slow? Well, sometimes you'll be shooting in situations that are so dark that you'll have no choice. You'll need to open the lens all the way and shoot at a very slow shutter speed. So, the slower you can manage, the better the chance of getting the shot. We'll discuss low-light shooting in more detail in Chapter 9.

Objects in your scene that are moving might still be blurry when shooting with such a slow speed, but you shouldn't see an overall softening of your image due to camera shake.

REMINDER: Steady As She Goes

When trying to hold the camera steady—which is especially important when using a slow shutter speed—remember to gently squeeze the trigger. Use the posture tips we discussed in Chapter 1, and *don't* hold your breath. Holding your breath actually makes you shakier. If possible, try to find something to lean against or that you can use to steady the camera.

Changing the ISO

In the previous chapter you learned that the ISO setting controls how light sensitive the T1i's sensor is. A higher ISO number means the camera's sensor is more sensitive. This means it can gather light more quickly, which allows you to use shorter shutter speeds and smaller apertures. For times when you need lots of motion-stopping power or a deep depth of field, the ability to increase your ISO can make the difference between getting and missing the shot. But in addition to creative latitude, increasing the ISO also means you can shoot in much lower light. In fact, the image sensor in the T1i is so sensitive that you can shoot effectively in much lower light than you could ever manage with film.

But, in addition to creative latitude, increasing the ISO also means you can shoot in much lower light. In fact, the image sensor in the T1i is so sensitive that you can shoot effectively in much lower light than you could ever manage with film.

As you learned in Chapter 5, ISOs are measured using a standard scale. The T1i offers a default ISO range from 100 to 3200 in whole-stop increments. So, the entire range of ISO settings goes like this:

100 200 400 800 1600 3200

In addition to these modes, the camera also lets you select Auto ISO. With Auto ISO activated, the camera will automatically choose an ISO for you. (Note that you can select an ISO only when shooting in Program, Shutter Priority, Aperture Priority, or Manual mode.)

So, if a faster ISO offers better low-light performance and the ability to shoot with really fast shutter speeds and narrow apertures whenever you need them, why shouldn't you just leave the camera on ISO 1600 all the time?

In Chapter 5, you learned that the camera increases the sensitivity of the sensor by boosting the amplification of the voltages that are read off the sensor after an image is shot. Unfortunately, any time you amplify any type of electrical signal, you increase any noise in the signal along with the data you're trying to read. Noise is just what you think it is—the extraneous, staticky signals that you hear on a radio. Noise is generated by components in the camera, by other electrical sources in the room, and even by the stray cosmic ray that might be passing through you and the rest of the planet. The practical upshot of this is that as you increase the ISO of the camera, you also increase the *noise* (grainy patterns that sometimes look a lot like film grain) in your image.

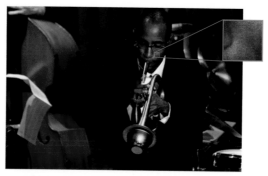

This image was shot at ISO 1600 and suffers from a tiny bit of noise—a speckly pattern that occurs predominantly in shadowy areas.

Because of this noise, you always want to shoot at the lowest ISO that you can to ensure that you don't introduce extraneous noise. But, on the T1i, you'll probably find that there's very little difference in the amount of noise you see in an ISO 100, 200, or 400 image. So, you can safely choose these ISOs and see no discernible noise increase. And, although you may be able to see a noise increase at ISO 800 and 1600, the T1i produces so little noise, and it's such a nice quality, that you probably won't mind; even ISO 3200 is very clean and usable. Sometimes a bit of texture can add a lot of atmosphere to an image. Most importantly, just because noise is visible on-screen doesn't mean it will show up in print. By the time you've scaled your image to your desired output size and the printer has processed it, the noise might be far less visible.

Setting ISO

By default, the T1i uses an Auto ISO setting. This means the camera is free to change the ISO any time it thinks it needs to do so to get a better exposure or an exposure with a shutter speed that's fast enough for handheld shooting.

At times, though, you won't want the camera to change the ISO. For example, if you're trying to shoot with very specific shutter speeds or aperture settings, you might find you need to lock the ISO down to get the exposure settings you want.

Or, if you're shooting in a dark venue that has bright lights, such as a stage or concert hall, you might want to lock the ISO on a very high value to ensure that the camera doesn't get confused by the occasional very bright light and end up shooting with an ISO that will leave the darker parts of the image very noisy.

Finally, some people just prefer to stay away from auto settings because they like to know exactly what settings are being used so they aren't surprised by something later.

To change the ISO, press the ISO button, which is located just behind the Main dial. The camera will present the ISO speed menu.

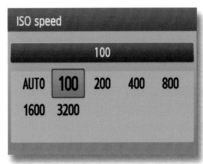

The ISO speed menu lets you select an ISO, which can make the camera more sensitive in low light.

Use the Main dial or the arrow buttons to select the ISO you want, and then press the Set button. The current ISO is displayed on the rear status display, as well as on the in-viewfinder status display. In fact, you can easily change the ISO without taking your eye from the viewfinder, since the ISO button and the Main dial are located just behind the shutter button and are easily found by feel.

> **TIP:** ISO Expansion
>
> As you'll see in Chapter 12, the Rebel T1i supports an additional ISO setting of 6400. We'll cover how to activate that feature when we look at the camera's "Custom Functions."

A Real-World ISO Change

Let's say you're trying to shoot a close-up of a flower on a windy day. Your meter has recommended 1/125th of a second at f3.5. This is great because it gives you the shallow depth of field that you want, but it's so windy that 1/125th of a second is resulting in an image that's too blurry. If you increase the shutter speed by three stops to 1/1000, the image will be underexposed, because the camera's aperture can't be opened any further.

But, if you increase the ISO from 100 to 800 (a three-stop difference), you'll have enough exposure latitude to make your shutter speed change and get your shot.

White Balance

Although your Rebel T1i is an incredibly sophisticated imaging instrument, it still pales in comparison to the human eye. Your eye has better autofocus, can perceive a much wider range of tones and colors, and has the amazing ability to autocorrect color under different types of light.

That last one may not sound that difficult, but think for a moment about your street corner. During the daytime, it's covered with sunshine (unless it's a cloudy day), but at night, it's lit up by a street light. The street light is very yellow, whereas sunshine is much "cooler"—closer to the blue end of the spectrum—and cloudy light cooler still.

Similarly, the light you're sitting in right now might be an entirely different color. It will vary if you're sitting under a fluorescent light or a tungsten light. Or maybe you have the book under a tungsten desk lamp, with fluorescent overhead lighting while sunshine streams through a nearby window.

Throughout all of this, your eyes still register the pages of this book as white. For the most part, no matter what light you move the book into, you'll still perceive the pages as white—they might be brighter or darker, but your sense of color will remain consistent, until the light level drops below a certain threshold, at which point your ability to perceive any color will be compromised.

We have yet to develop a technology that is as good as your eyes are when it comes to correctly rendering color under any type of light. Different types of film have to be specially formulated for different kinds of light, which is why you buy special "daylight" film when you're shooting outside. Similarly, your Rebel T1i must be calibrated to the type of light you're shooting in, a process called *white balancing*.

To understand the fundamental principles of white balance, you need to think back to elementary school. At some point, you probably learned how a rainbow works—how the droplets of water act like tiny little prisms that scatter the light that passes through them. And from this you learned that the light we see is actually made up of a bunch of independent color components, the Roy G. Biv collection of red, orange, yellow, green, blue, indigo, and violet. These colors combine to create the white light that we normally see.

So, the idea with white balancing is that if you can accurately represent the color white, then you get an accurate representation of every other color, since all other colors combine to make white.

White Balance Presets

By default, your Rebel T1i is set up to use the Auto White Balance feature, which uses complex algorithms to analyze the color in your scene to determine what's what and then calibrates itself to those white values. This is the only white balance option that's available in Full Auto mode, but in Program mode, you can override the Auto White Balance and opt for some more manual control. Why would you ever want to do this? Because as good as the Auto White Balance is, it can be confused. Consider this image:

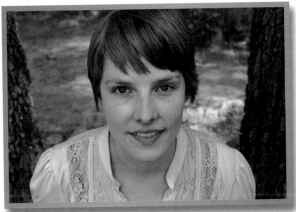

This image was shot under shade, using the camera's Auto White Balance feature.

This was shot in nearly complete shade, and although the color doesn't look wildly bad, it's rather cool and unflattering. The woman is too blue, and the image's overall cast is too cold.

In this case, the Auto White Balance has not been able to properly calibrate the camera for the light we're shooting in. To correct for this, we need to change to a white balance preset that has been designed for a specific type of light.

To select a white balance preset, press the WB button on the back of the camera. The camera will display the White balance menu.

There are different white balance presets for six different types of light, as well as a full Auto White Balance and a full Manual white balance. Use the arrow buttons to select the appropriate white balance, and then press the Set button.

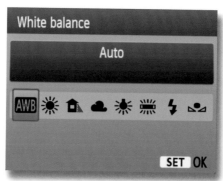

The White balance menu lets you select, from left to right, Auto White Balance, Daylight, Shade, Cloudy, Tungsten, Fluorescent, Flash, or Manual.

Shade is the best white balance choice for our previous example. It's similar to the Cloudy white balance, and it's often worth trying both. Since our subject is in the shade, I decided to go with that.

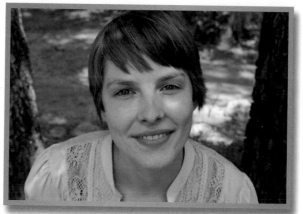

With Shade white balance, our image looks much more color-accurate.

While the Auto White Balance shot you saw before didn't look terrible, the Cloudy white balance shot makes the weakness of the previous shot a little more apparent.

In general, with the Rebel T1i, you'll probably find that Auto White Balance works very well. However, it's best to get in the habit of noticing whenever you enter a cloudy or shady area or an area that's predominantly lit by tungsten lights or by fluorescent lights. In these instances, you'll probably get better results with Manual white balance.

If you're unsure what the best setting is, when you get into a new lighting environment, you can easily preview different white balance settings using Live View.

1. Press the Live View button (⬛).

2. Press the Set button. A small menu will appear on the left side of the screen.

3. Use the up/down arrows to select the White balance menu item.

4. Turn the Main dial to cycle through all of the different white balance settings. With each one, the screen will update to show what that white balance setting looks like.

The screen on the T1i is not terrifically color accurate, but it is good enough for you to see the difference between white balance settings.

> **REMINDER:** Don't Forget to Change Back!
>
> One of the trickiest things about white balance is that you must remember to change it when the light changes. So, if you move into shade and switch to Cloudy white balance but then move back into daylight, you *must* remember to switch back to Auto or Daylight white balance. Correcting a bad white balance in an image editor is extremely difficult—and often impossible—so it's important to get white balance right.

Custom White Balance

For the most accurate color, you'll want to use a custom white balance. Custom white balance is also the best choice when you're in a lighting situation for which there is no preset, such as a mixed lighting situation (sunlight falling into a fluorescent-lit room, for example). Auto White Balance works by identifying something in your image that's probably white, usually a bright highlight. This area is then used as the basis for the camera's white balance analysis. White balance presets don't analyze the current scene at all. Instead, they're simply preset values that Canon has determined are good for each specific lighting type.

When you use a custom white balance, you point the camera at something white and tell it to use that as the reference for its white balance calculations. Because you're in control of what the camera is using as a reference and because that reference is reflecting the actual light in your scene, you get a very accurate white balance calculation.

To perform a custom white balance, you first need something white, like a piece of paper or a white T-shirt. It's very important that the white object be in the same light as your subject. For example, if you're standing in shade and your subject is 10 feet away in bright sunlight, don't hold the white object directly in front of the lens, because the camera is actually in very different light from the subject.

Once you've positioned the object in your scene, take a picture of it. Try to fill the frame with as much of the white object as you can. At the very least, it needs to fill the circle that appears in the middle of the viewfinder.

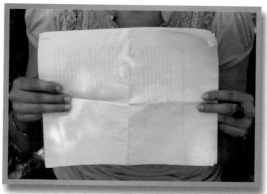

White paper defines a Custom white balance that produces very accurate color.

Next, press the WB button on the back of the camera, and select Custom white balance. Now you need to tell the camera which image you want to use for the white balance analysis. Press the Menu button and choose Custom WB from the second shooting menu.

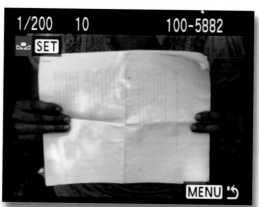

Using the Custom WB menu command, select the shot that contains our white object. The camera will use this as the basis for its white balance calculations.

The camera will immediately appear to go into playback mode, but note the White Balance Set icon in the upper-left corner. If the shot of your white object is not showing, navigate to it just as you would navigate within playback mode. When you've found your white object photo, press the Set button. The camera will present a dialog box that says "Use WB data from this image for Custom WB?" Select OK. You are now configured for Custom white balance.

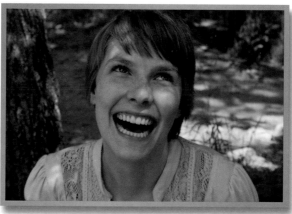

After Custom white balance, the same shady scene has more accurate color and a nice touch of warmth.

Unfortunately, it's difficult to make any hard and fast rules about which white balance setting will work best for you. In a tricky lighting situation like shade or clouds, you'll probably want to try Auto, the appropriate preset, and Custom, just as we have here. The human eye is very sensitive to changes in flesh tone color, so it's very important to get white balance correct when shooting portraits.

TIP: Gray Is Even Better Than White

While a custom white balance works fine with a white object, it works even better with a gray object. However, it needs to be a spectrally neutral gray object, meaning it needs to be a true gray with no hint of other hues in it. It's best to use a white object unless you have a gray card designed specifically for white balance, like the WhiBal card from *www.whibal.com*. It's spectrally neutral and is gray all the way through, so if it gets scratched, you can just sand it off and still have a usable gray. What's more, it floats if you accidentally drop it in a stream. If you use custom white balance a lot, the WhiBal card is a very good investment.

White Balance Shift

Sometimes neither Auto White Balance nor the white balance preset is quite right for your situation. If a custom white balance is not an option (perhaps you don't have a white reference available), then you can always use the T1i's White Balance Shift feature.

This is a fairly advanced option that is intended for shooters who are used to balancing light using colored filters. Such a topic is beyond the scope of this book, but even without an understanding of filter use, or *mireds* (a unit of measure used for specifying color filter density), White Balance Shift might still be handy. To apply white balance correction, choose WB SHIFT/BKT from the second shooting menu. The White Balance Shift page shows a grid with two axes.

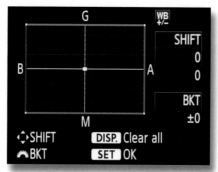

White Balance Shift lets you tweak and adjust your white balance setting so as to bias it toward a particular color range.

In the center of the grid is a white dot that you can move around using the four arrow buttons. The vertical axis shifts the white balance in your image from green to magenta, and the horizontal axis shifts from blue to amber. Note that these adjustments are very subtle—too subtle to show up in the printing process used in this book. But they can still serve to improve the overall color tone of your image if you're printing on a photo printer. Use the arrow buttons to set the correction you want, and then press the Set button.

To deactivate the White Balance Shift correction, press the DISP button. The white dot should return to the center of the grid. If you've spent any time using an image editor, you might think, "Why would I do this here when I can make this adjustment much easier in my image editor?" If you were just shooting a single shot, then you'd be right. Using the White Balance Shift feature wouldn't make a lot of sense.

But let's say you were shooting an event. When you got to the location, you might take a couple test shots to determine what white balance looks best in that lighting. If you determine that all the images are a little too cool, are too warm, or have a weird color shift of some kind, then you could dial in a White Balance Shift and all of your images would be correct when you shot them, saving you a tremendous amount of time in your image editor later. To be honest, this is not a feature you will use very often, if it all, but it's worth knowing about.

White Balance Bracketing

At times you'll come into a lighting situation that you know is going to trip up the T1i's Auto White Balance and for which there's no suitable white balance preset. Obviously, the ideal solution in these instances is to use a custom white balance, but this isn't always possible. White balance bracketing is another good option for these instances.

Bracketing is the process of shooting multiple exposures of the same scene with slightly different settings. It's usually used for varying exposure, but the Rebel T1i includes an option for bracketing white balance.

When you turn on white balance bracketing, the T1i shoots the first shot with your chosen white balance (Auto if you're on Auto, a preset if you've chosen a preset, or your specified custom white balance if that's what you're currently using). The next shot you shoot will be shot with the same white balance but one that has been shifted to be more blue/amber. The next shot will be biased toward magenta/green.

In a tricky white balance setting, your chances of getting a good white balance are improved with white balance bracketing, simply because you're shooting more coverage with more variation.

To enable balance bracketing, choose WB SHIFT/BKT from the second shooting menu. You'll see the same page you saw in the previous "White Balance Shift" section.

You can control how much bracketing you want by turning the Main dial. There are three different levels of correction for both the blue/amber shot and the magenta/green shot. Turn the Main dial to the right to set the amount of blue/amber adjustment and to the left to adjust the magenta/green adjustment. One, two, or three squares will appear for each adjustment. The more squares, the stronger the adjustment. Press the Set button to accept the adjustment.

To cancel the white balance bracket, press the DISP button.

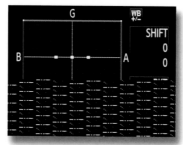

Here I've dialed in a white balance bracket that ranges from blue to amber.

Note that when you're using white balance bracketing, your maximum burst speed during continuous shooting will go down, and the number of shots you can take before the camera's buffer starts to bog down will be reduced to one-third of its normal amount. This shouldn't be a huge problem, though, because if you're shooting a rapidly changing situation, you won't want to be using white balance bracketing anyway, as each shot will have a different white balance.

> **TIP:** Avoid White Balance Altogether with Raw
>
> One of the great advantages of shooting in Raw mode rather than the default JPEG mode is that you can alter white balance later, in your image editor, making many of these issues moot. We'll discuss Raw mode in detail in Chapter 11.

Drive Mode and the Self-Timer

By default, the T1i shoots in single-frame mode. When you hold the button down, it takes only one picture. But you can change the camera to Drive mode, which will cause it to keep shooting frames as long as you have the button held down.

The obvious application for Drive mode is shooting action scenes such as sporting events or wild animals, or any moment where you're concerned that your reflexes won't be fast enough to grab the decisive moment. With Drive mode you can shoot a burst of images and pick out the best one later.

But Drive mode can also be useful for more everyday events, especially shooting candid shots of people. People's expressions can change very subtly from one moment to the next, and with a burst of images you can capture a range of expression and pull out exactly the right shot later.

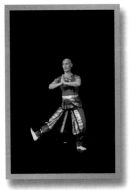 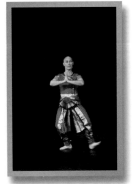 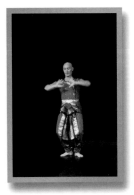

Drive mode is great for shooting action sequences, since it allows you to shoot a burst of images to capture a specific moment.

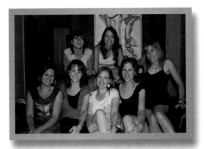 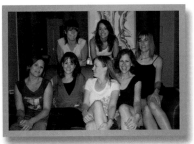

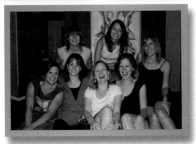

With groups of people, it can be difficult to know the precise moment when everyone's eyes will be open, when everyone will have a good expression, and so on. Drive mode can ease this by letting you quickly gather a burst of images.

To activate Drive mode, press the Drive mode button ( ) on the back of the camera. The Drive mode menu will appear.

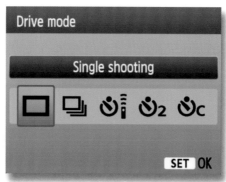

The Drive mode menu lets you choose single shooting, continuous, self-timer with remote control, 2-second self-timer, or continuous self-timer.

Press the right arrow once to select Drive mode (or turn the Main dial), and then press Set. The current Drive mode is shown on the T1i's rear status screen.

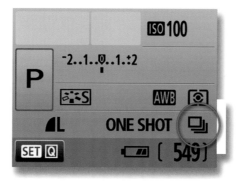

The current Drive mode is displayed on the camera's rear status display.

To shoot with Drive mode, you do all the same things you do for ordinary, single-mode shooting. Press the shutter button halfway to autofocus, make sure the camera is focused properly, and then press the button the rest of the way to take the shot. Now, though, as long as you hold the shutter button down, the camera will continue to shoot, bursting away at a maximum of about 3.5 frames per second. In the viewfinder status display, you'll see a number that counts down as you continue to shoot.

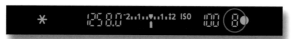

On the right side of the viewfinder status display is a number showing how many shots are available in the camera's buffer.

When this number reaches zero, you have filled the camera's buffer, and it will have to pause as it writes data out to the card. The camera does not wait until the buffer is full before it starts writing; it is continuously writing as you shoot. But when the counter hits zero, you've overrun the buffer. As soon as some space is available and the counter returns to one, you can shoot again, but you'll get only one shot before you experience another pause.

In practice, this won't be a huge problem, because we don't tend to shoot really long bursts. But it's still a good idea to keep an eye on this number and to shoot small bursts with breaks in between. If the "big play" is about to unfold, don't just start bursting with the idea that you'll get the whole thing. Wait until the critical moment is as close as possible, and then begin your burst. Not only will this improve your chances of getting the shot you want without incurring a pause, but you'll have fewer images to wade through later, when you start processing your images.

When shooting in Drive mode, the camera does *not* display each image on the LCD screen. Instead, it waits until you're done with the burst and then displays the last image you shot.

Using the Self-Timer

Cameras have had self-timers for years, and we've probably all experienced the process of setting the timer on a camera teetering on the edge of a car hood and then scrambling into the shot before the camera fires. The Rebel T1i also includes this feature, allowing you to bring your hasty scrambles into the digital age.

You access the self-timer from the same screen that you used to set Drive mode. From the Drive mode screen, select the appropriate self-timer:

Self-timer/remote control Sets a 10-second self-timer.

Self-timer: 2 sec Sets a 2-second self-timer.

Self-timer: Continuous Sets a 10-second timer that fires a burst of shots. By default it shoots two, but you can increase this up to ten.

Once you've set a self-timer, frame your shot and half-press to focus; then press the shutter the rest of the way. Upon fully pressing the shutter, the camera will *not* take the picture. Instead, it will begin the timer. The Rebel T1i will beep, flash the self-timer lamp on the front of the camera, and display a countdown on the rear LCD screen. When the elapsed time has passed, it will shoot.

There are some things you should consider when using the self-timer. First of all, if you won't be looking through the viewfinder when the camera finally fires, you should use the eyepiece cover. Without your face in front of the viewfinder, light can enter the viewfinder and interfere with the camera's exposure calculations.

While the use of a 10-second timer is fairly obvious—with 10 seconds, you have plenty of time to get into position in front of the camera—the 2-second timer may seem less practical.

The two-second timer is not for self-portraits but for when you want to take a shot with minimal camera contact. Any time you handle the camera, you risk introducing shake that can cause your images to be soft, especially with long exposures. So, with a longer exposure, you'll get the sharpest image if you put the camera on a tripod and use the two-second self-timer.

That way, your hands will be completely off the camera while the shutter is open. This approach is good for low-light photos, astrophotography, or photos where you're using a small aperture for a deep depth of field and so must use a long shutter speed.

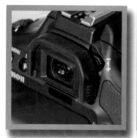 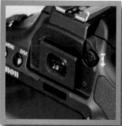 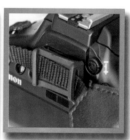

To use the eyepiece cover, first remove the eyepiece. Fit the eyepiece cover (attached to the strap) over the eyepiece mount. When you're done, replace the eyepiece.

If you want to shoot a solo self-portrait, bear in mind that focus can be tricky. If your goal is to stand in an open area, then you have a focus concern. When you half-press the shutter button, the camera will focus on whatever might be behind you, which could be a long way away. After you press the shutter button down all the way and run in front of the camera, the focus won't change—focus is locked with the half-press.

To compensate for this, tilt the camera down and focus on the spot on the ground where you plan to stand. In fact, you might want to mark the spot beforehand. Press the shutter halfway to lock focus, frame your shot, and then press the rest of the way to start the timer.

Now run to the marked spot, and you should get good focus. To improve your chances, select a small aperture to increase depth of field. That way, if the focus is off by a foot or two, your image will still most likely be in focus.

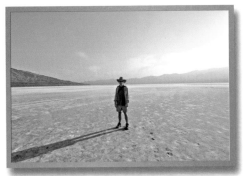

To shoot this self-portrait, I first focused on the spot on the ground where I would be standing. Then I switched the camera to manual focus and set the self-timer.

> **TIP:** Canceling a Self-Timer Shot
>
> Be sure to turn off the self-timer feature when you're done using it. If not, you may be frustrated later when you press the shutter button to take a shot, only to have the camera start beeping through a self-timer shot. If you get caught in a timer, just turn the camera off and on, and turn off the self-timer.

Choosing an Image Size and Format

The Rebel T1i's image sensor has roughly 15 million pixels on it. When shooting at maximum image size, it produces an image that's 4,752 pixels wide by 3,168 pixels high.

When shooting at maximum image size, you will be able to fit approximately 184 JPEG images on a 1 GB card. Although this is a lot of images (equivalent to about five rolls of 36-exposure film), there will be times when you need to save space, and so you might want to shoot images that don't take up as much storage. The T1i provides two options for controlling the size of the images it captures.

First, if you choose Quality from the first shooting menu, you'll be presented with a menu of size and format options. From this menu you can choose from three different image sizes: L, M, and S.

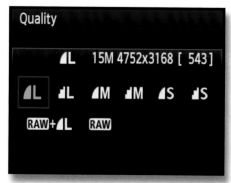

The T1i gives you a choice of three different sizes—L, M, and S—each with a choice of two quality levels.

Second, for each size, you can choose from two different levels of compression. You can also choose to shoot raw. Raw format offers a number of advantages over JPEG modes, and we'll cover it in detail in Chapter 11. The last options on the menu are a combination of raw and JPEG.

For now, it's best to stick with one of the JPEG options because this will allow a speedier workflow when you take your images into your computer.

You can set image size and quality options only when in Creative Auto, Program, Shutter Priority, Aperture Priority, Manual, or Auto Dep mode. The other modes do not give you a quality option.

To select a size and compression option, use the arrow keys to navigate to the option you want, and then press the Set button.

Why Choose a Different Size?

The size of the image affects two things: how large a print you can make and how much you can blow up a detail in an image.

To print a large image, you want to have as many pixels as possible. Although an image-editing program can do a good job of enlarging an image, there's no substitute for actual pixel data, and the T1i can capture a lot of pixels.

Usually, the only reason you would choose to shoot at a smaller size is if you're running out of space on your card or you know that you will only ever print an image at a certain size. For example, if you've never printed an image larger than 4 x 6, then you might argue that you won't ever need more than the smallest size, because that's more than enough data to print a 4 x 6.

FOOD FOR THOUGHT

WHAT IS JPEG COMPRESSION?

To help fit more images onto your storage card, your T1i offers two levels of *JPEG compression*. JPEG compression is a computational process that compresses the data that makes up your image so that it takes up less space. JPEG is a *lossy* compression scheme, meaning that it *does* degrade your image quality. However, the highest-quality JPEG setting on the T1i is *very* good, and you'll be hard-pressed to spot any image degradation.

Your eye is more sensitive to changes in brightness than it is to changes in color. So, a JPEG compressor first separates the color data in your image from the luminance data. It then takes all of the color data and divides it into a grid of 8 x 8–pixel chunks. The color in each of these 8 x 8 grids is then averaged so that the values of each pixel in the grid are the same. This averaging means that the color data can be very effectively compressed using an algorithm that is similar to the ZIP compressor you might use on a personal computer. Finally, the color and luminance data are put back together. Because the luminance data—the stuff your eye is most sensitive to—has been left untouched, you most likely won't notice any loss of quality. However, if an extreme amount of JPEG compression is applied, you may be able to see an 8 x 8–pixel blocky pattern in your image.

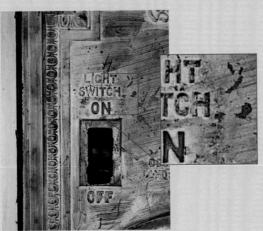

Too much JPEG compression can leave boxy artifacts in your image. So, be very careful about saving and resaving your images as JPEGs.

Shooting at a smaller size will afford you more space, but can you be absolutely *certain* that you'll never want to print at a larger size? Storage is cheap now, so it's not unreasonable to keep full-res images, and having access to the maximum size will ensure that you can repurpose your images for any use that you may come across.

So, if you're really in a crunch for space, you might want to increase the level of compression rather than reducing the image size. The T1i's low-quality compression is still very good, but if you're planning on enlarging your images, then the resulting JPEG artifacts might be visible once you've blown up your image.

However, if you're sure that the only thing you'll ever use your images for is low-res output—a web page, for example—then shooting with a smaller image size will allow you to fit far more images on your card.

Summing Up Program Mode

Program mode is probably the mode you'll use most often on the T1i, and the reasons why should be becoming clear to you. Like Full Auto mode, Program mode can automatically focus and choose an exposure, white balance, and ISO for you. But, unlike Full Auto and Creative Auto mode, you can take control of all of these parameters, and choose a shutter speed or aperture that's better suited to your creative goals and adjust ISO if you need more latitude for your exposure settings.

You can override the camera's autofocus mechanism to ensure that the subject you want is in focus and even tell the camera to track moving objects.

You can control white balance to a very refined degree, allowing you to shoot better, more accurate color in a broader range of lighting conditions, and you can maximize the use of your storage card by adjusting image size and compression settings.

As you've been playing with the camera, you've probably begun to get a better feel for the T1i's interface and for Canon's clever design. In Program mode, using just the Main dial and ISO button, you can easily select a shutter speed, aperture, and ISO, all without ever taking your eye from the viewfinder.

We'll be staying in Program mode for another couple of chapters, because there are still more features for you to learn about. However, with what we've covered here, you should now have a little more creative latitude, and so you should experiment with shutter speed, aperture, and ISO control, as well as the different focusing options.

Creative Auto Mode

Between Full Auto and Program mode on the Mode dial is Creative Auto mode, which looks like this: ⒶⒶ. As you would expect, Creative Auto tries to split the difference between Full Auto and Program modes. It still makes most critical decisions for you, just like Full Auto, but affords you a simple method for taking a little more creative control.

When you activate Creative Auto mode, the display on the back of the camera will change. Shutter speed and aperture will still be shown on the top of the display, along side flash mode and some other parameters.

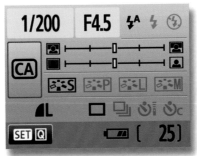

In Creative Auto mode, the status display on the back of the camera will change.

But notice the two sliders. The top one allows you to control how blurry or soft the background is, and the bottom slider lets you change how bright or dark the image is.

To change a parameter, press the Set button. The flash controls at the top of the screen should be highlighted, and "Auto Flash" will appear at the bottom of the screen. Press the down arrow button to move to the next parameter, the first slider control, which is labeled "Background: Blurred <-> Sharp".

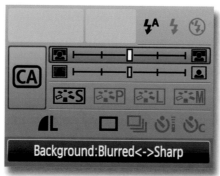

In Creative Auto mode, you can use the Background slider to control how blurred or sharp the background is.

With the Background slider selected, turn the Main dial to adjust the slider. Turn the dial to the left and the background will become blurrier. Turn it to the right, and the background will become sharper. What should be obvious to you now is that the slider is giving you control over aperture. The four different positions let you go from a wider aperture on the left to a smaller aperture on the right. The lower slider is the same as Exposure Compensation. It allows you to specify that you want the image under- or overexposed.

In the first draft of this book, I introduced Creative Auto mode immediately after Full Auto. Like Canon, I thought this might be a way to introduce some more advanced concepts without having to get too technical. After writing those sections, though, I realized that this is really not the best way to learn these essential exposure concepts. Although Creative Auto definitely provides a simple interface, the fact is that depth of field is not controlled only by aperture. As you learned in Chapter 5, focal length and camera position have a huge impact on depth of field. So, it would be very easy to move the slider to "blurrier" in Creative Auto mode and still have deep depth of field.

Ultimately, I decided that if you're going to the trouble of reading this book, you're serious about wanting to learn how exposure really works. As such, I'm going to recommend that you don't bother with Creative Auto mode. It doesn't provide any capability that you can't get in Program mode (or the other modes we'll be looking at later), and it doesn't offer as much flexibility as what you'll get from the T1i's more sophisticated shooting modes.

CHAPTER 7

Advanced Exposure

LEARNING MORE ABOUT THE T1i LIGHT METER
AND EXPOSURE CONTROLS

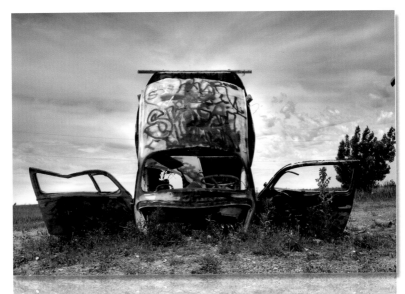

There's more to exposure than what we've seen so far. In addition to motion and depth of field control, exposure control also lets you control tonality in your image. Your exposure control is very dependent on your light meter, though, so to really understand exposure, you have to learn about some of the workings of the T1i's light meter. In this chapter, we'll go deeper into metering and exposure and explore some of the T1i's image-processing options.

The Light Meter Revisited

In Chapter 1, we looked at the T1i's light meter, which analyzes the light in your scene to determine an exposure that will yield an image that's neither too light nor too dark. The light meter is activated every time you half-press the shutter button, and while the automatic metering in the T1i is very good, it *can* be confused and won't always calculate the best exposure for every scene. For example, consider this image:

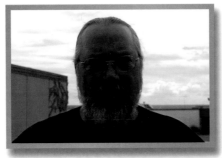

Bad backlighting is leaving the subject's face in shadow.

We've looked at a bad backlighting problem before. Because of the bright background, the camera is biasing its metering toward the brighter portion of the image, and the resulting exposure leaves the person underexposed. But you'll find that other problems can also crop up from mismetering, most notably an inability to render black tones as real black. We'll look at both of these problems and see how they can be easily addressed using a few simple tricks and controls. Let's start with the backlighting problem.

Metering Modes

Because different lighting situations present different problems, the Rebel T1i provides four different light meters. You may not switch amongst these very often, but when faced with a troubling exposure, these extra meters can be very handy.

⊡ Evaluative metering

By default, the T1i uses an *evaluative meter* system for its light metering. The T1i's evaluative meter divides your scene into a grid of 35 zones. The brightness of each zone is measured, as well as the contrast between zones, the size of your subject, the brightness of your subject, the contrast between your subject and the other zones in the grid, and more. (It determines what is "your subject" by looking at which focus points were selected when the camera autofocused.) It then analyzes all of this data and tries to come up with exposure settings that will properly expose your subject, without blowing out the highlights in the image and while preserving as much shadow detail as possible.

For most scenes, evaluative metering works very well, and it's the most consistently accurate meter on the camera. This is why Full Auto mode uses evaluative metering. If you just want to point the camera and shoot, evaluative metering stands the best chance of giving a good result. However, evaluative metering can be confused, as shown in the previous example. So, while evaluative metering will probably work well for most shots, the T1i provides a few other metering modes that you can employ in tricky situations.

The metering mode you have currently selected is shown on the status display on the back of the camera.

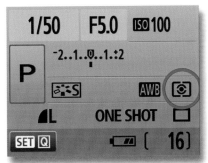

The metering mode is shown on the status display on the back of the T1i.

⊡ Partial metering

If you're shooting a scene that has a background that is significantly brighter than the foreground, then the evaluative meter could get confused, resulting in your foreground being overexposed. *Partial metering* analyzes only a small area in the center of the image and ignores the metering zones in the rest of the frame.

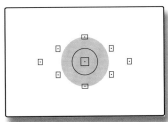

Partial metering uses the gray zones to determine exposure.

In the description of partial metering of the Rebel T1i manual, Canon says, "The gray area in the figure is where the metering is weighted to obtain the standard exposure." While this implies that other zones in the image are considered, in practice you'll find that areas outside the partial metering circle have no bearing on the final metering. (If you're curious, this circle covers about 9% of your scene.)

Partial metering provides an easy fix for the backlighting problem we showed earlier. Because the partial metering circle meters only our subject, the bright backlight is ignored, and we get a good exposure for our model. To change to Partial metering:

1. Select "Metering mode" from the second Shooting menu.

2. Use the left and right arrow keys to select the metering mode that you want.

3. Press the Set button to change modes.

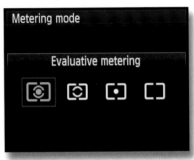

The T1i's four metering modes, shown on the Metering mode menu.

Note that the Metering mode menu displays the name of each mode as you select it, so you don't have to memorize the somewhat arcane metering icons.

Partial metering is a good solution to this problem. The face is better exposed, and although the background is blown out, there's really no way around that without using the flash.

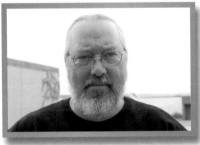

With partial metering, our subject's face is better exposed.

However, with a flash, the camera could meter for the background, which would underexpose the face. But then the flash would fire, which would add fill light that would brighten the face. (You'll learn more about this later.) For times when flash is not appropriate or your subject is too far away, switching to a better metering system can be your only option.

⊡ Spot metering

The spot meter is just like partial metering, but it meters a very narrow area in the center of the frame. When you want to ensure that a very specific area is metered properly, use spot metering. Spot metering is also effective for backlit situations or for ensuring that detail in a specific location in your scene is metered properly and, therefore, visible. (And, for those of you who have been keeping track, the T1i's spot meter measures a circle that's about 4% of your scene.)

⊡ Center-weight average metering

Center-weight average is a lot like partial metering. But, where partial pays strict attention to the center circle of zones, center-weight average analyzes the whole scene, just like evaluative, but gives more weight to the center. In the case of this image, it yields about the same results as partial. In a less extreme backlit situation, it might very well yield the best results.

Metering and Auto ISO

If you set the T1i's ISO setting to Auto, then the camera will adjust the ISO as well as the shutter speed and aperture when it meters. Because there's little difference in noise from ISO 100 to 400, Auto ISO helps ensure that you have a shutter speed that's suited to handholding and an aperture that will yield good focus.

WARNING: Don't Use Evaluative Metering When Focusing and Reframing

Earlier, you saw the technique of using a single, centered focus spot to focus on an object and then reframing your scene. When using this technique, you might find that you get better results if you *don't* use evaluative metering. If you're using evaluative metering, then areas of the frame that won't be in your shot will be factored into the camera's final metering. Most of the time, this won't matter, but in a scene with high dynamic range—a dark foreground and bright sky, for example—it could get you into trouble. Instead, if you want to use evaluative metering, after focusing, set your lens to Manual focus to lock focus, and then frame your shot as desired and meter.

For most of your shots, Evaluative metering will be your meter of choice. The only time you will switch to a different meter is if evaluative metering is yielding bad results—one part of your image is over- or underexposed, for example. If it's not immediately obvious which meter you should switch to, don't worry, that's normal. It's absolutely fine to experiment with different metering options. After each try, consult the histogram to determine how your exposure changed. Over time, you'll get a better idea of which meters are good for which types of problems.

Exposure Lock

So far, you've been doing all of your metering using Evaluative (⊡) metering. You've seen how, when you press the shutter button down halfway, the camera takes a meter reading and then locks that metering. If you reframe your shot, the camera will still use the metering that got locked in when you half-pressed the shutter buton.

In Partial, Spot, and Centerweight metering, the camera will still meter when you half-press the shutter button, but if you reframe your shot, the T1i will *re-meter* as you move the camera around.

For example, say you're facing a bad backlight situation, like in the previous example. You could use the spot meter to fix the problem, but suppose you want to frame your subject on the edge of the frame. If you put the spot meter on your subject and half-press the shutter, the camera will meter. But when you reframe to place the subject on the edge of the frame, the camera will calculate a new metering based on the new center of the frame.

To fix this problem, you need to use the Auto Exposure Lock button, located on the back of the camera. After you meter, press the Auto Exposure Lock button, and the T1i will keep its exposure locked, no matter how you reframe.

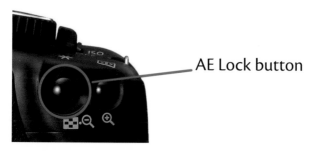

AE Lock button

Use AE Lock so that your exposure doesn't change when reframing while using Spot, Centerweight, or Partial metering.

When you press the AE Lock button, an asterisk will appear in the viewfinder status display to indicate that your exposure is now locked.

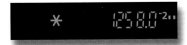

The asterisk indicates that the exposure is now locked.

As you'll see later, there are some ways to customize the behavior of the shutter and AE Lock buttons so that they better-suit your style of shooting.

> **TIP:** Exposure Lock Timeout
>
> When you meter with the T1i, if you release the shutter button, the camera will remember that metering for about four seconds. Even if you've locked exposure, the reading will eventually time out, and the viewfinder status will go dark. So, once you've locked exposure, it's a good idea to keep the button half-pressed, or press the button halfway down every second or so to preserve the locked exposure.

What Your Light Meter Actually Meters

Has this ever happened to you? It's a nice snowy day, you take a picture, and when you look at the image, the snow seems much dingier than you remember. Surprisingly, this is not the camera doing something wrong. It's actually metering exactly the way it was designed. To understand what it's up to and how to fix it, you need to understand a little more about how a light meter works.

Your light meter doesn't know anything about color; it measures only luminance, or brightness. Perhaps the strangest thing about your light meter is that it always assumes that everything you're pointing it at is 18% gray. That is, it's assuming that everything you're pointing it at is reflecting 18% of the light that's striking it. What's even *stranger*, though, is that most of the time what you're pointing at *is* reflecting 18% of the light that hits it.

Consider these alternating black and white bars:

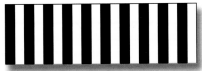

Although there are an equal number of black and white bars here, this image reflects only 18% of the light that strikes it.

There are an equal number of these bars, 10 each. Because half are black and half are white, you might assume that this pattern is reflecting 50 percent of the light that's striking it—half reflected by the white and half absorbed by the black. But, because of the physics of light, this pattern is actually reflecting only about 18%.

In fact, it turns out that the majority of the scenes in the world reflect 18% of the light that strikes them. Therefore, if your camera *assumes* that it's pointed at a scene that is reflecting 18% of the light that strikes it (photographers refer to this as a scene that is *18% gray*) and it calculates a metering that is correct for 18% gray, then the odds are that its calculated metering will be correct for your scene.

Most of the time this works. But, sometimes 18% gray assumption is incorrect. The field of white snow is a great example. Since the camera is assuming that it's pointed at something that's 18% gray, it calculates an exposure that will represent the field of snow as gray rather than white. Fortunately, the T1i's meter is so sophisticated that it will usually recognize a strong white object as white and calculate an appropriate exposure.

Nevertheless, when subjects are bright white, you want to carefully review your images to make sure the white doesn't appear gray. If it does, then you'll need to *overexpose* your shot to render white objects as true white. We'll look at how to do this in just a bit.

> **TIP:** Very Good Metering
>
> It's important to understand the overexposure concept I just discussed, in case you ever end up with images with dingy whites. However, thanks to the excellent metering on the T1i, you'll probably rarely encounter this problem. Keep an eye on your whites until you get some more experience with how the camera meters and renders bright tones. If whites end up dingy, you'll need to overexpose.

Exposing So That Black Looks Black

Black objects are more likely to trip up the T1i's meter than are white objects. Again, if you point the camera at a black object, it will assume that the object is actually 18% gray and so will concoct exposure settings that will properly render that object as gray. Consequently, black objects can sometimes appear ashen. For instance, in this shot of a black car, the blacks are not as black as they could be, because the meter assumed that the car was actually gray and so chose exposure settings that yielded an image that looked more gray than black.

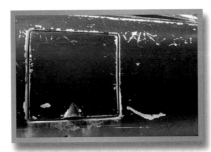

The light meter assumes that it's pointed at something that's 18% gray, so it calculates an exposure that renders the black tone of this car a little grayish.

By *underexposing* we can accurately represent the black tones in the image as black. As I mentioned earlier, the T1i's meter is sophisticated enough that it often figures out these problems on its own. However, it's important that you don't become too dependent on the camera's ability to get it right. Learn to recognize when a scene might need to be over- or underexposed. If you're not sure, then review the image and reshoot if you need to.

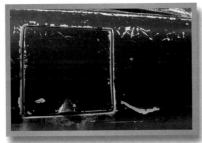

With one stop of underexposure, the black car is rendered a true black.

Using Exposure Compensation to Over- or Underexpose

Now that you've seen some of the occasions when you might want to over- or underexpose, we'll look at one of the ways that you can tell the camera to make such an exposure adjustment. There are many ways of controlling exposure on the T1i, but the easiest method is to use exposure compensation.

These days, almost all cameras have an Exposure Compensation control, which simply lets you make a *relative* exposure change. That is, you can tell the camera, "I don't care how you metered the scene; I just want you to go up from there by one stop."

Try using exposure compensation now:

1. Frame a shot.

2. Press the shutter button down halfway to meter your scene (the camera will also autofocus and take a white balance reading).

3. After the camera beeps, the viewfinder and status LCD will show you the shutter speed and aperture settings that it has calculated.

4. Take the shot.

5. Now frame the same shot, and again press the shutter button halfway down to meter the scene.

6. Using your thumb, press the Exposure Compensation button on the back of the camera.

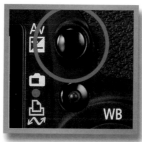

Dial in a specific amount of over- or underexposure.

7. Rotate the Main dial until the Exposure Compensation display in the viewfinder indicates a one-stop overexposure. (If you haven't changed the camera's defaults, then this will be three clicks on the dial.)

8. Take the shot.

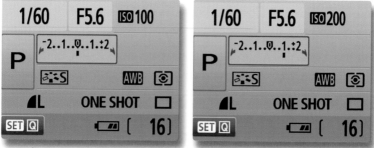

The Exposure Compensation display highlights. Turn the Main dial to increase (brighten) or decrease (darken) the setting.

FOOD FOR THOUGHT

WHAT'S WRONG WITH OVER- OR UNDEREXPOSING?

Of course, once you start tinkering with the camera's carefully concocted exposure settings, you run the risk of over- or underexposing your scene to the point where bright things blow out to complete white or where dark shadows fall to complete black. When an area in your image goes to all white or all black, it becomes an area with no detail. Detail in a photo is constructed from contrasting tones, and when part of an image is one color, it looks like a flat surface.

In the case of shadows, this isn't so bad. A black shadow simply looks like an area that's too dark to see. Unless there's some detail in the shadowy area that you really want to keep visible, letting a shadow darken is not too terrible. Overexposed highlights, though, are almost always distracting. An area of complete white acts like a magnet for the viewer's eye and can sometimes upstage your subject.

However, at times it's worth overexposing a highlight to get better tonality on your subject. Also, a little bit of overexposed bright spots—small bits of chrome on a car, for example—won't necessarily be noticeable. While there are no hard and fast rules about how much over- or underexposure is too much (and many times, overexposing an image can be an effective stylistic choice), it's important to understand the risk and make an intelligent decision.

Now go into playback mode and look at the two images. The second one should be much brighter than the first one. This is the image that was *over*exposed. Note that you didn't tell the camera a specific shutter speed or aperture. Instead, you simply told it to go up one stop from whatever it thought was the correct exposure. The T1i has an exposure compensation range of -2 stops to +2 stops. By default, the control moves in 1/3-stop increments.

When you use exposure compensation, you don't actually know exactly *how* the camera will achieve its over- or underexposure, but the camera does follow a predictable method. It will always try to achieve its change in a way that doesn't involve a shutter speed that might be too slow for handheld use.

Remember, a slower shutter speed means that the shutter is open longer, which means that your images are more susceptible to the blurring and softening caused by shakiness in your hand. If you have the ISO set to Auto, the T1i will often effect the change by altering the ISO setting, but it will never do this to the point of introducing noise into your image. Because there's no visible difference between ISO 100 and 400, the T1i has two stops of ISO latitude to play with, meaning it will often keep the shutter speed and aperture the same as you change exposure compensation.

The black car example that you saw earlier is a prime example of using exposure compensation. I knew that the black probably wouldn't render properly, so I set exposure compensation to underexpose by one stop to get an image that had a more accurate black tone.

Exposure Compensation and Program Shift

In Chapter 6 you learned about Program Shift, which lets you automatically switch between reciprocal exposure settings after the camera has metered. Program Shift makes it easy to quickly switch to a different shutter speed or aperture while maintaining a good exposure. However, because Program Shift always changes to a reciprocal exposure, it never gives you an over- or underexposure, but you can dial in an exposure compensation for that, and you can easily use these two features in concert.

For example, you might meter and then use Program Shift to switch to a faster shutter speed, but maybe you're shooting something white and want a little bit of overexposure. If you dial in +1/3 of a stop, you'll still get both your faster shutter speed *and* overexposure. In many cases, these two controls will provide all the manual power you need, and you can drive them both while looking through the viewfinder thanks to the T1i's powerful interface.

Controlling Color Tone with Exposure Compensation

It should make sense that a slight underexposure will make black tones appear more black than gray (and vice versa for white tones). You've seen already that an underexposed image is darker than a regular exposure, so a bit of underexposure can be just what you need to restore a dark object to its true tone.

Like black and white, color also has a tone. Some reds are darker than others, for example. Consequently, it's possible to adjust the saturation of a color in your image by over- or underexposing. For example, consider this image, which I shot using the camera's recommended metering and with a 1/3-stop underexposure.

Notice that the colors are a little bit more saturated and generally richer. This is because they have a slightly darker tone that needs to be underexposed to appear correct.

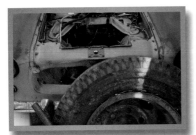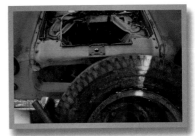

After I dialed in a 1/3-stop underexposure, the camera rendered richer colors.

In general, when shooting in bright daylight, you might find that leaving your exposure compensation set to -1/3 gives you better saturation and deeper color. However, be aware that you'll run the risk of losing detail in the very darkest parts of your image, and lighter tones may render a little gray.

REMINDER: Slide Shooting Techniques at Work in the Digital World

If you have ever shot slide film, this last recommendation might sound familiar. In general, when shooting in JPEG mode on the T1i, you should keep all of your slide film exposure habits.

Using the Histogram

One of the great things about digital photography is that you can see your images onscreen right away. In fact, we're now well into a generation of kids who've never known cameras to work any other way and for whom the idea of waiting to see an image makes about as much sense as having a guy deliver blocks of ice to the house.

And while the image on the T1i's LCD *does* provide a great way to check your composition, it offers very little help when it comes to assessing your exposure choices. It's very important to understand that the color and contrast shown on the back of the T1i screen is not very accurate. This is not due to any ineptitude on Canon's part. Just the opposite, actually. The T1i screen needs to be visible in many different situations, including bright sunlight. To make this possible, the T1i intentionally pumps up the brightness and saturation on the images that are shown on the camera's screen. This makes the image easier to see in bright light, but it also means you won't have an accurate view of color and contrast.

Fortunately, the camera includes an additional feature that provides a tremendous amount of information about exposure and that will repeatedly save you from returning home with poorly exposed shots.

You have already caught a glimpse of the *histogram* when we explored the T1i's different display modes. Go into playback mode on your camera, and press the DISP button until you see a display that looks like this:

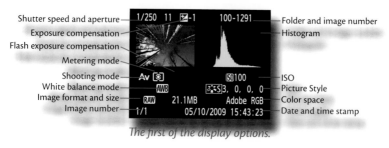

The first of the display options.

This is one of two screens designed to help you better assess the exposure of an image. Scattered around the screen is a lot of status information, including shutter speed, aperture, and ISO. The camera also shows the date and time the image was shot, as well as your balance setting, shooting mode, metering mode, picture style, image format, size of the final image, and color space of the image, but it's the shutter speed, aperture, ISO, and histogram display that are going to ease your exposure headaches in the field.

The histogram is that graph-looking thing in the upper-right corner. Although it may look complex and scientific, it's actually quite simple.

A histogram is nothing more than a bar chart that shows the distribution of tones in your image, with black on the left and white on the right. If there's a lot of black in your image, then there will be a lot of bars on the left side of the image. If there's a lot of white, then there will be a lot of bars on the right side of the image. If there's a broad range of tones, then there will be data across the histogram.

The height of each bar in the histogram simply tells you how *much* of a particular tone there is. So, in the image shown earlier you can see that the image has a good range of tones from black to white, with most of the tones in the shadow and highlight areas and a smattering of tones spread across the middle.

This next part is very important: *the shape of the histogram is irrelevant!* You are not trying to get a particular shape; the histogram is simply showing you what's in your image, and two masterfully exposed images might have very different histograms, because they might contain very different subject matter.

What the histogram is good for is showing you when you've over- or underexposed and how much contrast you've captured.

Recognizing Over- and Underexposure in the Histogram

When an image is overexposed, there will be a big spike on the right side of the histogram, as in this image:

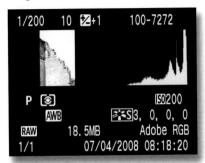

Because this image is overexposed, the histogram shows a spike on the right side.

Here, we've overexposed the shot, and the highlights in the image have gone to complete white. That overexposure appears in the histogram as a big spike on the right side. In addition, the T1i will flash overexposed pixels in the image thumbnail, making it easy to tell which parts of the image are overexposed.

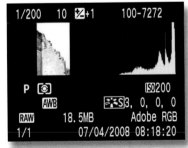 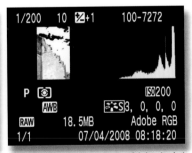

The T1i will flash overexposed pixels in black, making it easy to see which pixels in the image have blown out to complete white.

Underexposure shows in the histogram in just the opposite way, with a big spike on the left side of the image. Underexposed pixels do *not* flash in the thumbnail display.

With this simple tool you can immediately determine whether you need to dial in an exposure compensation or change your exposure strategy. If you see a big spike on the right side, consider underexposing.

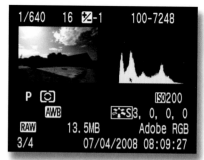

1/640   16 ☒-1   100-7248

P ⊙
AWB
RAW   13.5MB   Adobe RGB
3/4   07/04/2008 08:09:27
ISO200
✷✷S3, 0, 0, 0

This image is underexposed, so its histogram shows a spike on the left side.

DEFINITION: Clipped, Blown, and Other Terms

You'll hear photographers use several different terms to refer to a highlight that has been so overexposed that it results in a spike on the right side of the histogram. *Clipped* and *blown out* are the most common.

Recognizing Contrast in the Histogram

An image with more contrast has a broader range from the darkest tone to the lightest tone. As such, it will have a histogram with data that covers a broader range.

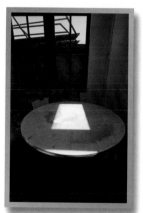
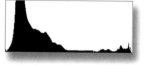

This image has a lot of contrast, with a wide tonal range from black to white.

Some images will have more contrast simply because your subject is more contrasty. A penguin, for example, is more contrasty than an emu that's a single shade of brown.

At other times, though, your image will have low contrast because of your exposure choice. For example, I shot this image with the camera's suggested metering and then looked at the histogram. (For the sake of clarity, I'm showing a histogram from Photoshop, but you'll see the same information on the T1i histogram.)

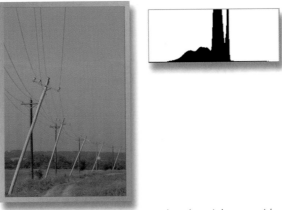

This low-contrast image sports a histogram that doesn't have a wide spread of data. There's little distance from the darkest to the lightest tones.

It appeared to me that the image should have a little more contrast, so I tried overexposing by one stop and shot again, and I got this histogram:

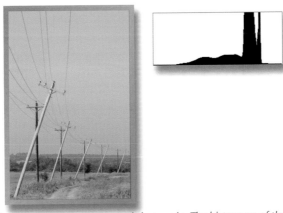

I dialed in a 1-stop overexposure and shot again. The histogram of the resulting image shows more contrast. This greater amount of data means I'll have more editing latitude when I start making adjustments and corrections.

Again, there are no right or wrong histogram shapes. Nor are there right or wrong distributions across the histogram. However, the histogram can be a very useful tool for spotting over- or underexposure, as well as contrast range. An image with more contrast has more tones across the histogram that I can brighten or darken in my editing program, which means I'll have more latitude to make changes later.

The Three-Channel Histogram

If you press the DISP button one more time after seeing the first histogram, you'll get to the second histogram page.

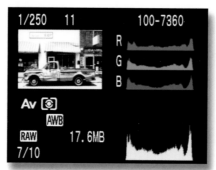

The T1i's three-channel histogram display shows a separate histogram for the red, green, and blue information in your image.

This page shows the same histogram you saw before, along with an additional three-channel histogram. In Chapter 5 you learned that an image is made up of three separate channels of color information: one red, one green, and one blue. The three-channel histogram lets you see a separate histogram for each of these channels. This can sometimes be useful for spotting white balance troubles that could otherwise be difficult to see on the LCD screen. In an image with good white balance, all three channels are usually fairly "registered." That is, similar.

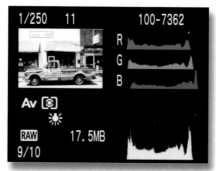

The same image as before, this time shot with a tungsten white balance. Notice that the separate channels are now shifted away from each other.

Obviously, if you're shooting a still life of separate red, green, and blue Christmas ornaments, then the histograms for each channel will be very different. But in a typical image, the highlights in a three-channel histogram should fall mostly in the same place. If they don't, you'll want to consider switching to a white balance preset, switching to a custom white balance, or using the white balance shift to correct the image.

Using Priority Modes to Control Exposure

The Exposure Compensation and Program Shift controls are both great ways to control exposure, but there will be times when you'll want more direct control. Shutter and Aperture Priority let you select specific shutter speeds or apertures and leave the camera on those settings. So, for example, if you're shooting land-scapes and know that you're going to want a deep depth of field all day long, you can set the camera on Aperture Priority, dial in f/11, and be assured that every shot will be taken with that aperture. Or, if you're shooting a sporting event and know that you want lots of motion-stopping power, you can select Shutter Priority and set the shutter speed to something quick, like 1/1000th of a second.

Aperture Priority

To use Aperture Priority, set the T1i's Mode dial to Av. In Aperture Priority mode, you select the aperture you want, and the camera automatically chooses an appropriate shutter speed, based on its metering. In Aperture Priority mode, the rear LCD will display the current aperture setting in a gray box, with arrows on both sides to indicate that you can change this parameter. Turn the Main dial to change the aperture. When you half-press the shutter to meter, the camera will display the shutter speed that it has chosen.

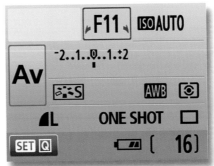

In Aperture Priority mode, the current aperture is displayed in a box on the rear LCD screen.

Different lenses have different aperture ranges, and with a zoom lens, the wide end of the aperture range is often variable. For example, on the 18–55mm lens that Canon bundles with the T1i, the wide end of the aperture range varies from 3.5 to 5.6. That is, when you're zoomed out all the way to 18mm, the lens has a maximum aperture of 3.5. When you zoom in all the way to 55, the maximum aperture is a slightly smaller 5.6 aperture.

The maximum aperture varies in between these extremes. So, if you find that you sometimes can select a wider aperture than at other times, this is because you're probably shooting at different focal lengths.

Depth of Field Preview

To ensure a viewfinder that's as bright as possible, the T1i keeps its aperture open as wide as possible all the time. Even if you or the camera have chosen a very small aperture, the aperture stays open all the way until you actually take the picture. Then the aperture closes down to the specified setting, and the sensor is exposed.

In addition to letting as much light into the viewfinder as possible, the fact that the aperture is always wide open means you're possibly seeing less depth of field in the viewfinder than what your final picture will actually have. Trying to shoot with a very deep depth of field can be tricky because, as we learned earlier, depth of field is centered around the point of focus, and there's more depth of field behind that point than in front.

If you want to see what the depth of field in your scene will actually look like, you can use the Depth of Field Preview button.

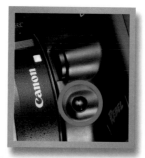

The Depth of Field Preview button lets you see the actual depth of field of your scene in the T1i viewfinder.

Unfortunately, as the viewfinder gets darker, it can be harder to see fine focus details. However, if you let your eyes adjust to the darker scene, you'll probably be able to get a good idea of what is in focus and what isn't. Depth of field preview will work in any mode on the T1i and is a great way to determine whether you've chosen an aperture and focus point that yield the depth of field you want.

Note that, depending on your lighting situation, you can't always pick any aperture that you want. In a low-light situation, if you pick a very small aperture, the T1i may not have a shutter speed that's fast enough to yield a good exposure. In these circumstances, the camera will flash the shutter speed readout to indicate that your image will be underexposed. You'll need to choose a wider aperture or increase the ISO until the camera indicates that it can get a good exposure.

> **WARNING:** Pay Attention to Shutter Speed
>
> Just because you now have complete control of aperture, and just because the camera is choosing a shutter speed for you, that doesn't mean you don't have to think about shutter speed at all. You still need to pay attention to the handheld shutter speed rule. If you pick an aperture that yields a shutter speed that's too slow for handholding or motion stopping, you may end up with an annoyingly blurry image. The T1i will display its selected shutter speed any time you meter.

Shutter Priority

Select Shutter Priority mode by turning the Mode dial to Tv (and no, this isn't the most intuitive abbreviation—think "Time Value"). In Shutter Priority mode, you select the shutter speed you want, and the T1i will automatically choose an appropriate aperture.

In Shutter Priority mode, the T1i will display the shutter speed in a box on the LCD screen, with arrows to indicate you can change it. Turn the Main dial to select the speed you want.

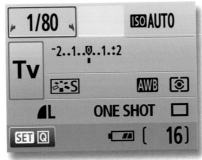

The T1i picks an appropriate aperture after it meters.

As you may have already discovered, you can choose slower and slower shutter speeds, until eventually shutter speed is measured in whole seconds.

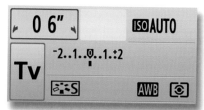

The T1i offers shutter speeds up to 30 seconds long (longer if you use Bulb mode). Here it's indicating a six-second exposure. You might use such a shutter speed to take shots at night, by moonlight.

FOOD FOR THOUGHT

KNOWING YOUR APERTURE SWEET SPOT

Many people assume if they want a shallow depth of field, they should just choose the widest aperture (smallest number) that they can, and if they want a deep depth of field, they should choose the smallest aperture (largest number).

Obviously, these aperture extremes can yield shutter speeds that may not be suitable, but there's another price to pay for this simplified approach to depth of field. Every lens has an aperture "sweet spot." If you go outside of this sweet spot, the lens will yield slightly softer images.

On the 18–55mm lens that ships with the T1i, if you go much past f11, you'll start to see a drop-off in sharpness. Depending on the size you choose to print at, this loss of sharpness may not matter, but by the time you get to f16 or f22 and beyond, you'll probably start to see a drop in sharpness at any size.Do some tests with your camera to determine where the aperture sweet spot is, and keep these apertures in mind when shooting.

TIP: Priority Modes and Exposure Compensation

You can use Exposure Compensation with either shutter or aperture priority mode. The camera will never alter the parameter you've selected, but will instead change the other exposure parameter, as well as ISO, to achieve the compensation you want. If it can't get a proper exposure, it will flash the non-priority value to indicate that your shot will be misexposed.

Manual Mode

For the ultimate in control, you'll want to use Manual mode, which lets you adjust both aperture and shutter speed. To activate Manual mode, move the Mode dial to M. The LCD screen will show both the shutter speed and aperture, with a box around the shutter speed.

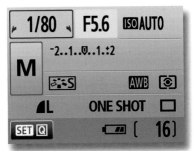

In Manual mode, you can change both shutter speed and aperture. The menu highlights which parameter is currently editable. Here, we're changing shutter speed.

You can change shutter speed by turning the Main dial. If you want to change aperture, press and hold the Exposure Compensation button (⊞) while turning the Main dial.

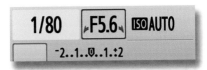

Still in Manual mode, we're now altering aperture.

If the exposure settings you choose are over- or underexposed, the camera will indicate the misexposure by flashing a bar under the Exposure Compensation meter. So, if you're one stop underexposed, for example, it will flash a bar under the -1 stop notch on the Exposure Compensation readout. If you're two or more stops over- or underexposed, it will flash beneath +2 or -2, respectively.

Manual mode can be handy for times when you want to ensure very specific results. Perhaps you're shooting a still life and so want a deep depth of field. You might switch to Aperture Priority to select a smaller aperture. But say it's dim lighting and the camera doesn't yield a shutter speed that's appropriate for handheld shooting. You can switch to Manual mode and dial in both the shutter speed and aperture you want. The results might be underexposed, but you might be able to brighten the image in your image editor later.

FOOD FOR THOUGHT

A-DEP MODE FOR MAXIMUM DoF

If you're shooting a landscape and want to ensure as much depth of field as possible, you have to choose settings that will yield a deep depth of field *and* focus at a point that will ensure that your depth of field covers the area you want.

A-DEP is a special mode that will automatically try to calculate settings that will yield the maximum depth of field for your scene. To use it, switch the Mode dial to A-DEP, then frame your shot as you normally do, and press the shutter release halfway down. When you activate A-DEP, the T1i automatically switches back to autofocus point selection and activates all autofocus points. It will use its autofocus mechanism to determine the nearest and farthest points in your scene and then choose a focus point and exposure settings that will render the entire range in focus.

For A-DEP to work, you want the upper focus point to be on the farthest point in your scene and the lowest point to be on the nearest. You might need to use the focus and reframe technique that we saw earlier to get the points positioned properly. For landscape shooters, A-DEP can be an easy way to ensure that large vistas are in sharp focus.

Exposure Bracketing

Now that I've thrown all this exposure theory at you and loaded up your head with all these things to remember, it's time to learn the easy solution to the whole exposure thing: rather than worry about trying to nail the exposure with one shot, just shoot the same shot a few times with different exposure settings. This process is called *bracketing*.

Bracketing is very simple. You shoot one shot at the camera's recommended metering, then another shot underexposed, and another shot overexposed. How much to over- or underexpose depends on how tricky the scene is and how cautious you are.

For example, if you're in a situation where you're not sure of the exposure—maybe there's a big mix of bright and dark tones—then you might want to bracket your shots. Or, if you're shooting a very bright or very dark object and aren't sure how to expose to properly render the tones, then bracketing can be the answer.

With exposure compensation, it's very easy to bracket. Shoot a shot, set exposure compensation down, shoot another, and then dial it up and shoot a third.

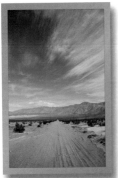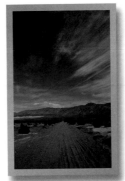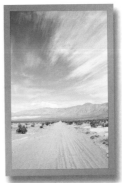

Here's a bracketed set of the same scene. The left-most image was shot as the camera metered it, the second image is underexposed by one stop, and the third image is overexposed by one stop.

Bracketing does *not* make you a wimpy photographer! It does *not* mean you don't know what you're doing or that you're not serious. Some of the best photographers in history bracketed very heavily.

Obviously, bracketing is not viable when you're shooting action shots or any sort of fleeting moment. But for landscapes, still lifes, portraits, and other static scenes, it can mean the difference between a usable shot and one with exposure troubles.

Auto Bracketing

The T1i includes an auto bracketing feature that will perform an automatic exposure change for you, making it simple to take a bracketed set of shots.

1. To activate auto bracketing, choose Expo.Comp./AEB from the second shooting menu "Expo Comp" stands for "Exposure Compensation," which you've already learned about. "AEB" stands for "Auto Exposure Bracketing." When you select Expo.Comp/AEB, you'll be taken to a new screen that lets you specify both a bracketing amount and an exposure compensation amount.

2. Use the Main dial to define a bracket amount. As you can see, the bracketing scale is divided into stops, with 1/3rd-stop increments. In the figure below, you can see a bracket that defines three steps, each one stop apart. (Note that auto brackets on the Rebel are always three steps.)

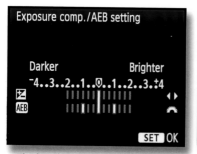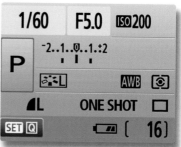

The bracket you've selected will be shown on the rear LCD as well as in the viewfinder status display.

3. When you've selected the bracket that you want, press Set. Note that a half-press of the shutter button will not confirm your selection; you must press Set.

4. Now take a picture. That shot will be exposed as the meter recommends, and the camera will automatically be adjusted to underexpose by the amount indicated in the AEB setting.

5. Notice after you take the first shot, the bracketing indicator on the T1i status displays begins flashing. This indicates that you're currently in the middle of a bracketed set. When these indicators are flashing, you know that your next shot will either be over- or underexposed, depending on where you are in the bracket.

6. Take another picture. That shot will use your underexposed setting, and the camera will automatically be adjusted to overexpose by the AEB amount.

7. Shoot a third and final shot. This will end your bracketed set.

Your next shot will be fired as metered, because now you're into a new bracketed set. In this way, you can easily fire off three shots and have a fully bracketed set.

Deactivating auto bracketing

To deactivate auto bracketing, just go back to the AEB page and press the left arrow button until the bracket is gone. If you decide in the middle of a bracketed set that you *don't* want auto bracketing, just turn it off in the AEB menu.

Auto bracketing and Drive mode

An even easier way to shoot a bracketed set is to turn on AEB and then activate Drive mode. Now press and hold the shutter button until it takes three shots. Because AEB was activated, those three shots will be bracketed.

Auto bracketing and exposure compensation

When you define a bracket using the auto bracketing feature, you can also use the left and right buttons to shift the entire bracket left and right. This lets you specify that the entire bracket should be over- or under-exposed. After you've defined the bracket, and are shooting, you can still use exposure compensation. When you dial in an exposure compensation, the entire bracket will be shifted up or down.

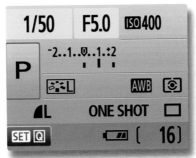

With auto bracketing enabled, using exposure compensation will shift the entire bracket up or down.

Note that when bracketing is turned on, the exposure compensation range expands to -4 to +4. However, the largest bracket you can define is still -2 to +2 stops. The expanded exposure range gives you more room to place that four-stop bracket range.

> **T I P :** Auto Bracketing and Power
>
> If you turn the T1i off, the auto bracketing setting will be canceled. This is one of the few T1i settings that doesn't persist when the power is cycled, and it gives you a speedy way to deactivate auto bracketing.

Peripheral Illumination Correction

Sometimes a lens will yield an image with dark corners, a phenomenon most commonly referred to as *vignetting*. This is most prevalent in wide-angle lenses (or zoom lenses that are being used at their widest angle). For some reason, Canon has chosen to call this *a drop in peripheral illumination*, and so they have built a *peripheral illumination correction* feature into the Rebel T1i. Whatever you choose to call the problem, the ability to correct it in-camera is very handy.

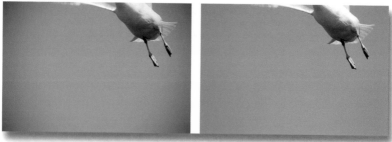

The image on the left suffers from vignetting, what Canon calls a "peripheral illumination" problem. Fortunately, the T1i can correct this trouble in-camera.

To enable peripheral illumination correction:

1. In the first shooting menu, choose "Peripheral illmin. correct". The T1i will show you a status display that includes the name of the attached lens. The T1i includes a database of the peripheral illumination characteristics of roughly 25 lenses. If the camera recognizes your lens, it will indicate that correction data is available.

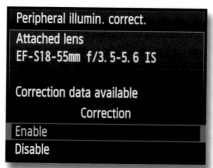

Enable peripheral illumination correction to fix vignetting.

2. Choose Enable to activate peripheral illumination correction. Shoot as normal.

You'll want to be sure to turn this feature off when you don't need it, as it might result in a brightening of the corners in your image. As you might expect, the Rebel's internal lens database includes only Canon lenses, so if you're using a third-party lens, don't expect to find correction data.

With the DPP software that is included you can see a list of which lenses the camera has data for, and possibly add more correction data. When it's activated, peripheral illumination correction is automatically applied to every image that you shoot in JPEG mode. It cannot be applied to images that you've already shot. In raw mode, things work a little bit differently, but you'll learn about that later.

FOOD FOR THOUGHT

JPEG IMAGE PROCESSING

Earlier, you learned the basics of how the image sensor in your Rebel T1i works. You learned that the image sensor can measure the light that strikes each pixel on its surface, and that to calculate color, a complex interpolation process is employed. In fact, though, there's actually a lot more that goes on in the camera when you shoot in JPEG mode (which is the only type of shooting we've done so far).

After reading the data off the sensor, amplifying it, and interpolating the color values, the T1i must do a lot of additional processing before a usable image is produced. After performing its initial color computations (which involves *demosaicing* and then performing *colorimetric interpolation*, for those of you who want some fancy terms to throw around at your next cocktail party), it then maps the data into a *color space*.

Here's the trouble with color: it's *very* subjective. If you've ever gotten into an argument with someone over a color—one of those "How can you say that's mauve when it's *plainly* maroon"–type arguments—then you've experienced firsthand how different people can see colors in very different ways. Things are further compounded because different types of devices can record and interpret different ranges of colors. For example, your eyes can perceive a *much* larger range of tones and colors than the Rebel T1i can, but the T1i can capture and store *far* more colors than any printing technology can print.

So, the T1i image sensor may analyze its data and discover that one pixel is 100% maroon, but what does "100% maroon" mean? Is it a really dark maroon or a lighter maroon or a maroon that leans toward the red side? Or the magenta side? To address this issue, scientists use something called a *color space*. You can think of a color space as simply being an agreed-upon scale that is used when measuring color.

So, for example, in the sRGB color space that the T1i defaults to, "100% red" is defined as being a very specific shade of red. Photo nerds will argue the merits of one color space over another, saying that some are too small (meaning that the full range of colors a camera can capture aren't represented), whereas others are too large (meaning that your image might suffer from some strange color problems).

– Continued

FOOD FOR THOUGHT

JPEG IMAGE PROCESSING (continued)

So, after your camera calculates color, it maps those colors into the specified color space. (Later, we'll look at how to change the color space.)

With the color stored, the camera turns to an issue of contrast. Your senses are *nonlinear* in the way that they respond to stimuli. For example, if you double the amount of light in the room, your eyes don't register a 200% increase in brightness. Instead, the brightness increase is *attenuated*, or rolled off. This effectively makes your eyes more sensitive to changes at the extreme bright and dark ends of their range.

The image sensor in the T1i, though, is *linear* in its response to light. A double of brightness results in the sensor registering twice as much light. The practical upshot of all this is that your eyes see much more contrast than does your Rebel. For example, here's the same scene as your eye would see it and as the T1i's image sensor sees it:

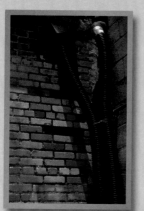 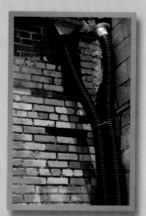

Contrast-wise, the left image is fairly close to how your eyes would see this scene. The right image shows how your camera sees the scene.

Although the difference isn't huge, the linear image is definitely a little duller and lacks some of the punch of the nonlinear image. To make the linear image more like what our eyes are used to seeing, the camera applies a mathematical curve to the values in your image to make them nonlinear. This process is called *gamma correction*.

– Continued

FOOD FOR THOUGHT

JPEG IMAGE PROCESSING (continued)

After gamma correction, the camera corrects the color according to the white balance settings on the camera. At this point, you have a very good-looking image that is recognizable as a quality color photo (assuming you exposed well). But the camera still does more.

Using the equivalent of an in-camera image-editing program, the T1i adjusts the contrast, color saturation, and color tone in your image, and then finally applies sharpening. These adjustments have nothing to do with any exposure parameters you've chosen; they're simply image-editing operations of the same kind you would apply using an image editor such as Photoshop.

Earlier, you learned about pixels, and we discussed how you can represent a greater number of colors if you dedicate more bits of memory to each pixel. Basically, with more bits you can count higher, which means you can represent a greater number of colors. The Rebel T1i stores 14 bits of data per pixel, which represents a *lot* of colors. Unfortunately, the JPEG format supports only 8 bits per pixel, so after all of this image processing, the next thing the camera must do is discard a bunch of its color data. The images is converted from a 14-bit image down to an 8-bit image.

Finally, the image is JPEG-compressed and stored on the media card.

While most of this process is out of your control—it's simply a few billion calculations that the camera performs automatically in the split second after you shoot a picture—the amount of contrast, color saturation, and color tone adjustment that the camera applies *is* something you can alter.

Scene Modes Revisited

In Chapter 1 you learned about the T1i's scene modes, those special automatic modes that are designed for shooting in specific circumstances. Let's take another quick look at those with your new understanding of exposure.

Portrait mode tries to choose an exposure that will blur out the background. So, you now know that it's trying to choose an exposure with a wide aperture (lower f-number), since a wider aperture produces a shallower depth of field. And, you also now know that if it's using a wider aperture, then it must use a faster shutter speed to compensate (a wider aperture lets in more light, so you need a shorter exposure time).

Landscape mode does the exact opposite from Portrait mode. It uses a smaller aperture (bigger number) to increase depth of field. This will usually result in a slower shutter speed. When the shutter speed drops below what the camera thinks is appropriate for handholding the camera at your current focal length, then it will flash the shutter speed readout as a warning.

Close-up mode opts for a shallower depth of field, just like Portrait mode. So, this means wider aperture.

Sports mode aims for motion-stopping power, which you now know means faster shutter speed. It also activates Drive mode and Servo focus.

Night Portrait mode activates the flash but also sets a shutter speed that's appropriate for exposing the scene *without the flash*. So, the flash fires to expose your subject in the foreground, but the long exposure properly exposes the background.

Scene modes offer no manual overrides. You cannot use exposure compensation or change the ISO, white balance, metering, or focus point in any scene mode. If you do, the camera will display a warning.

Scene modes are great when you're starting out or if you're really in a hurry, but as your skill grows, you'll probably find yourself using these modes less and less as you learn to accomplish the same shots with more customization, using manual overrides.

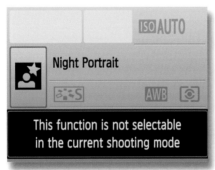

Not all features are available when using a scene mode.
If you try to use one that's not allowed, the camera will issue a warning.

Picture Styles

You've now seen how changes in exposure can affect the tones in your image, as well as the saturation. But the T1i has some other ways to alter the contrast, saturation, and color in your image.

Picture styles allow you to change the way the camera processes its images, with direct control from the camera of sharpness, contrast, saturation, and color tone in your image. These processes are very different from what happens when you change exposure, and to understand how they work, you need to know a little more about how the camera makes an image.

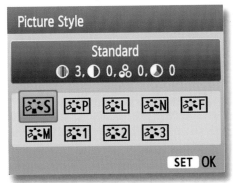

The Picture Style menu.

Selecting a Picture Style

A Rebel T1i picture style is a collection of image-editing directives. A picture style can contain detailed color correction instructions that affect specific hues, as well as global corrections to contrast, saturation, color tone, and sharpness settings.

By default, the T1i uses the Standard picture style, which is a general-purpose style that delivers nicely balanced saturation and accuracy to deliver attractive color that's still realistic.

To change picture styles, press the down arrow button on the back of the camera. Notice that it has a Picture Style icon next to it. Select the picture style you want, and then press Set. The camera displays the current picture style on the rear LCD status page.

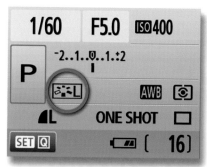

Your current picture style choice is shown on the T1i's LCD screen.

Each picture style affects your image as follows:

Portrait lowers the sharpness that's applied to the image in an attempt to smooth skin tones. It also boosts certain tones to make skin tones more realistic. This is similar to the way that Kodak Gold film used to make skin tones more golden to give them a "healthy glow." Obviously, this feature is biased toward Caucasian and lighter skin tones. Bear in mind that Portrait picture style has no impact on the camera's exposure choice. Unlike the Portrait shooting mode, the Portrait picture style does not impact the camera's aperture choice. However, this picture style is automatically selected when you choose Portrait shooting mode.

Landscape increases the sharpness that's applied to the image so as to bring finer detail to landscape scenery. Landscape style also boosts green and blue tones to create richer skies and more vivid foliage. This style is automatically selected when you choose Landscape shooting mode.

Neutral deactivates sharpening and most in-camera color correction altogether. If you prefer to process your images yourself, then Neutral is a good way to go. It's possible to edit an image too much, resulting in visible artifacts in your image. So, if you're serious about editing, you might not want the camera to "use up" too much of your editability. Images shot with Neutral will appear more subdued.

Faithful is what you'll want to use if you're a stickler for color accuracy, assuming you're shooting in daylight. With this style, images are adjusted with an eye toward more accurate color reproduction. Like Neutral, images shot with Faithful appear to be a little dull.

Monochrome converts your images to grayscale (or *black and white*, if you prefer the more traditional term). Grayscale conversion is a very subjective process, so although this picture style is handy, if you're serious about black-and-white photography, you'll be better served by shooting in color and performing your conversion by hand in an image editor.

Adjusting Predefined Picture Styles

You can tweak the six predefined picture styles by adjusting saturation, color tone, and contrast within the camera. Each of these parameters has a range from -4 to +4, whereas Sharpness has a range from 0 to 7.

While you can't edit all of the effects of a picture style, these four parameters give you a fair amount of adjustment latitude.

1. To edit a picture style, select Picture Style from the second shooting menu.

2. Navigate to the picture style you want to edit, and then press the DISP button.

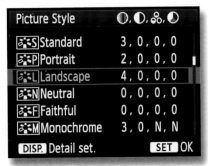

You can choose a picture style to edit.

3. From the "Detail set." page, you can dial in Sharpness, Contrast, Saturation, or Color tone. Simply select the parameter you want to edit, and press the Set button. You can then use the arrow keys to move the slider for that value. Press Set again when finished.

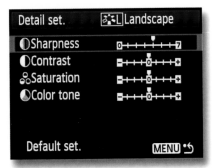

Choose how you want to adjust the selected picture style.

CREATING YOUR OWN PICTURE STYLE

The T1i supports up to three user-defined styles. You edit these just like you would any other style. From the Picture Style menu, select User Def. 1, 2, or 3, and hit the DISP button. You can now edit the same four parameters for each setting. These user-defined picture styles appear on the Picture Style menu when you press the down arrow key, just like any other picture style.

If you're really serious about picture styles, you'll want to look at the Picture Style Editor application that's included on the EOS Digital Solution Disk. The Picture Style Editor gives you far more control than what you can get from the four in-camera sliders. Working from any example image you choose, you can select colors and then adjust their hue, saturation, and lightness. You can edit dozens of colors and, when you're done, export the resulting picture style to your camera.

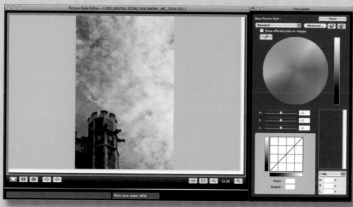

You can define your own picture styles for use when shooting JPEG images.

Before you dive into learning the application, think a little bit about your work-flow. Picture styles are very handy if you want to be able to quickly crank out images without doing any postproduction editing. For wedding and event shooters, this is a great feature. But for most of us who are willing to spend some time editing individual images, it makes more sense to work over our image in an image editor, rather than trying to define some sort of "global" editing adjustment that will be applied to every image we shoot.

Creating a Better Exposure with Fill Flash

I want to take a quick moment to introduce you to the simplest—and most-often used—form of flash photography. Most people think that a flash is for shooting in low light, but flash can be just as important when shooting in direct sunlight. In fact, since the built-in flash on the Rebel T1i is not especially powerful and can't be pointed in specific directions, you may find you use it more in bright daylight than you do in low light situations.

For example, if you're shooting someone standing under a tree, the tree will shade her face, while full sunlight brightens up the scenery behind her. This is just like the earlier example of shooting someone in front of a window. The camera will most likely meter for the background, rendering the foreground underexposed. In the window scenario, we used different metering modes to properly expose the foreground at the expense of overexposing the background. If you don't want to blow out the background, and if your subject is within range of the flash, you can use the pop-up flash to fill in the foreground to create an even exposure.

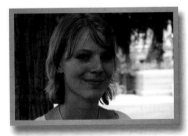 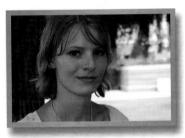

Before and after fill flash.

Similarly, someone wearing a hat can have a face cast in shadow. Fill flash can easily open up these shadows to produce a better exposure.

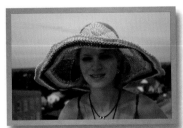 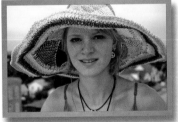

In the image on the left, the hat is shading the woman's face. With a fill flash, we even out the exposure, throwing more light onto her face while maintaining a natural, sunlit look.

In fact, fill flash would have been a fine alternative to the bright window scene that we struggled with earlier. To shoot with fill flash in Program mode, simply press the flash button to pop up the flash, and shoot as normal.

A Word About Dynamic Range

There is a range from very dark to very bright wherein your eyes can see detail. Below this range, things are too dark, and above this range, things are painfully bright. This is called *dynamic range,* and in humans, it's about 18 stops wide. That is, there are about 18 doublings of light from darkest to lightest.

Unfortunately, like all cameras, the Rebel T1i has a much smaller dynamic range than what the human eye can perceive. About half the range, actually. This means that, with a single shot, you cannot capture some scenes in the way your eye sees them. For example:

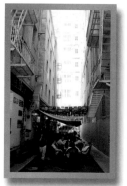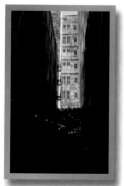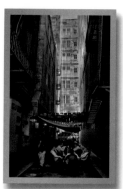

The image on the right has such a huge dynamic range that it couldn't be captured in one shot. Instead, I had to shoot an image exposed for the shadows and one exposed for the highlights and then combine them in an image editor.

This image has a very large dynamic range. There are details in the shadows and details in the highlights. It was not actually possible to capture this in one shot. Instead, I had to take two shots, one exposed for shadows and the other exposed for highlights, and then combine them in an image editor. Unfortunately, performing this kind of combining is not always possible, either because your subject is moving, you didn't think to take multiple shots, or the postproduction work is too hard. Most of the time, when shooting a scene like this, you simply have to decide whether you want to shoot for highlights or shadows.

As discussed earlier, it's usually better to preserve details in highlights, because areas of solid white are distracting. Areas of solid black just look like dark shadows that we can't see into.

Which Mode Should You Choose?

Many people have a misconception that using one mode or another will open up a tremendous amount of imaging power that's not available in other modes. But there's no hierarchical organization to the T1i's shooting modes. Program mode does *not* yield less power than priority modes, and choosing priority modes over Manual mode does *not* cut you off from some greater photographic potential. For the most part, any picture that you can take in one mode you also can take in another.

The secret to maximum creative power is to understand aperture, shutter speed, ISO, depth of field, camera position, focal length, and post processing, and learn how all of these factors are balanced and played off of each other to create specific effects.

We've covered a few reasons why you might choose one mode over another, but the simple upshot is that when you need more control of one parameter, then one mode might make dialing in that control a little easier. If you need control of both parameters, or if you are intentionally under- or overexposing in a way that your camera is not predisposed to, then Manual mode will be your best choice.

CHAPTER 8

Finding and Composing a Photo

EXPLORING THE ART OF PHOTOGRAPHY

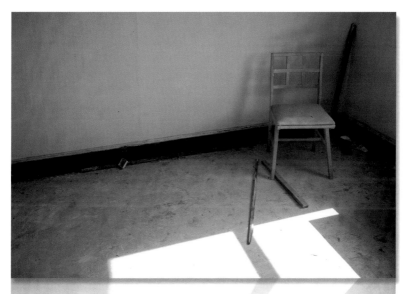

As with most creative endeavors, you can divide your photographic study into two areas: craft and artistry. Craft encompasses your technical understanding of photographic process—how different parameters affect your image and how you use the controls on your camera to set those parameters. Artistry is the process of using your craft skill to represent a scene, person, or moment as a photographic image—ideally an image that evokes something of the "truth" of your subject that you felt when shooting. In this chapter, we're going to focus on the artistry side of things and explore how you visualize and compose an image.

Learning to See Again

If you're like most people, you've probably experienced something like this: You can't find your keys (or your sunglasses, your favorite pen, your wallet, or whatever), so you look on your desk, in your pockets, in your coat, and on the kitchen table. You try to retrace your steps to determine where you might have been when you last had your keys. You look and look and then, finally, an hour later, you see them sitting out in the open in the middle of your desk—right there in the first place you looked.

This type of maddening situation happens because, while it's very easy to look at something, it can be far more complicated to actually *see* it. We tend to use the words *look* and *see* synonymously, but for a photographer, there are very important differences between the two terms.

Let's return to the lost key scenario. How is it that you can look at the desk, specifically trying to find your keys, and not see them? The answer has to do with the fact that your eyes are far more than a simple optical instrument. It's very easy to draw a parallel between a digital camera and your eye: they both have lenses with irises, and they both have separate receptors for red, green, and blue light. But the optical system in your head has a very important additional component attached to it, in the form of a human brain. While we like to think of our eyes as camera-like devices that capture whatever scene is in front of us, our brains dramatically alter our perception of what we're seeing. Not seeing the keys on the desk in front of you is a prime example of this phenomenon, and there's a good reason your brain has evolved to work this way.

Think about crossing a busy street while running an errand. You know there are cars bearing down on you, and you know how far each car is, how fast it's going, and how to navigate across the street without getting hit; and most likely you know all of this while also thinking about your errand and how it will go and what you'll do afterward. However, despite this huge amount of information, when you get to the other side of the street, if someone were to ask you the color, make, and model of each car you passed, you probably wouldn't be able to recall. If you're a car freak, you might be able to, but if pressed to go further and tell the gender of each driver, you'd probably be out of luck. Even though your eyes were taking in all of this information—just as a camera would—your brain was editing it away.

Processing visual input requires an incredible amount of your neural bandwidth —bandwidth that you need for other things, such as keeping track of errands, and so forth. So that you aren't overwhelmed with visual information, your brain tends to edit or "abbreviate" your visual experience. So, when crossing the street, rather than seeing a "large metal vehicle resting on four wheels, with a clear glass window on top, six dead grasshoppers stuck to the front grill, a license plate that reads 'ILUVNY', and a middle-aged woman in curlers behind the wheel," you very often just register "car." By reducing the complexity of a large vehicle down to a simple concept, and a simple iconic image, you don't have to spend so much time registering all of the details that you end up getting run over. Instead, your brain takes a shortcut that allows you to get on with your day, albeit in a way that makes the world possibly less visually rich.

When looking for your keys, you will look at the desk, and your brain will decide that it already knows what it looks like, not bothering to register details that it feels it already knows. There normally aren't keys sitting there, so you don't see them. This is why someone who's not so familiar with your desk might walk in the room and spot the keys immediately.

Little kids are different. Because the world is a new place for them, they notice every detail of the objects around them. They have to because they haven't yet learned to abbreviate the visual complexity of the world down to simple symbols like "car" or "desk." But for a photographer, the "visual complexity" that makes up the world is also the raw material for your photographs. So, you don't *want* your brain to be abbreviating your experience; you want to see every detail. In other words, you want to learn to *see* again as you did when you were a kid.

Unfortunately, the older you get, the more knowledge of the world you have, so the more your brain can fill in a lot of blanks for you, relieving you from the hassle of seeing. So is it possible to make it stop doing this? Recent research has shown that the longer you look at a scene, the less contrast you are able to perceive in that scene. An image or scene will increasingly go flatter, contrast-wise, as your brain devotes fewer resources to it. The theory is that if you're looking at something for a while and it hasn't killed you, your brain decides that there's no need to devote precious resources to higher-quality visual processing of that scene.

So, to a degree, your brain stands in the way of you seeing accurately. However, you can still do many things to try to open up your senses and learn to better spot the interesting visual matter around you. The more you do this, the more you will discover raw material that can be transformed into photos.

INTENTIONALLY CONFUSING YOUR VISUAL PROCESSING

Another way to see how much your brain is involved in the visual process is to look at optical illusions, even something as simple as this line rendering of a transparent cube:

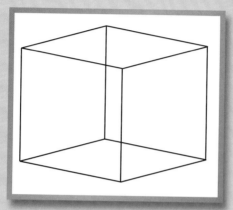

When you look at this two-dimensional representation of a cube, it appears to flip back and forth in space. This is an example of your brain failing to properly interpret the visual data that your eyes have collected.

Your eyes are properly registering a series of lines on a flat piece of paper, but your brain is stepping into the process. It notices that the arrangement of these lines usually represents a particular 3D object—a cube—as if they were truly a three-dimensional shape. Because it isn't actually a cube, your brain gets confused, and the orientation of the cube appears to flip around. This is a prime example of how your brain manipulates your visual experience after your eyes have already gathered up raw visual data.

Seeing Exercises

Just as a musician can train his ear to recognize pitch, intervals, and chords, a photographer can train his eyes to be more open and receptive to the world. In other words, you can practice and improve your ability to see.

One of the most important aspects of learning how to see is knowing what seeing feels like. However, if it's been a long time since your visual sense was really open, then it may be difficult to know what the difference is between seeing and not seeing. One of the easiest ways to get your eyes going is to go somewhere new. Perhaps you've noticed this when you travel or go on vacation. When you first get to someplace very foreign or new, you often notice lots of little details. This is partly a survival mechanism. You're a little more wary than usual, a little more alert, so all of your senses are going. It's also because you have lots of new stuff to see.

This is one reason that a lot of people think, "I want to do some photography. I need to go somewhere." They've recognized before that when they travel, they really see stuff. While it's sometimes simply because you're in an especially scenic place, I think it has as much to do with your visual sense being more charged and effective. Paying attention to what this feels like next time it happens to you is a good way to learn what it feels like to really see. Once you know the feeling, it can be a little easier to find it again.

Here are some ways to get your sense of seeing going, without having to travel.

Warm up

Don't assume you can work at your job all day and then dash out the door and suddenly be a photographer. You wouldn't expect to play a musical instrument without warming up and certainly wouldn't expect to do well at any kind of athletic event without warming up. While not tiring, the act of seeing is physical. It's not physically straining, but it's something you have to feel. It can take some time to calm down from the everyday stresses of your life and open yourself up to your visual sense.

When you first step out the door, take a picture. It doesn't matter what it is—take a picture of your foot, the light pole across the street, a manhole cover, a water meter in the sidewalk, anything at all. Taking that first shot will put you into the physicality of shooting. You'll see through the T1i viewfinder and be reminded of the frame shape and size you'll feel with the camera in your hands. All of this will help get you out of the distractions of your everyday life and into seeing and thinking about images.

Give yourself an assignment

I hear a lot of people say, "I'm going on vacation this summer, and that's when I'll take a lot of pictures." As discussed earlier, it's definitely easier to find images when you're somewhere new, especially if it's somewhere really photogenic. But photography takes practice, and you need to do it regularly. What's more, good pictures can happen anywhere, but only if you're open to them. If you can't work on your own block or around your own house, then there's no guarantee you'll be able to do good work in an exotic location.

One way to get yourself to practice and to breathe new life into familiar locations is to give yourself an assignment. Perhaps it's a subject—"old cars," "fire hydrants," "doorways"—or maybe it's a phrase or a word—"beauty and the beast," "contentment," "no pain, no gain." The subject matter or word doesn't have to mean anything to anyone else, and you can interpret it any way you want. The idea is to give yourself some way to frame your view of your location. This will often make you see familiar ground in a new way.

I keep three ongoing projects: "My street," "My neighborhood," and "San Francisco." Sometimes, when I have a moment to spare, I'll pick one of these things and go shooting. Confining myself to just my street is the hardest, while the neighborhood is easier, and having the whole city to work with is even easier. But trying to work on just my street is interesting, because it makes me look for unusual lighting or compositions amongst very familiar locales.

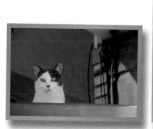 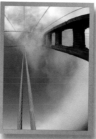 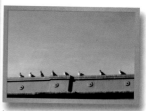

Images from my ongoing "My street", "My neighborhood", and "San Francisco" projects, respectively. Defining some projects for yourself can make it much easier to find things to shoot.

As with any creative endeavor, practice is the key. It's not just about memorizing what shutter speed and aperture do and how to control them, but practicing composition, seeing, and interpretation.

Look at other photos

Photography is a strange form because, whereas aspiring writers will all be able to easily name their favorite writers and books, I encounter very few aspiring photographers who know much about the history of their chosen form. Few can name a favorite photographer or pick up on references to famous, important works of photography. Familiarity with great works, though, is an easy way to improve your own shots.

Go to the library or bookstore, or do some Google searches, and find work by some of the great masters—Ansel Adams, Henri Cartier-Bresson, Paul Strand, Elliot Erwitt, and Alfred Stieglitz. Spend some time looking at their images with an eye toward both simply seeing how they make you feel and figuring out what was done technically to create the image. Pay attention to how the images are composed, and try to think about what the photographer might have done, exposure-wise, to achieve a given effect. By reverse-engineering their solutions, you'll learn a lot about how they saw a scene and what choices and decisions they made to turn that scene into a finished image.

> **TIP:** Study Other Photographers
>
> Looking at other works can be inspiring and energizing, and is a great way to practice seeing when you don't have the time or opportunity to go shooting.

Practice

I already mentioned this, but it's important, so I'm gonna mention it again: practice. Practice a lot. Not only will you learn your camera better, but you'll get better at seeing and recognizing images. If you want to take it to the extreme, you can do like photographer Joe Buissink who, if he doesn't have a camera but sees an image that he would like to shoot, says "click" or snaps his fingers. This "shooting without a camera" keeps him in the habit of seeing photographically, acknowledging when there's a shot he wants to take, and taking a moment to think about how he might compose it.

How to Make a Photo

Every so often my grandmother decides to go to a portrait studio. As with many people of her generation, she's always said that she's off to "have her picture made."

Nowadays, of course, we would say that we're going to have our picture "taken," but this is something of a misnomer, because a good picture is *made*. To "take" a picture implies that the subject is just there, as is, and that your camera records a perfect representation of it. But that's not actually how a good photograph happens.

The process of taking a good picture, whether it's a portrait, a still life, a landscape, a street shoot, or anything else, involves making a lot of decisions and solving a lot of problems. It also often requires you to shoot a lot of pictures as you experiment and try different ideas. Good images are not taken; they are *made* from the raw material of the scene you've decided to shoot. In the rest of this chapter, we're going to talk about the process that you go through to make a picture, from recognizing a scene to composing a shot to making exposure decisions.

Recognizing a Potential Photo

The photographic process begins, of course, by finding something that you want to take a picture of. While sometimes a subject is obvious—"Look! Godzilla is attacking the Eiffel Tower, I'd better get my camera!"—more often, interesting photos are hidden from those who aren't necessarily looking for a picture.

From beginning shooters, I often hear questions like, "How do you find stuff to shoot?" They think that you must go find interesting objects, stunning vistas, or beautiful landmarks. But good pictures usually begin with nothing more than a simple impulse based on something you've seen—a play of light, a beautiful color, an interesting piece of geometry. You might be walking down the street in the late afternoon and find a weathered door that the setting sun is throwing into deep, textured relief. Or perhaps you come across an otherwise mundane object that's being brightly lit by the sunset. Or maybe you find a curious piece of repeating geometry or some kids engaged in a very serious game of tag.

Sometimes you'll find scenes that you simply think are beautiful or interesting, and at other times you might see something in the corner of your eye that captures your attention but when you look directly at it find yourself unsure as to what it was that initially intrigued you. In *all* of these, that initial impulse—whether it's strong and obvious or fleeting and difficult to interpret—is "how you find stuff to shoot." Often, after that impulse, you'll immediately have an idea of the finished image in your head and can begin to work. At other times, you'll have no idea how to shoot the scene. In these instances, it's very easy to decide that your idea wasn't any good and not even try to take a picture. But don't give in to this self-doubt. Trust those initial impulses, and if you have even the foggiest notion that a picture might be possible, then start to work.

TIP: Watch the Light

All photos begin with light, and different types of light have different qualities. Excepting portraits, just about any subject looks better when it's struck by light that's coming from a lower angle. The angled light will reveal more detail and texture on the image. This means morning and afternoon are the best times for shooting. The midday sun produces a very flat light and rarely yields a good picture. Pay attention to the light! If you look out the window and see lots of beautiful contrast in the late afternoon, get outside with your camera! If you see a fascinating subject but find your pictures of it to be a little boring, try returning to that subject in the morning or afternoon. You may find that under better light, your subject really comes alive. Good photography often requires getting up *very* early, but this is how it is when your medium is light-based.

Look through that camera

Sometimes, on outings with a class, I'll have students who say they aren't getting any images. But when I watch them, I realize they aren't actually shooting very much, if at all. What they mean is that they're walking around looking but aren't seeing anything they think will make a good image. Unfortunately, what they're not understanding is that learning to view the world as a camera sees it takes a lot of practice.

If you find you've been walking around for a while in good light and you *aren't* seeing anything you want to shoot, you might simply be in a location that isn't providing any good material. However, it might also be that your eyes and brain just aren't seeing things photographically. Sometimes you have to look through your camera before you begin to see potential photographs. If you find yourself stuck, lift the camera up to your eye and start looking through it. The frame of your viewfinder often crops the world in ways that you can't visualize when you're walking around, and these crops often reveal interesting images. You may have to shoot your way through some unusable, outright bad images before your photographic senses get working. If you suffer through this process, though, you may find yourself seeing more things to shoot.

If you try this and *still* aren't finding things, then either there really isn't anything you're interested in shooting or your photographic juices just aren't flowing. Don't let this discourage you. Relax, give it a rest, and come back another day.

Photography as abstraction

While it's easy to believe that a photograph is a realistic representation of a scene, it's really not, for very obvious reasons. Photos are flat, two-dimensional objects, possessed of far less color or contrast than a scene in the real world; they convey nothing of the sound, smell, or feel of a scene, and they force a very cropped view.

Your job as a photographer is to try to figure out how to capture the feel of a moment or a scene with that flat image. Obviously, this is no small feat, but that's why great artistry is difficult to achieve.

Working Your Subject

Occasionally, *very* occasionally, you'll take a shot, and it will be exactly right. But don't expect this kind of good fortune very often. More often than not, you'll have to do some work to turn the scene you're shooting into a good image. You'll have to try different compositions, shooting from a variety of locations, and trying different exposure ideas, different focal lengths, and different vantage points. In the simplest terms, *working* a shot means trying as many different things as you can think of.

Even if you have a very clear vision of what the image should be, you should *still* try lots of different things because once you're looking through the lens, you might start to see things very differently and get new ideas.

Many people think if they can't get the image in one shot, then they must not be a good photographer. But this isn't how photography—or any artistic endeavor —works. Artistic expression is a process of experimentation and discovery, and as a photographer, the way you experiment and discover is to shoot lots of different compositions that explore many different ideas.

There are no rules to working a shot, other than to try anything and everything you can think of. However, it's almost always true that as you get in closer, your shot will improve. We'll discuss this more when we cover composition later in this chapter.

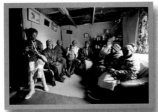
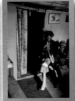
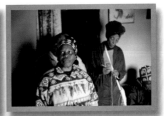

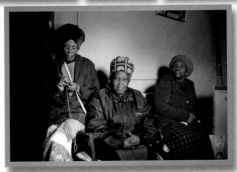

I tried many different angles and compositions before I finally found the shot that was "the keeper." Often, you'll find the right shot only by working your subject heavily.

TIP: Take Your Time

It can take time to make a good image: time to find the right angle and composition, time to thoroughly work your shot, time to figure out what it is about the scene that you're trying to capture. When possible, try to take your time and work through your options, and think about your exposure and composition strategies. Obviously, fleeting moments like the big play at a sporting event or a street shot involving moving people don't allow for repeated shooting. However, if you're shooting these types of moments for a while in the same location, then you'll have time to adjust your exposure strategy to the current lighting and to experiment with different angles on the action.

FOOD FOR THOUGHT

SHOOTING THROUGH FEAR

Unless you're a war photographer or you like to shoot in hazardous locations, photography is really not a dangerous endeavor. Nevertheless, people will succumb to all sorts of fear-based behavior when trying to take pictures. The most common one is that they will stick to the ideas that they know work, or that have worked before, rather than trying something new and risking the bad feeling that comes when something doesn't work.

This approach has two problems. First, what worked before in one shot might not work in another. But more importantly, this type of fear keeps you from exploring. It may be strange to speak of "courage" in a practice as harmless as photography, but often you have to muster courage to thoroughly work a shot. And what you have to be courageous about is failure.

The reason that most people don't work their shots enough is that they're afraid they'll get home, look at their shots, see that most of them are bad, and then feel, "Oh no, I'm a lousy photographer." So instead, they take the one or two shots that are safe—the shots that are obvious or that have worked before. These shots may not be bad, but after a while you will become very bored with them.

The process of working a shot is like sketching before a painting or drawing. Just as a painter sketches or a composer writes out motifs or ideas, you have to shoot some coverage of your scene from different angles, exploring different ideas, before you can zero in on the idea you like best. *All* good photographers do this, which means they *all* come home with a lot of images that are unusable, because many of these images were just process images that were required to get to the final shot.

Don't succumb to the fear of failure. Experiment, try things, get in close, and have the courage to take the shots that you don't normally take.

Choosing a Camera Position and Focal Length

Once you've spotted a subject and decided to start working it, you're ready to begin composing your shot. All composition begins with a choice about where to stand.

"But why do I need to think about where to stand?" you may be saying. After all, you've spotted the image; shouldn't you just take the picture? Not necessarily. The odds that you happen to have recognized a shot from the absolute best position in the world for shooting it are pretty small, and camera position can have a huge bearing on what your final image looks like.

Obviously, standing closer or farther, or off to one side or the other, can make a big difference in your shot. But camera position also affects your choice of focal length, and focal length can have a huge impact on the sense of space in your scene.

Understanding how focal length choice affects your image

While a zoom lens is a great convenience that keeps you from having to move around so much when you're shooting—rather than walk across the street, for example, you can just zoom in—it also tends to make for lazy photographers and to keep shooters from thinking about the right focal length for their scene.

Zooming a lens does much more than simply make a far subject appear closer. When you change focal lengths, a lot of things in your image change. Consequently, it's important to understand what a longer or shorter focal length does to your image.

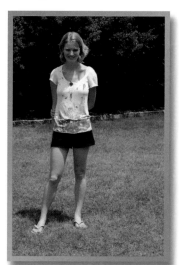 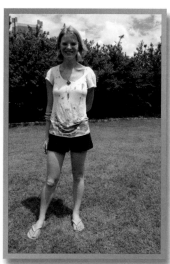

These two images are framed the same way, but the camera position and focal length changed, resulting in dramatic differences in the composition of the image.

My goal in both shots was to have my subject as large as possible. In the left image, I was standing farther away and so had to zoom in to get her to fill the frame. In the second image, I moved very close and so had to zoom out to a shorter focal length. While both strategies fill the frame with my subject, look at the huge differences in the background of the image.

In the left image, the background is filled with plants; in the right image, we can see some architecture and a fair amount of sky. Note, too, the difference in the sense of space in the image. In the left image, the plants in the background appear closer, whereas in the right image they look farther away and shorter.

When you zoom in (or, if you're using prime lenses, when you choose a lens with a longer focal length), the sense of depth in your scene gets compressed. Objects in the background will appear closer, and the overall composition of shapes, as well as sense of space, can be very different.

So, rather than standing in one place and zooming around to get your shot, it's important to pay attention to how different focal lengths affect the sense of space in your image. By choosing a different camera position and focal length, you can choose to make a space seem more spacious or more intimate (or, depending on the subject matter, more desolate or cramped).

Note that the compositional differences shown in those two images are all visible through the viewfinder, so you don't even need to take a shot to experiment with focal length changes.

Focal length and portraits

When shooting a portrait, it's also very important to pay attention to focal length because, just as the sense of space in a large scene changes dramatically depending on your focal length choice, people's faces can be similarly distorted. Again, here are two images framed with the subject taking up the same amount of space:

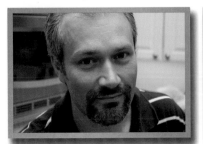 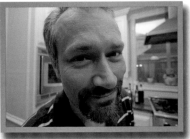

Focal length choice and camera position are also critical when shooting portraits.

The left image was shot with a slightly telephoto lens. For the image on the right, I switched to a wide-angle lens and moved in closer. Obviously, the wide-angle lens has greatly distorted the man's face. Note, too, the change in background. In the left image, the oven in the background looks very close, whereas in the right image it appears farther away. The wide angle lens has stretched the distance between his nose and ear and between his head and the background.

Portrait photographers typically use a focal length that's a little longer than a normal lens. On the T1i, 50mm is just about perfect for flattering portraiture. When combined with a large aperture, you'll get nice portraits with a soft background.

Composing Your Shot

Composition is the process of arranging the elements in your scene—the shapes and objects that comprise your foreground and background—to create a pleasing image.

Earlier we looked at some simple composition rules: fill the frame, lead your subject, don't be afraid to get in tight. These guidelines can greatly improve your snapshots and are relevant to all kinds of shooting. For more complex subjects and to produce more compelling images, though, you'll want to think about some additional compositional ideas.

There's no right or wrong to composition, but some compositions are definitely better than others. Rules are made to be broken, of course, and many compositions won't ascribe to any particular compositional theory or set of rules. However, when trying to make a photo—that is, when you've found an interesting subject and you're trying to figure out how to shoot it—remembering these compositional ideas will help you explore and experiment, and will probably lead you to better results.

Balance

One of the simplest compositional ideas is balance. Balance in a photo works just like balance in the real world. Different elements in your photo have compositional "weight," and you need to balance those against each other.

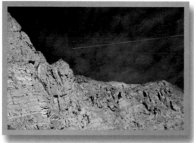 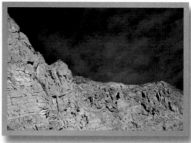

The contrail in the left image serves to balance the compositional "weight" of the cliff. If we remove the contrail, the image falls a bit out of balance.

Compositional balance is a tricky thing because you don't need elements of equal size to create balance. Just as a small piece of lead on a scale can balance a tremendous number of marshmallows, some small graphic elements can balance elements that are much larger. This is almost always true with people. We put a lot of import on people, and a single person in a frame can balance a huge amount of other compositional elements.

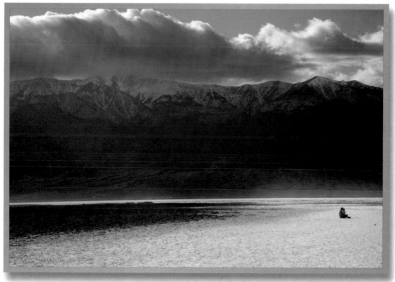

Humans carry a lot of compositional weight. Even a small figure can balance a very large element.

You won't always balance shapes in a composition. Sometimes you will find balance by putting tones—light and dark—against each other.

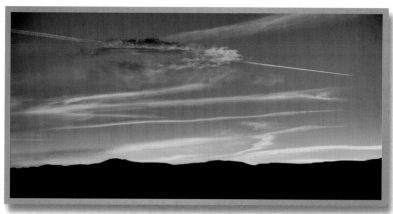

Here, the light line at the top of the image balances the dark shape at the bottom.

Sometimes, even empty space can create a balance. Consider this image:

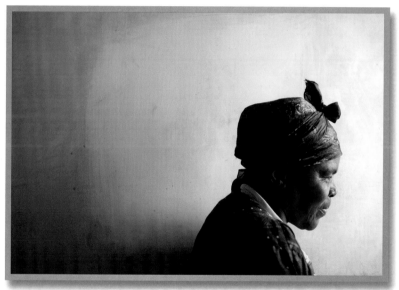

Sometimes you can balance an element in a scene using empty space.

This image is a good example of breaking a rule, because we're plainly break-ing the "lead your subject" rule. In this image, though, it works. The woman's pensive, reflective expression makes the empty space behind her more powerful. That space is evocative of emotional weight that is bearing down on her, or of her past. Graphically, the mostly empty space on the left balances out her presence on the right.

Geometry

Geometric shapes make great compositional elements and almost always make an image more interesting. Geometry can be anything from a strong line to a repeating pattern. You can see examples of geometry in some of the balance images we already looked at. The strong line of the airplane contrail makes for compelling compositions and packs a lot of compositional weight.

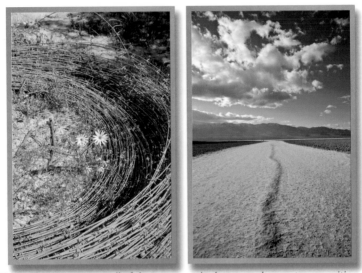

Circles, lines, patterns—all of these geometric shapes make great compositional elements that you can use to create more interesting images.

Sometimes, pure geometry itself can be interesting.

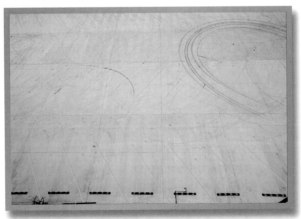

This fairly abstract scene is composed of pure geometry.

Repetition

Roughly akin to geometry is repetition. Repeating geometric or tonal patterns in an image are another powerful compositional device.

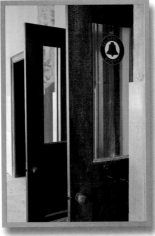

Repeating elements and textures almost always make for interesting compositions.

The rule of thirds

If you imagine a grid laid over your image that divides the picture into thirds, both horizontally and vertically, then the intersections of those grid lines make good places to put compositional elements. This is known as the *rule of thirds*, and it will often lead you to good compositions.

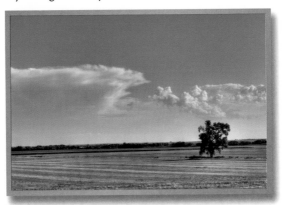

The rule of thirds can provide a good guideline for positioning elements in the frame.

TIP: Don't Be Afraid to Put Things in the Middle

It is possible to get *too* creative. When worrying about the rule of thirds, balance, and all these other things, you might be too clever and forget that, often, the best composition is to leave your subject in the dead center of the frame.

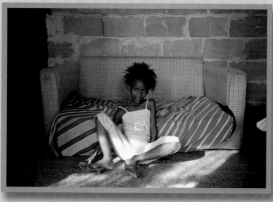

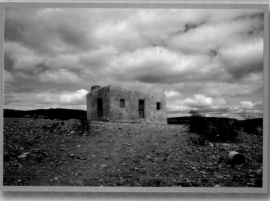

Foreground/background

If you've ever had someone stand you in front of a statue or a landmark, then you've experienced this rule: a photo needs a foreground and a background. Another way of thinking about this is as a subject and a background. What's more, the relationship between those two things is very important.

Earlier you learned about the idea of using the entire frame, or filling the frame. Choosing what to fill the frame with is an important part of good composition.

For example, here's a person standing in front of the Golden Gate Bridge:

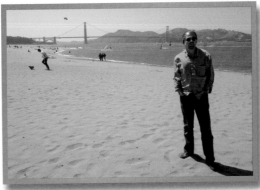

This image shows the whole bridge and the whole person, but showing everything isn't always the best approach.

Even though we've filled the entire frame and though we can see the entire bridge and the man's whole body, the image doesn't really have a strong subject. In fact, the bridge is as much the subject as the guy, who serves little purpose other than to indicate scale.

If we want this to be a picture of a person in front of the Golden Gate Bridge, we're better off framing tighter.

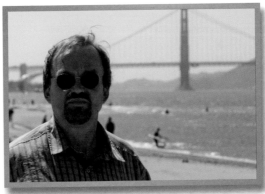

Here we have a tighter shot that's easier to read.

By filling the frame with more of the person, we know they are now definitely the subject of the image. Yes, we've had to crop the bridge, but the image still plainly conveys the person in their environment. If you want a picture of the bridge, that's a different subject, and a different photo, and you probably don't need a person in there at all.

Sometimes you'll come across a beautiful or compelling vista and it will be enough to serve as a subject all its own. You'll still want to think about framing and composition and consider some of the rules that we've discussed, but you won't have a definite foreground and background.

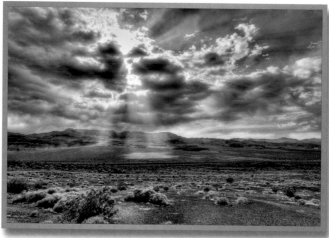

While this image doesn't have a definite foreground element, the scene itself is compelling enough to be a subject all on its own.

At other times you might come across a compelling vista but not be able to find a composition that feels right. This might be because the scene lacks a subject, so your eye doesn't really know how to "read" the image. If you can find something to use as a subject, you'll often find it's easier to compose.

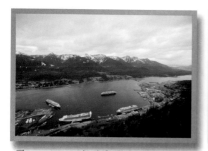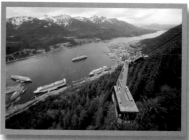

The scene on the left is much improved by waiting for the funicular to come into the frame and serve as a subject.

Sometimes, patience is the most important photographic tool at your disposal. If you find a nice background, wait and see whether someone walks into it to complete the composition or to serve as a subject.

Composing with light and dark

Earlier, you saw an example of a light airplane contrail balancing a dark horizon. Very often, you'll build composition out of light and dark, not just out of geometry.

Light is the raw material of photography, so don't forget to pay attention to light and dark elements within an image—they can make great compositional elements.

Also, don't worry if you can't find an exposure that reveals all the detail in a dark area. Often, a completely black shadow is just what an image needs. We don't need to see detail everywhere in an image, and choosing what to show and what to hide is part of the process of making a compelling image.

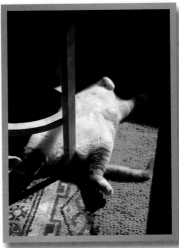

You can't see any detail in the shadow area of this image, but that's okay. The dark shadow makes the pool of light more pronounced, and any detail in the shadow would simply distract us from the sleeping cat.

Less is more

The world can be annoying in many ways, but for photographers, one of the biggest annoyances (after running out of media cards in the middle of a shoot) is that there's just too much stuff in the world.

Painters have it easy; they start with nothing and add only the things that they want in their scene. Photographers, though, have to contend with power lines, street signs, people who walk into their compositions, and trees that have one branch that's pointing in the wrong direction, and so on and so forth.

One of your most important jobs as a photographer is to find compositions that reduce the clutter in a scene so that the viewer is not confused about what to look at and so that her eye finds its way through the image.

If you work to fill the frame, as discussed in Chapter 1, you'll go a long way toward reducing extraneous clutter in your scene. When you're working a subject and trying to find different ways of shooting, one of the easiest variations is simply to get closer.

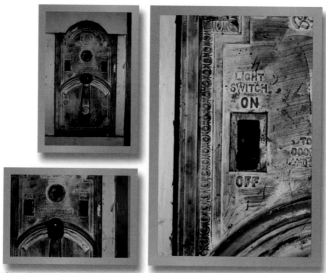

Though not always the case, getting in closer to your subject often will yield a more interesting image.

Closer usually yields a less-cluttered, cleaner image. When shooting people, getting in closer can be intimidating because you must move closer to your subject. Obviously, you don't want to make them uncomfortable, but don't be afraid to entertain the idea of moving a little closer when the situation feels right.

When shooting in public, closer often means separating yourself from the crowd and moving toward a scene. This can often leave you feeling like everyone is looking at you. In reality, they probably *aren't* (everyone is used to seeing people with cameras these days), but more importantly, so what? They notice you for a few moments and then go on about their day, while you return home with an interesting photo.

Some, all, or none

If you look back over the images I've used as examples, you'll find a lot of overlap of compositional ideas. For example, in the funicular picture, note that the funicular is positioned according to the rule of thirds.

You'll find that you can easily mix and match these compositional ideas to build up a good image, and as we've already seen, you might occasionally throw these ideas out altogether. Sometimes you'll be conscious of these rules; sometimes you'll simply go by feeling. If you practice these techniques, you'll soon come to find that even when you review images that you shot by feel, they still conform to many of these concepts. Studying the work of other photographers is also a great way to learn how they put these ideas to use, and sometimes such study makes it easier to understand another shooter's thought process and the choices he made.

Where these rules can be especially helpful is when you come across a scene that you want to capture but don't know where to begin. Start by thinking about camera position and focal length, and look through the lens to see how the sense of depth and space in the scene changes as you adjust position and focal length. Then start thinking about subject and background, and about geometry and pattern, repetition, and the rule of thirds. These can all serve as guidelines as you explore the scene through your camera lens.

Art and Craft

Throughout this whole process of working a shot and trying to make a composition, you will be constantly employing the technical concepts you've learned so far.

For example, you might be working a scene, moving around, getting in close, and then you find a focal length and camera position that creates a wonderful sense of space and that allows a composition that is balanced, with a nice subject/background relationship. But then you realize that what would make it perfect is to soften the background. So, you choose to go to a wider aperture using Program Shift, by turning the Main dial until an exposure set comes up that has a smaller f-stop number.

But then maybe you realize that your subject is very dark and so needs to be underexposed. So, you use exposure compensation to dial in a 2/3rd stop underexposure.

You shoot the shot and then review the image to check both your composition and the histogram, which will tell you how well your exposure has worked. In this way, your technical knowledge and handling of the camera combines with your artistic decisions.

Practice

Although it's possible to contrive guidelines for specific photographic situations—get down low while shooting kids, fill the frame when shooting portraits, etc.—as you've seen, the process of making a good photo requires a lot of decision making and a lot of choice and experimentation. Rather than learning specific rules for specific situations, it's better to learn what it feels like to see, what makes a good composition, and how your exposure settings affect your image. With these basic building blocks, you'll be able to go far beyond simple formulas for different situations. You'll be able to find your own solutions that better convey what you feel about a particular scene.

We can discuss all of these ideas and rules for hours, and the discussion can be very enjoyable and enlightening, but more than any lesson, more than any new piece of gear, more than any piece of postproduction software, the single thing that will do the most to improve your photography is practice.

You must practice seeing; practice composing; practice your understanding of the effects of exposure, camera position, and focal length; and practice with the controls of your T1i so that you can quickly adjust and adapt to any situation without having to think too much about the camera. You want your focus to be on composition. Practice will make all of these things possible. So, get out and shoot as much as you can, and pay attention to what works and what doesn't.

Because your camera records your exposure and focal length parameters for each shot you take, it's easy to review images and understand exactly what exposure you used for every shot. Paying attention to the effects of these choices will help you learn.

CHAPTER 9

Specialty Shooting

USING SPECIAL FEATURES FOR SHOOTING
IN SPECIFIC CONDITIONS

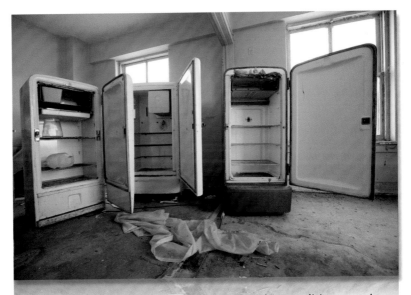

As you've already seen, different photographic conditions require different approaches. In this chapter, we're going to look at special features and techniques you can use for shooting concerts, panoramas, low-light shots, and more. The Rebel T1i provides all of the features you need for just about any type of shooting, even complex shots involving multiple exposures and special processing.

Using Live View

Though not a feature you'll use every day, Live View can be a lifesaver in certain tricky situations such as concerts, macro shots, or occasions when you need an angle that you can't get by holding the camera normally.

By this point in the book, you should be the type of person who can bandy about terms like *SLR* and *reciprocity* with ease. With your understanding of SLR mechanics, you should now be able to see why digital SLRs traditionally have not let you use the LCD screen as a viewfinder, the way you can do with a point-and-shoot camera.

To create an image to show on the LCD screen, the image sensor needs to be able to see out the lens. But in an SLR, there's a shutter and mirror between the sensor and lens, so the sensor is, effectively, blind. This means there's no way for it to see, and consequently it can't show you an image on the LCD screen. The T1i, though, provides a special feature called Live View that *does* let you use the LCD screen as a viewfinder.

Of course, one of the great advantages of an SLR is the high-quality, through-the-lens viewfinder that shows a bright, clear image and allows you to block out the rest of the world while you compose your shot. However, Live View can be useful in a few situations where a normal SLR viewfinder is difficult to use. Live View is ideal for:

Product and still-life shooting When you have your T1i mounted on a tripod and are trying to shoot a static composition, Live View can be a great boon. With it, you can easily arrange and adjust your camera position, subject, and lighting and see the resulting shot on the LCD screen. If the camera is mounted at a difficult angle, this can be much easier than trying to see through the viewfinder.

Macro shooting Shooting up close often requires you to hold the camera in strange positions—way down low or squeezed into tight, difficult-to-access locations. With Live View, you can line up your shot while keeping an eye on the LCD screen in order to see exactly what your final composition will be.

Concert and event shooting When you're shooting a crowded concert or event, it's often hard to get a good vantage point since crowded events tend to be full of people. With Live View, you can hold the camera over your head and see your framing on the camera's rear LCD.

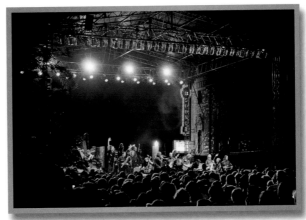

Shooting from within this crowd with Live View was easy, because I was able to hold the camera at arms length, over my head, and frame the shot on the LCD.

Activating Live View

You can use Live View in Program mode, Shutter and Aperture Priority Mode, and Manual Mode. To activate Live View, press the the Live View button (📷) on the back of the camera. You'll hear a clunk as the mirror flips up, and then the viewfinder will light up with your current scene.

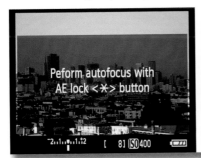
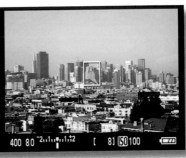

When you switch to Live View, the Rebel T1i first shows a focusing reminder screen, and then your current scene.

Believe it or not, it's easy to forget to focus when you're shooting in Live View. As you'll see, focusing your SLR in Live View mode is more complicated than focusing a point-and-shoot camera that has an LCD viewfinder. And because the screen's so small, you won't necessarily notice if an image is slightly out of focus.

So, when you first switch to Live View, the camera will put up a reminder to focus, as well as remind you of how to trigger autofocus. After a moment, the reminder will disappear, and your scene will appear.

> **TIP:** Dismiss the Focus Reminder
>
> If you're in a hurry to shoot and don't want to wait for the focus reminder to time out, give the shutter a half-press to dismiss the reminder screen.

The camera shows status information, including current ISO, number of shots remaining, and exposure compensation. After you half-press the shutter button, you'll also see shutter speed and aperture. Just like in playback mode, you can press the DISP button to see additional status information. As with normal shooting, a half-press of the shutter button will meter your scene and display a shutter speed and aperture. However, note that it doesn't focus.

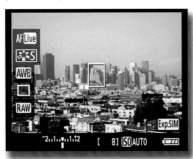 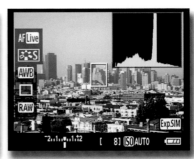

Pressing the DISP button toggles through other Live View display options.

> **QUESTION:** What If Live View Doesn't Activate?
>
> If you press the Live View button and Live View doesn't activate, then go to the first Tools menu and choose the Live View function settings. Then, change the Live View Shoot setting to Enable. Also, note that Live View doesn't work when you're using a Scene mode (except for Movie mode).

Focusing in Live View

The problem with focusing in Live View is that the camera's autofocus sensors are located in the top of the camera, where the pentamirror is. In Live View mode, since the main mirror is flipped up, the autofocus sensors can't "see" out the lens. Therefore, to focus, you have to choose one of several options.

Manual focus

If you switch your lens over to manual focus, you can manually focus the camera in Live View, just as you would if you were looking through the viewfinder. However, the LCD screen is not quite as clear and bright as the optical viewfinder, which can make it difficult to see if you're in focus, so Canon has built a focusing aid into the system. When in you're in Live View, you can press the Zoom In button (the same one you use in playback mode) to see a magnified view of the center of the image. Press it again and magnification will increase. Press it a third time and you'll go back to the normal view. With the magnified view, manual focus becomes much easier.

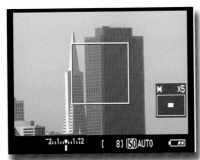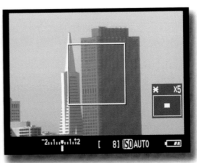

You can use the Zoom In function to see a magnified view of your image.

However, if you're shooting in low light, even a highly magnified view can be difficult to see. Fortunately, the T1i also offers some autofocus options for working in Live View.

Autofocusing in advance

One way to use autofocus in Live View is to focus *before* you activate it. Look through the viewfinder and half-press the shutter just as you always would. The camera will autofocus and lock. Then press Set to activate Live View. As long as the distance to your subject doesn't change, your image should be in focus.

Using Live mode for autofocusing

The T1i actually *can* use autofocus, using two different schemes to work around the fact that its autofocus sensors can't actually see when in Live View mode. Live View provides three different autofocus modes, with the default set to something called Live Mode.

With Live mode enabled, you'll see a big square in the middle of the screen. This is the area that the camera will focus on. By using the arrow keys on the back of the camera, you can move the box to any position on the frame that you want.

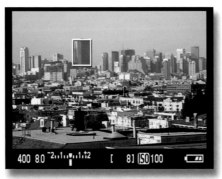

A square on your LCD display indicates where the camera will focus.

To autofocus, press the ✳ button and hold it in. The camera will work to focus, and when it succeeds, the camera will beep and the white box will turn green.

In Live Mode, the camera is not using the autofocus sensors that it normally uses. Instead, it is analyzing the image data that's being caught by the image sensor. Because of the amount of data that must be processed, focusing this way can take a while, and might not always succeed. For this reason, some other focus modes are provided.

In order to change modes, you'll need to go to the second Tools menu, where you'll find an entry called "Live View function settings". Choose this, and you'll be taken to a number of different Live View options. The AF mode option lets you switch between the camera's three focusing modes.

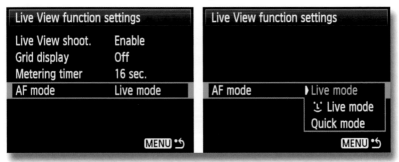

Use the Live View function settings menu to choose a focusing mode.

Focusing in Quick Mode

Quick mode autofocus uses the camera's autofocus sensors, just like autofocus does when you're shooting normally. However, to use these sensors, the mirror must be flipped up temporarily, so that the sensors can "see." To autofocus in Quick mode:

1. Frame your shot.

2. If you want to change to a different focus point, press the Set button, and then use the the Main dial to select a focus point.

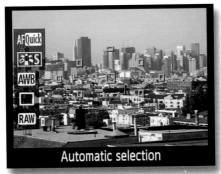

You can select a focus point in Live View mode,
just as you do when shooting normally.

3. Press the ✱ button to autofocus. The mirror will flip up, which means your screen will go black temporarily (with the mirror up, the image sensor can't "see," and so no image can be generated for the LCD screen). When focus has been achieved, the camera will beep, the mirror will flip back down, and the camera will be ready to shoot.

4. Press the shutter button to take your shot.

Quick mode focus is faster and more accurate than Live mode, but if the screen blackout bothers you, then you may want to stay with Live mode. However, with all of these modes, as long as your subject isn't moving, you'll probably need to focus only once.

Focusing in Face Detection Live mode

Face Detection Live mode works just like normal Live mode – the mirror stays up, so that your screen doesn't black out, and the camera's image sensor is used to calculate focus. However, rather than identifying one of the normal focus points, in Face Detection mode, the camera searches the frame for what appears to be a face, and then focuses on that point. A box appears around the face to indicate where the camera has chosen to focus, and the normal focus confirmation is given when the camera achieves focus lock.

Like Live mode, Face Detection mode can be a little slow, but it's worth playing with, to see if you find it practical for normal use. To use Face Detection Live mode:

1. Press the down arrow key to select Face Detection mode and press the Set button.

2. Then press the Menu button to exit the custom function page.

3. Finally, make sure your lens is set to autofocus, not manual focus.

Other Live View Options

As you've seen, you can press the Set button to manually move the Live Mode focus point around. But you might have also noticed that when you press the Set button, a menu pops up on the left side of the screen. This menu gives you a readout of the current Picture Style, white balance, drive mode, and image format settings. Use the up and down arrows to view each setting.

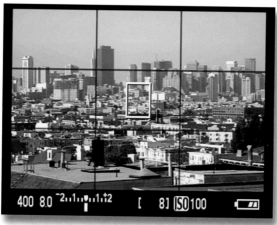

Live View lets you superimpose one of two grids over your image.

In the Live View function settings menu that you saw earlier, you can use the Grid display option to superimpose one of two grids over the viewfinder. This can make it easier to shoot level shots. Finally, the Metering Time setting lets you control how long the metering information is displayed on the screen.

What You Don't See in Live View

Although Live View is very handy for the circumstances mentioned earlier, there's one thing to bear in mind when using an LCD screen as a viewfinder. As we've discussed, your eyes can see a much wider range of tones than your camera can capture, and good photography is often about how you choose to represent these different tones. When you look through a normal viewfinder, you can see the whole scene, just as your eye really sees it.

With Live View, however, your view of the scene is inherently limited to the dynamic range of the camera. For the image shown in Live View, the Rebel T1i will try to preserve the highlights so that they don't blow out to complete white. This usually means that shadow areas in your image will go very dark and show very little detail.

Also, bear in mind that Live View is more like a video camera than a still camera. The Rebel T1i must keep 30 frames per second delivered to the screen, which means it's not possible for it to take long exposure shots that might reveal brighter shadows. So, while your image may have a very different exposure than what you see in Live View, the camera will have time to do a longer exposure when it actually shoots the shot (of course, this is also true when looking through the normal viewfinder).

Live View's limited dynamic range can make composition a little trickier because some compositional elements that you see with your eye may be obscured in Live View. With practice, you can learn to work around this, and at first you may not even notice it, simply because you don't miss what you can't see.

But ultimately, composing with a real viewfinder almost always allows a better view of your scene —and therefore more creative options—than a view on an LCD viewfinder. This is not a deficiency of the Rebel T1i; you'll find this problem in any camera that uses an LCD screen as a viewfinder.

Shooting Panoramas

No matter how wide your lens might go, there will still be times when you face a vista that just can't be captured in one frame. In the old days, your only choice would have been to shoot and layer a series of images together to create a collage.

Nothing is wrong with this technique, and it can actually be quite evocative, but thanks to digital image processing, we have another option. Now you can take those same images, and, rather than layering them together as a collage, you can digitally merge them into a single seamless image.

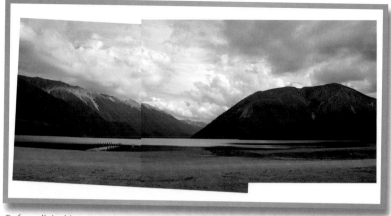

Before digital image processing, the only way to create a photographic panorama from multiple shots was to make a collage.

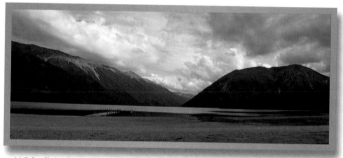

With digital stitching software, we can seamlessly merge individual images into a completed panorama.

Shooting this type of panoramic image requires a combination of shooting technique and special software. You must shoot your images in a particular way to ensure that they contain the information you need to construct a good panorama and then use special *stitching* software to create the seamless merge. Your EOS Digital Solutions Disk includes a panoramic stitching program called PhotoStitch.

Choosing a Focal Length for Panoramas

Making a successful panoramic shot begins by shooting usable images. A lot can go wrong when you're shooting a panorama, so you have to take care to shoot your source images carefully to ensure the best result.

First you must choose a focal length. If you choose a shorter (wider angle) focal length, then you won't need as many shots to cover the width of your panorama.

However, as we've already seen, a shorter focal length will have a deep depth, which will render many objects in your scene very small. Also, a super-wide angle might confuse some stitching programs.

If you choose a longer focal length, distant objects will appear larger, but you'll have to shoot more frames, which will increase your chances of making an error and ending up with unusable source material.

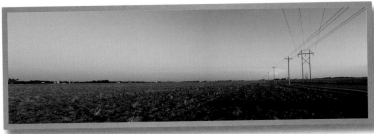

This panorama was shot with a shorter, wider-angle focal length. While a wider angle lets you cover a wider area with fewer shots, it means the distant objects will be smaller.

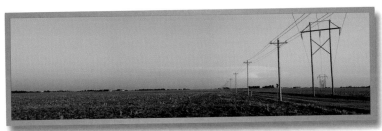

This panorama was shot with a longer, more telephoto focal length. It took more images to cover the scene, but objects in the foreground and background are larger and more prominent.

Consequently, your best option is to aim somewhere in the middle and choose a moderate focal length that reveals the details you want to see but is still wide enough that you don't have to shoot a lot of frames to cover your scene. Once you've selected a focal length, it's time to think about exposure.

Panoramic Exposure

From a panoramic photography standpoint, one of the things that's really annoying about the world is that it's not lit perfectly evenly. This problem is much more pronounced when shooting a panorama than when shooting a single frame.

If you look at most any panoramic scene in the real world, you'll probably find that one end is brighter than the other. The reason this is a drag for panoramic shooting is that the area that's brighter will expose differently than the area that's darker, and when you try to stitch your images together, you could very well end up with weird color bands in the sky.

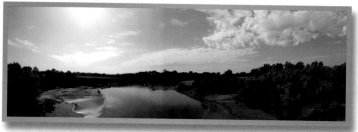

This panorama was not evenly exposed. The vertical bands in the middle of the image are the result of the stitching program trying to reconcile the different exposures.

To compensate for this, you'll want to use the same exposure for all your shots. This will ensure that all the components of your panorama have the same overall brightness and tone and will stitch together smoothly. On the T1i, this is easy to achieve, thanks to the AE Lock button located on the back of the camera.

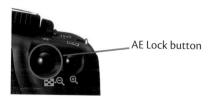

AE Lock button

Use AE Lock to ensure all your images use the same exposure.

Using AE Lock

Try this: Point your camera in a predominantly bright direction and half-press the shutter to take a meter reading. Note the shutter speed and aperture that are chosen. Now point the camera in a darker direction and take a reading. The camera chooses different exposure settings, which makes sense since you're looking into an area that's darker. Now return to your initial bright scene and half-press the shutter again to meter. After you meter, press the AE Lock button. An asterisk should appear in the viewfinder status display to indicate that your exposure is now locked.

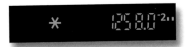

The asterisk indicates the exposure is now locked.

Release the shutter button and point the camera at the dark area you looked at earlier. Half-press the shutter button and the camera will focus, but notice that the exposure has not changed. Since the exposure is locked, the T1i will use the same exposure settings you used when you metered the bright area. (Obviously, these settings are not ideal, and your final image will probably be dark and underexposed.) Thanks to exposure lock, it's possible to shoot a whole panorama of images, all with the same exposure.

> **TIP:** Exposure Lock Timeout
>
> When you meter with the T1i, if you release the shutter button, the camera will remember that metering for about four seconds. Even if you've locked exposure, the reading will eventually time out, and the viewfinder status will go dark. So, once you've locked exposure, it's a good idea to keep the button half-pressed or press the button halfway down every second or so to preserve the locked exposure. You might need some time to compose your panorama after you've locked exposure, so you don't want the lock to time out. Another option is simply to take note of what the exposure is, switch to Manual mode, and dial it in. This will buy you all the time you need to compose and ponder.

Choosing an exposure

While it's easy enough to use the AE Lock button to lock your exposure across an entire panorama, you still have to choose *which* exposure to lock onto. Locking on the brighter end will cause the camera to stop down and use a fast shutter speed, thus possibly underexposing the darker end of the panorama. Or should you meter off the darker end and risk blowing out the bright side of the panorama? Obviously, the easiest way to balance these two problems is to split the difference and meter off of some place in the middle. Pick a mid-range point in your panorama, frame it with your chosen focal length, and press the shutter button halfway down to meter. Then press the exposure lock button to lock your exposure, swivel to the starting end of your panorama, and start shooting.

As mentioned, the AE Lock setting can time out. If you find you don't have enough time to get your entire panorama shot, take note of the shutter speed and aperture you're using, and then switch to Manual mode and dial them in by hand. With the camera now locked on those settings, you can take all the time you need to shoot your panorama.

Shooting Panoramic Frames

In theory, shooting a panorama is very simple. You work from one side to the other, panning the camera and shooting frames that overlap by at least a third on each end. In practice, it's a bit trickier than this because, to get usable frames, you need to be sure that you're not tilting the camera when you turn to the next frame. Also, it's essential that you pan *the camera* and not your body.

Panning tips

Personally, I find it easiest to work from left to right, but sometimes you might want or need to go the other direction. So, after you've assessed your exposure needs and locked exposure (if necessary), choose the end you want to start on and frame your shot. After taking the shot, rotate the camera and shoot the next frame. Again, aim for about one-third of the frame to overlap the previous shot. To achieve this overlap, just use something in the frame as a reference point.

Try to hold the camera level—parallel to the ground—as you rotate. Most importantly, though, be sure to rotate the camera! The camera needs to be rotated around its focal plane, but if you simply rotate at the waist, then you're rotating the camera around the middle of your head. This can cause troubles later when you try to stitch. So, instead of just pivoting your body, hold the camera where it is and rotate it independently of your body. You may have to move your feet to rotate yourself around the camera while you do this.

It can take practice to get good at shooting straight, usable panoramas, so you'll want to shoot multiple tries to improve your chances of getting something useful. Also, before you start shooting, it's a good idea to rotate through the whole panorama to ensure that your focal length choice fits everything in the scene.

Also, panoramic shooting will get easier after you've stitched a few panoramas and seen the effects of different problems. So, it's a good idea to practice shooting at home, where you can stitch right away, before you head off to an exotic panoramic location.

TIP: Panoramic Tripod Heads

If you're really serious about panoramic shooting, then you might want to invest in a special panoramic tripod head. In addition to holding the camera level throughout its rotation, a panoramic head will provide ratcheted stops that ensure proper overlap. Check out *www.kaidan.com* for more info.

Stitching a Panorama

Once you've shot your panoramic frames, you'll be ready to stitch. Copy the pano frames to your computer using your method of choice. If you haven't already installed Canon PhotoStitch from the EOS Digital Solutions Disk, do so now and then launch the program.

Click the Open button on the left side of the PhotoStitch toolbar. In the Open dialog box that appears, select the file you want to stitch. Hold down the Shift key to select multiple files. PhotoStitch will display your chosen images side by side. You can use the Arrange, Switch, Clear, and Rotate buttons to get the images in the right order, with the right orientation, and use the Enlarge and Reduce buttons to zoom in and out.

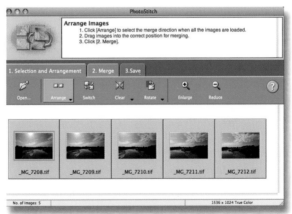

You begin the process of stitching in PhotoStitch by importing your source images.

Next, click the Merge tab and press the Start button. PhotoStitch might prompt you to enter the focal length you used when you were shooting. The program expects 35mm equivalency, so multiply the focal length you used by 1.6. For landscape panoramas, where you're panning and shooting, the Panning technique is the best option. Click the OK button, and PhotoStitch will stitch your image.

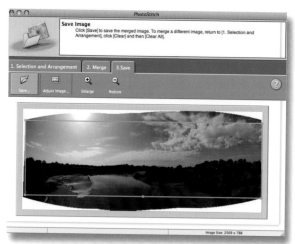

You'll need to crop your image before saving.

When it's done, click the Save tab to view the crop of your final image. Stitching always requires cropping, and you can easily adjust the crop by dragging the cropping handles. When you have the crop that you like, click the Save button to save your image as a TIFF, JPEG, BMP, or PICT. TIFF files are best if you want to edit your image further somewhere else.

> **TIP:** Better Stitching Software
>
> PhotoStitch is fast, easy, and does a good job of stitching, and for free software, it's a great deal. However, you'll find that the latest version of Photoshop does a much better job of stitching.

Low-Light Shooting

A lot of new shooters think that low light means shooting with the flash. And while the flash can often yield good pictures in low light, with your Rebel T1i, you have far more low-light options, thanks to its excellent high ISO capability. You must use care when shooting in low light, but with a little practice you'll probably find that there's a whole world of subject matter that reveals itself when light levels dim.

When to Use Flash in Low Light

Your flash works well when you have a subject that's close to the camera and you want it lit up very brightly, using a light source positioned where you're standing. But flash photos can often look weird or even outright bad. If you're not careful with your exposure, then your subject can look harshly lit, while your background may not be lit at all. We'll discuss flash exposure in detail in the next chapter.

Another problem with flash shooting with the camera's built-in flash is that it washes out the natural light in your scene. Very often, when you're out at night, what might strike you about a particular scene are the unique colors that are created under street lights or other lighting sources that appear only at night.

Finally, many times shooting a flash is inappropriate or simply not allowed. Concerts and performances, art galleries, or any situation where you don't want to be intrusive all rule out flash shooting as a way to get a shot in a low-light situation. For all of these situations—and simply to have more tools in your creative arsenal —you'll want to learn about other low-light shooting techniques.

Shooting in Low Light at High ISO

You've seen how you can increase the T1i's ISO setting to buy yourself more exposure latitude when choosing a shutter speed or aperture, but you'll most often increase ISO when you want to shoot in lower light. Very often, this won't be extreme dark but rather just a small change to compensate for lower light indoors. For example, if you move indoors in the late afternoon, even into a room with windows, you might need to increase your ISO to 200 or 400.

On the T1i, you can easily shoot at up to ISO 1600 without suffering a noticeable noise penalty in your final image. So, if you're shooting indoors and notice that your shutter speed is staying very low, crank up the ISO and you should see a marked increase in shutter speed. However, although the T1i's keeps the noise low at higher ISOs, it's still best to always shoot at the lowest ISO you can manage.

In extreme low light—outside at night, in a concert, or in a performance—you'll need to go to higher ISOs: 800 to 3200. While these settings will yield a little more noise in your image, it's an attractive noise that looks very much like film grain.

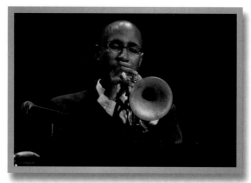

If you're shooting in very low light, you can increase the T1i's ISO

Depending on your final output, you may not even be able to see the noise. For example, if you're printing at 4" x 6", a lot of the noise will be sampled away as the image is downsized.

By default, the T1i shoots high ISO images with very low levels of noise, but you can reduce this further by changing Custom Function 5, High ISO Speed Noise Reduction, from Standard to Strong. This will apply additional noise reduction processing to images shot at higher ISOs. However, because this extra processing takes time, the maximum number of shots you can shoot in a burst will greatly decrease. So, if you're planning on burst shooting, you'll want to leave this feature off. Note, too, that this feature disables white balance bracketing. Also, noise reduction can soften an image. If you find you don't like how soft your images go when High ISO Speed Noise Reduction is applied, then you can use Custom Function 5 to set the feature to Low, or to disable it altogether.

How do you know when to go to higher ISOs like 800, 1600, or 3200? The same way that you choose to go to 200 or 400. If you can't get a shutter speed that's fast enough to shoot handheld in low light or fast enough to suit your creative goals, then increase the ISO to 800 or 1600.

> **WARNING:** Don't Forget to Change Back!
>
> If you spend an evening shooting in low light at ISO 1600, be sure to set your ISO back to Auto or something less noisy, like 100–400. Shooting in bright daylight at ISO 1600 won't hurt anything, but your images will have slightly more noise, and your camera will bias toward faster shutter speeds.

ISO Expansion

In addition to the range of ISOs that you've already seen, the Rebel T1i can shoot two stops beyond ISO 3200: ISO 6400 and 12,800. By Canon's standards, these settings are unacceptably noisy, which is why they're not included on the normal ISO dial. Images you shoot at these higher ISO settings will definitely be grungy, but for times when you absolutely *must* get a shot in low light, and it's too dark for a usable shutter speed at ISO 3200, then these faster settings can be very handy.

To activate these higher ISOs, you must enable *ISO expansion*, which you'll find under Custom Function 2. When ISO expansion is enabled, the ISO menu will show two additional entries: 6400 and H. ISO H is really just 12,800, which makes it two stops faster than ISO 3200. And no, no one knows why they call it "H."

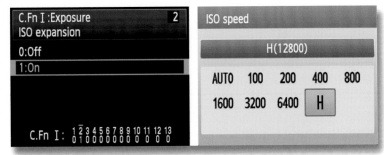

If you activate Custom Function 2, ISO Expansion, then two additional ISO settings will appear in the ISO menu.

Shooting Techniques for Low-Light Situations

Unfortunately, shooting in low light is a little more complicated than just choosing a high ISO and shooting away. Your main concern is to be aware of shutter speed. Remember the handheld shooting rule (shutter speed should never go below 1/*effective focal length*), and keep an eye on the shutter speed in the viewfinder status display. Note too that you can usually hear a slow shutter speed, if you're paying attention. If the "click" of the camera takes a bit longer than you're used to, you might want to check in and see what your shutter speed is set to.

Shooting with a long shutter speed

Sometimes the light is so low that you have no choice but to use a slow shutter speed. Although this may not make for ideal shooting, a slow shutter speed image is usually better than getting no image at all. When shooting at longer shutter speeds, remember the following:

- You'll want to take extra pains to shoot a stable shot. Remember your posture, find something to lean on, find a place to set the camera, or carry a tripod.

- Remember that while you might do a great job of holding still, if your subject is moving, it might come out blurry.

Sometimes, intentionally blurring your subject can be evocative, but if you're trying to document an event, such as a dance performance, then long shutter speeds won't be appropriate.

If you're shooting a landscape or other nonmoving subject, then you can choose an extremely long shutter speed. The T1i lets you select up to 30 seconds for a shutter speed, or you can use Bulb mode to keep the shutter open for as long as you want.

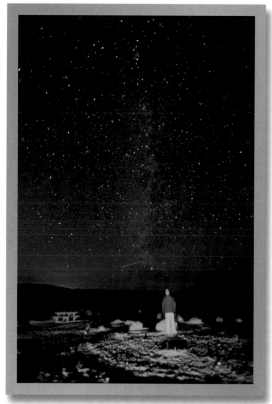

Using Bulb mode, I was able to shoot this extremely low-light shot.

For this image, I used a 90-second exposure. Obviously, the camera must be mounted on a tripod when you're shooting such a long exposure. Bulb mode was required to get the long exposure, and because I didn't want to stand there with my finger on the shutter (both because it's uncomfortable and because it risks introducing camera shake), I used a remote control to trip the shutter. Canon makes both wired and wireless remote controls that are ideal for this type of shooting.

Long exposure noise

When you shoot with very long exposures, you run the risk of introducing an additional type of noise to your images. When the shutter is left open for a long time, some pixels on the image sensor can get "stuck." These pixels will appear in your final image as bright white specks. Fortunately, the camera has a built-in mechanism for handling this situation. If you go to custom functions, you'll find that Custom Function 4 is called *long exposure noise reduction*. Set this function to Auto, and the camera will automatically employ a special noise-removal algorithm any time you shoot with a shutter speed of more than one second.

One caveat about long exposure noise reduction: on an extremely long exposure, the noise reduction processing time might take as long as the actual exposure, and you will not be able to use the camera while it processes. So, a 30-second exposure might require an additional 30 seconds of noise reduction processing. If you're using *extremely* long exposures, measuring in the minutes (or hours), you'll want to factor this extra time into your shooting plan.

Use Mirror Lockup for long exposures

When shooting a very long exposure, you'll want to be especially careful of camera shake. Be sure to use a tripod, use a remote control to trip the shutter, and activate the camera's mirror lockup feature.

As you know, when you press the shutter button, the T1i must raise its mirror out of the way before it opens the shutter and then lower it again. This process can actually vibrate the camera enough to induce softness in a long exposure image. Using Custom Function 9, you can enable Mirror Lockup.

When Mirror Lockup is turned on, pressing the shutter button will raise the mirror but *won't* take a picture. It takes an additional shutter press to take a picture, after which the mirror will come back down. Half-pressing the shutter before the initial press will autofocus and meter, as normal.

> **WARNING:** Beware of Heat
>
> Noise levels in your high-ISO images will increase as the camera gets warmer. It takes a fair amount of heat to create a noticeable change in noise, and the most significant source of heat is usually the camera itself. Try to avoid Live View and extensive use of the LCD screen when shooting high-ISO images, because the LCD screen can heat up the camera significantly. Also, *don't* try to cool the camera by putting it in a refrigerator. The sudden change in temperature can damage internal components.

Aperture control for low-light conditions

Low-light shooting almost always precludes any kind of aperture control, because the only way to get a shot at all is to have the lens wide open. So, don't expect to shoot a lot deep depth of field shots unless you have a tripod and are shooting a nonmoving subject. In these instances, you can stop the lens down and shoot a very long exposure.

Shooting Sports or Stage Performances

Even though sporting events are often held at night and stage performances are often in dark auditoriums, these events are not necessarily "low-light" events. A football field, for example, is usually well lit. However, even with all the floodlighting, you still probably won't be able to get away with shooting at ISO 100 or even 400. Also, for a sporting event you'll probably want some motion-stopping power in your exposure and so will be using a longer shutter speed. This means you'll most likely be shooting at ISO 800 or 1600.

The T1i's Sports shooting mode is very good, but if you want more power, you'll want to switch to Shutter Priority, crank the ISO up, and set a shutter speed that's fast enough to freeze the action. Ideally, you'll have a long telephoto lens with image stabilization. Good sports shots are often the result of anticipation. If you know when the big play is about to transpire and know who the key players are, then you'll want to get focused on them early so that you can get the shot when the action unfolds. To improve your chances of getting the precise moment of interest, switch to Drive mode and put the focus mode on AI Servo.

Press the shutter button just before you think the key moment will transpire and burst through. Remember, the camera's shooting buffer can fill up if you shoot for a long time, so try to keep the length of your bursts low.

If you're shooting in an auditorium, your lighting challenge will be a little more difficult because a stage usually alternates between very bright areas and very dark areas. As with sports shooting, your main concern will be to try to freeze action, so set the camera to a high ISO, use Shutter Priority, and choose a shutter speed that's fast enough to freeze motion—at least a 30th of a second for normal speed motions, faster if performers are moving quickly. In extreme low light, this shutter speed may result in your images being severely underexposed. Don't worry about this, because you can always brighten the images later using an image editor. This will result in noisier pictures, but the only alternative is to shoot with a longer shutter speed and risk blurring motion.

Both of these situations are well-served by a "fast" lens, meaning a lens with an aperture that can open extremely wide. An f2.0 telephoto, or a super-fast prime, such as the Canon 50mm 1.2, 1.4, or 1.8, make ideal low-light event lenses.

Low-Light White Balance

Low-light situations can play havoc with color, both in your eyes and in your camera. Your eyes, of course, see very limited color in low light. As the light dims, the color receptors in your eyes cease working, and your vision shifts over to black and white only. While your vision won't actually look like a black-and-white photo, you will have markedly lower color sensitivity than you would in brighter light. Color reproduction is difficult for your camera in low light because low-light situations are usually lit by an odd assortment of lighting types (for instance, the intentionally colored lights in a stage performance), the combination of which confuses your camera's white balance.

Depending on your situation, you won't necessarily have an in-camera fix for this problem. For example, if you're shooting a stage that's lit by lights that change color, then there's no way to get a manual white balance. Or, perhaps you're shooting far enough away from your subject that you can't get a white balance card into the scene to pull off manual white balance. In these situations, your best bet might be to try to fix color in your image editor. Shooting in raw will make this process much easier, as you'll see later.

Shooting Video

Although your T1i is an excellent still camera, it's also a very capable video camera that can shoot three different sizes of video (with sound), from standard definition all the way up to 1080p HD video.

To shoot video with the T1i, follow these steps:

1. Set the Mode dial to Movie mode ('🎥').

2. Frame your shot and focus, just as you normally do when using Live View.

3. Press the Live View button (📷) to start recording video. When video is recording, a red dot will appear in the upper-right corner of the LCD screen. (This dot matches the red dot on the Live View button, which is how you can remember which button to press to start and stop video recording.) Just to the left of the Flash button, on the left side of the camera, are four small holes. This is the camera's microphone. Be very careful not to cover it up while shooting.

4. Press the Live View button again to stop recording.

When in Movie mode, the shooting menu includes a "Movie rec. size" item, which lets you choose one of the T1i's three frame sizes: 1920 × 1080, 1280 × 720, and 640 × 480.

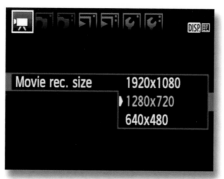

The T1i provides three different video sizes.

The default setting is 1280 × 720, which has a 16:9 aspect ratio. This is the same aspect ratio as a high-definition television. At this size, you can fit 18 minutes of video on a 4 GB card. The 1920 × 1080 resolution is also the same aspect ratio as an HD TV, and if your TV is capable of display 1080 resolution, then you'll possibly see a finer level of detail when shooting in this mode. However, note that when shooting in 1920 × 1080 mode, the frame rate will drop to 20 frames per second, which can make movement in the frame less smooth. In the other modes, you'll capture a full 30 frames per second. You can store a maximum of 12 minutes of video on a 4 GB card when shooting in 1920 × 1080 mode. (Note that YouTube now accepts 1280 x 720 video compressed in the H.264 format. This is precisely the size and compression that the T1i uses, making it ideal for YouTube postings.)

In these modes, the LCD screen is cropped at the top and bottom, to show you the true aspect ratio of the resulting image. (The Rebel T1i's screen and still images have a 3:2 aspect ratio.)

The 640 × 480 mode provides the same 4:3 aspect ratio as a standard definition TV, and the camera records a full 30 frames per second in this mode. You can store a maximum of 24 minutes of video on a 4 GB card. If you're shooting video that you only intend to post online, then this will be the best choice. No matter what mode you're shooting in, or how big your storage card is, the camera will automatically stop shooting if the movie size hits 4 GB. You can start it again with another press of the Live View button.

For best results when shooting video, you'll want to use a fast memory card. If you use a slow card, the camera may have a hard time dumping its data to the card with enough speed to maintain shooting. At that point, a thermometer-type indicator will appear on the right side of the screen; this display indicates how much data still needs to be written to the card. If it fills up, movie recording will automatically stop. If you run into this problem consistently, you'll need to get a faster card. Canon recommends using SDHC cards with at least a Class 6 rating.

Video Shooting Tips

Shooting video with your T1i is a little different than shooting video with a point-and-shoot camera, mostly because of the focusing issue. The T1i does not continuously autofocus as you, or your subject, moves around. So, if the distance between you and your subject changes, there's a chance that your subject will go out of focus.

The only workaround for this is to try manually focusing while shooting, which can be difficult, both because it's hard to see when the image is in focus and because handling the camera can be tricky. You can also press the ✳ button to force the camera to autofocus, but this is usually not a good idea, as there's a chance that the camera will first swing way *out* of focus before finally coming back into focus. The same autofocus modes that you find in Live View are also available in Movie mode, and you can select them from the shooting menu.

From the shooting menu, you can also choose to activate grid displays, to ease level shooting; turn sound recording off (to save space); or enable a remote control, which will allow you to remotely start and stop recording. If you press the Set button while in Movie mode, a menu will appear that allows you to change picture style and white balance mode, and shows you the amount of recording time remaining on the card. To change either picture style or white balance, use the up/down arrows to navigate to that menu option, then turn the Main dial to change to a different setting.

> **WARNING:** Heat Equals Noise
>
> It's very important to understand that the longer you leave the camera in movie mode, the warmer the camera will get. Running the LCD screen simply generates a lot of heat. Unfortunately, as the camera gets hotter, your images will get noisier. If the camera gets too hot, it will display a small thermometer icon. At this point, you should shut the camera off and let it cool down for a while.

With regard to sound, note that because the microphone is in the camera body, the sound of *all* camera handling will be recorded. Every button press, lens movement, and bump of the camera will be recorded as a fairly loud thump. So, if audio is critical, you'll want to be very careful about handling the camera while shooting, or you'll want to record audio on a separate recording device, and re-sync it later.

Finally, note that you can continue to shoot stills while recording video. Just press the shutter button just as you normally would, and the camera will write out an image. However, still shots will cause a roughly one-second pause in your video recording.

> **WARNING:** Avoid Any Sudden Pans
>
> Be very careful about making very quick pans with the camera (called *whip pans* in the video and movie trade). Sometimes, if you pan too quickly, the top of the frame will pan faster than the bottom, resulting in an image that looks like it's made out of Jello. This problem is known as *rolling shutter*, and it can sometimes affect fast-moving objects within your frame.

Exposure Control for Video

You can use the T1i's Exposure Compensation control when shooting video, just as you do when shooting stills. If bright objects in your scene are blowing out to complete white, you might want to dial in a negative exposure compensation. Similarly, if a bright sky is causing shadow areas to underexpose, then you might want to dial in a positive exposure compensation.

Note, too, that as you pan the camera around, it might re-meter, which can cause your image to suddenly brighten or darken. If you don't want this to happen, press the ISO button to lock the exposure. Once exposure is locked, you can press the ISO button again, to re-meter. So, as you pan the camera around, you can continue to re-meter your scene. Movie mode always operates in Auto ISO, and the Rebel will display its current ISO setting at the bottom of the screen.

Unfortunately, there's no way to choose a shutter speed or aperture when shooting video, which means you can't force the camera to shoot with shallow depth of field. If you're really serious about video, then there is a workaround to this problem, which is to buy an old Nikon lens (that's right, Nikon) that has a manual aperture ring, and then fit it to the Rebel using a Canon to Nikon adapter. This will allow you to control aperture manually.

Honestly, at this point, you're probably better off with a real video camera. With its long-duration shooting limitations and its awkward handling, the Rebel is really aimed at simple movie recording, not complex production.

Movie Playback

To play back a movie you've shot with the T1i:

1. Press the Play button (▶) to go into Playback mode.

2. Use the left and right arrows to find the movie you want to play.

3. Press the Set button to activate a set of on-screen playback controls.

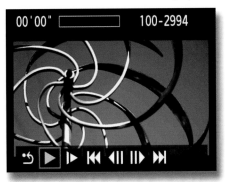

You can play back your video files on the T1i's LCD screen.

4. Use the arrow keys to select the button you want to press, and then click Set to activate it. For example, to play the movie, highlight the Play button (as shown above) and press Set.

During movie playback, you can adjust the volume of the movie by turning the Main dial. When watching movies on the camera, be aware that movies can be played only when shown at full screen size. If you've zoomed out to view a thumbnail display of multiple images and movies, you won't be able to access movie playback features.

You can view your movies on a TV monitor, just as you do with still images. Note, though, that if you have a monitor connected to the Rebel *while* you're shooting video, the image on the screen will be smaller than the actual image that's being recorded. Also, the TV will not play any sound from the movie. When you play back the image, though, it will play with sound, and at full size.

CHAPTER 10

Flash Shooting

USING A FLASH AND OTHER TOOLS FOR BETTER
CONTROL OF THE LIGHTING IN YOUR SCENE

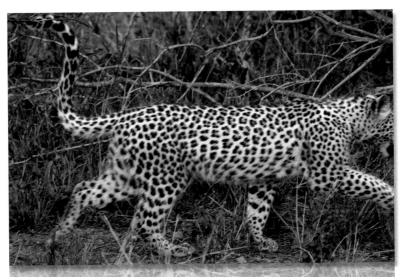

Using a flash is not hard, but it *is* something that sometimes requires
a little bit of extra thought and planning. In fact, one of the most
important things to learn about your camera's flash is when *not* to
use it. You've already learned some low-light shooting tricks that
provide you with additional strategies for shooting in dark situations,
but sometimes you simply need more illumination to get a good
shot. The Rebel T1i has a capable built-in flash, as well as support for
Canon's entire line of external flashes. In this chapter we'll look at both
built-in and external flash use, as well as some additional ways that
you can control light, regardless of whether you choose to use a flash.

Controlling Existing Light

Before we get into a full discussion of flash shooting, let's look at some simple non-flash-related strategies you can employ to control the light in your scene.

In Chapter 7, you learned about fill flash and saw how you can use the T1i's built-in flash to fill in some of the more shadowy areas in your scene to create a more even exposure. Although the flash can work well for this situation and is definitely easy to carry, sometimes a better alternative is to use a reflector.

Consider this image:

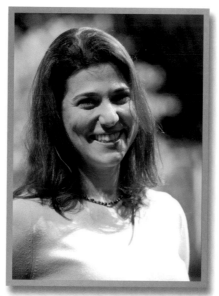

The lighting in this image, direct sunlight, is pretty harsh and contrasty.

The direct sunlight is so bright that we're getting deep shadows under her eyes, cheekbones, chin, and hair. In general, the image has too much contrast. We could use a fill flash to even out the exposure a little bit, but then we'd run the risk of the image looking a little flat. If we have the time, gear, and personnel to pull it off, we can choose a different solution. Using a diffuser, which is a piece of sheer white fabric, we can diffuse the sunlight to create a much softer look.

The diffuser serves the same function as a cloud. It diffuses the sunlight so that it's not as harsh, and the result is an image with lighter shadows and highlights that are not as small and bright.

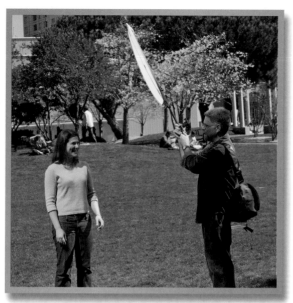

Here, a diffuser is placed between our light source
(in this case, the sun) and our subject.

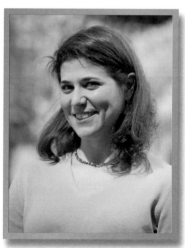

With the diffuser in place, we get a much gentler light that softens the shadows
under the eyes, chin, and hair.

While this image is much better, we can still do more. The shadows under the eyes and chin are still a little prominent, so we'll use a reflector to bounce some light up into them, rather like our fill flash would.

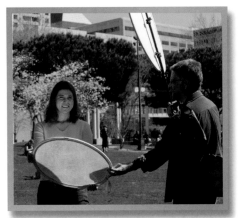
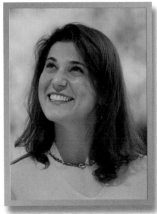

Here we're using a diffuser to cut the intensity of the sunlight and a reflector to add some fill light back onto our subject.

Using a reflector like this is not difficult. Just try to put it at a 45° angle to the light source—in this case, the sun. You'll be able to see the difference in person as you move the reflector around. Just watch the shadows, and when you see them lighten, you know you've positioned the reflector properly. Expose and shoot normally.

If you don't have a friend to help hold the reflector, then you can use a tripod and a remote control to trigger the shutter, or you can use the self-timer. You'll need to get in place quickly, so you'll probably want to experiment with the reflector position before you take the shot.

You can use any large piece of reflective material. While a large piece of white cardboard or foamcore isn't the easiest thing in the world to carry, any photo store will carry collapsible reflectors that fold into a small circle, usually about a foot in diameter. These can pack easily into a backpack or suitcase. What's more, these reflectors come in different colors, from white to silver to gold, allowing you to get more or less *reflectance*, or reflected light that has a color tint to it.

As mentioned earlier, you can sometimes use your camera's flash instead of the reflector to get the fill. However, if you're standing farther away from your subject —perhaps so as to use a more flattering focal length—your flash might be out of range, especially on a very bright day. Because a reflector is close to your subject, it might actually provide more illumination than your flash can.

Using the T1i's On-Camera Flash

In Chapter 7, you saw how you can use the on-camera flash to even out an exposure by brightening a dark subject when your background is too bright. You've also seen how you can use fill flash to even out darker shadows in a scene.

But there will be times when you're in a dimly lit room and simply need some extra light. In these snapshot-type situations, the T1i's onboard flash can do a good job of illuminating your scene, but you might need to take a little more control to get a good shot.

Flash Exposure

When you half-press the shutter button while the flash is popped up, the T1i calculates an exposure, just as it does when the flash is down. However, with the flash up, it bases its exposure on its understanding of how much light the flash will be able to add to the scene. In Program mode, the camera will never pick a shutter speed slower than 60, to ensure handheld shooting. It will also never pick a shutter speed faster than 200, because it's not possible for the entire sensor to be exposed to the flash if the shutter speed exceeds 200.

When you take a shot after metering, the camera will turn the flash on. When it sees that enough light has been added to the scene to properly expose it at the current settings, it then turns the flash off. In other words, although it might appear that the flash is always just a quick flash of light, the T1i is actually carefully monitoring the situation and firing the flash for longer or shorter periods of time.

> **WARNING:** Waiting for Recharge
>
> Before the flash can fire, it must charge up, a process that is usually very speedy. As your battery weakens, though, flash recycle time can worsen. The T1i will display a busy indicator in the viewfinder while the flash is charging. When the busy indicator is displayed, you'll still be able to shoot, but the flash will not fire.

Flash with Priority and Manual modes

If you're using the flash in Shutter Priority mode, then the camera will not let you select a shutter speed faster than 1/200th. As always, it will automatically calculate an aperture that's appropriate for your speed.

In Aperture Priority mode, no matter what aperture you pick, the camera will never choose a shutter speed faster than 1/200th.

In both modes, though, you can have shutter speeds that are much slower than 1/60th. This allows you to achieve the same slow-sync shutter effect that the Night Portrait scene mode creates (you learned about this mode in Chapter 1). *Slow-sync shutter* means the camera combines a flash shot with a long exposure to create a scene that has good exposure in both the foreground and the background.

If you haven't read the "Understand Flash Range" section in Chapter 1, you should do so now.

The Night Portrait mode is an easy and effective way to get slow-sync effects, but if you're shooting raw or want more white balance or ISO control, then you'll need to use Aperture Priority or Shutter Priority mode.

> **REMINDER:** Tell Your Subject Not to Move
>
> As with Night Portrait mode, when you shoot using a slow-sync shutter, it's important to tell your subjects not to move until you say it's okay. Most people will move as soon as the flash fires, but if the camera is set for a very long exposure, this can create blur.

In Manual mode you can select any combination of shutter speed and aperture, but as you would expect, you can't choose a shutter speed faster than 1/200th of a second. As always in Manual mode, if you dial in exposure settings that would result in an over- or underexposure, the camera will warn you by flashing the Exposure Compensation display to indicate the amount of exposure error.

Flash Exposure Compensation

In addition to changing the shutter speed and aperture settings as you normally would, you can also tell the camera to add more or less flash to your scene. For example, consider the flash exposure compensation image at the top of the next page.

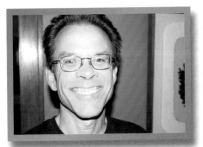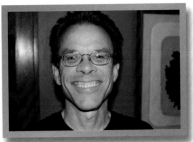

The flash in our left exposure is too bright, but we can dial it back using flash exposure compensation to produce the right image.

The flash has added a lot of brightness to the scene, but in the process, our subject has overblown highlights on him that make him look too harshly exposed. By using *flash exposure compensation* we can tell the camera to use less flash so that more of the natural light in our scene is used, and the harsh highlights are reduced. I shot the image on the right using a flash exposure compensation of -1 stop.

To activate Flash Exposure Compensation, choose Flash Control from the first Shooting menu, then choose "Built-in flash func. setting". You'll find Flash Exp. Comp in the resulting menu, just below Shutter Sync. You specify flash exposure compensation in stops, just like you do normal exposure compensation.

The image on the right has much better exposure and lacks the overblown highlights. A quick check of the histograms of the images confirms that the second exposure is better (it lacks the overexposure spike on the right side).

I didn't know ahead of time that 1/3rd of a stop would be enough, but because you can review your image and histogram as soon as you take the shot, it's easy to find the right exposure. So, if you go into a situation like a party in a dark room and plan on shooting flash, you might want to try a few tests right away to determine a proper flash exposure. Then you can shoot with those settings as long as the lighting doesn't change significantly.

> **TIP:** Don't Forget the Histogram
>
> Because the T1i's LCD screen isn't a perfectly accurate representation of exposure, it's important to check the histogram if you think there's a chance of overexposure. If you see a white spike on the right side of the histogram, then you'll need to adjust your flash exposure compensation and shoot again.

Improving flash range

Flash exposure compensation also lets you increase the amount of flash that gets added to a scene. However, this increase does not improve the range of your flash. Remember, all your camera can do is control how long the flash is on, but just as a desk lamp doesn't light up a bigger area if you leave it on for longer, your T1i's flash doesn't get a longer reach with an increased exposure setting.

However, you can effectively improve the range of the flash by increasing the camera's ISO. Light intensity falls off as it travels farther from its source, and when the camera's image sensor is dialed up to a higher level of light sensitivity, it will be able to pick up the fainter levels of light that have traveled farther away. Page 62 of the Rebel T1i instruction manual provides a chart that gives you an idea of how much of a range increase you can expect at different focal lengths.

In that chart, you'll see that at ISO 1600, with an 18mm lens, you can expect a range of about 50 feet. But remember, that doesn't mean objects 50 feet out will get the full flash exposure. You'll still want to review your images carefully and consider using a slow-sync flash exposure.

> **TIP:** Consistent Flash Overexposure
>
> If the display consistently blinks when you try to shoot a flash exposure, try lowering the ISO. If you've left the ISO at a very high setting and then go into a bright situation and try to use fill flash, the camera will probably not be able to get a good exposure. Dialing down the ISO should help.

Red-Eye Reduction

If you've spent a lot of time shooting flash snapshots with a point-and-shoot camera, then you've probably seen *red eye*, that creepy phenomenon that causes your subject's eyes to glow red. The red glow is nothing more than the reflection of the flash's light off the back of the subject's irises. (Dogs' eyes, by comparison, reflect blue light.) Although image-editing tools can remove this effect, it's often better to try to solve the problem while shooting to save editing time later.

The closer the flash is to the lens of a camera, the more likely it is that you'll get red eye, because the light from the flash can bounce straight off of your subject's eyes and back into the camera. Because the T1i has a flash that sits a ways from the lens, the chance of red eye is far less than it is with a point-and-shoot. However, it still can happen, which is why the Rebel T1i has a built-in red-eye reduction feature that can very effectively eliminate the effect.

To activate red-eye reduction, select the feature in the first Shooting menu, and turn it on.

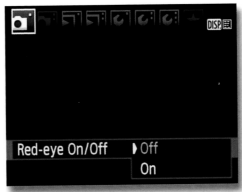

You can activate the built-in flash's red-eye reduction from Shooting menu 1.

When red-eye reduction is activated, every time you half-press the shutter, the camera will activate the red-eye reduction lamp, the one that flashes when you use the self-timer. The idea is that the lamp will cause the irises in your subject's eyes to close down, thus reducing the chance of red eye. For this to work, you must be certain that your fingers don't block the lamp.

Obviously, the lamp can be a bit distracting and in some venues might be very inappropriate, so you'll most likely want to turn the feature off when you're not using it.

> **WARNING:** Don't Shoot Too Close with the Flash
>
> Even if you dial flash exposure compensation down two stops, the flash will still put out a good amount of light. When shooting with the flash, it's best to stay at least three to four feet from your subject. Any closer can severely overexpose them.

Using an External Flash

On the top of the camera sits a *hotshoe*, a fairly standard camera interface that allows you to use a number of different accessories. It's called a hotshoe because it's an interface that provides electrical contacts through which the camera can communicate with an attached accessory (as opposed to a coldshoe, which has the same type of mount but provides no communication between the camera body and whatever is in the shoe).

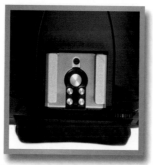

You can attach an external flash to the hotshoe on the top of the camera.

You can use the hotshoe to attach special wireless or wired remotes, levels (for ensuring your camera isn't tilted), umbrellas to keep your camera dry, and other specialized accessories. But hotshoes are most commonly used for external flash units.

Even though the T1i has a built-in flash, there are a number of reasons to use an external flash. They're more powerful, so they can cover a longer range and offer more latitude for exposure adjustment. Flash units all provide a specification called a *guide number* that indicates how powerful the flash unit is. For example, on page 214 of the Rebel T1i's instruction manual, you'll find a listing for Guide Number: 13/43 (ISO 100, in meters/feet). This number represents a constant that you can use to determine the range of the flash at a given aperture. For example, a guide number of 43 indicates that the flash can fully illuminate an object roughly 10 feet away when shooting at f4. (Ten feet multiplied by 4 is 40.)

These numbers used to be important for calculating manual exposures and for figuring out how to expose when using multiple flashes. If that last paragraph didn't make sense to you, don't worry, because you really don't need to keep track of this stuff anymore: the camera and flash will do it all for you.

Canon sells three different flash units that are compatible with the T1i, as well as two special flash attachments for macro shooting. You can see these on page

196 of the instruction manual. The Speedlight 430EX II has a guide number of 141 feet/43 meters, whereas the Speedlight 580EX II, Canon's largest external flash unit, has a guide number of 191 feet/58 meters. So, if you're willing to spend the money (and carry an extra component), you can pack a lot of illumination power into your camera bag.

Having the extra power doesn't just mean you can light up a subject farther away. With a larger flash, you'll be able to fill a larger area with more light.

External flashes also offer the advantage of being able to *slave* multiple units together. With multiple flashes, you can create complex lighting solutions. You've seen how you can use a fill flash to improve images shot under direct sunlight. With multiple flashes you're in control of several light sources, allowing for a tremendous amount of lighting creativity. The use of multiple flashes is far beyond the scope of this book and is something that most shooters don't need.

However, external flashes also give you the option to tilt and bounce the flash, rather than aiming it directly at your subject. This is probably the greatest advantage of an external flash, and when combined with the stronger power of these units, the tilt/swivel capability allows you to create very natural-looking lighting.

One of the biggest problems with flash pictures is that the flash is always located in the same location as your camera. In other words, the main source of illumination for your subject is located just a little above your head. This is very rarely how real-world light sources work, so flash pictures always look like…well, flash pictures.

In the real world, we're used to light coming from overhead, and we're also used to those light sources being larger than a single bulb the size of the T1i's flash head. Lighting that shines onto the front of a person, from a very small source, simply doesn't look natural to us.

Bouncing a Flash

When we speak of *bouncing* a flash or a light source, it's easy to think of that bouncing as being billiard-ball-like, or like bouncing a laser off a bunch of mirrors. With this analogy, then you might think you have to worry about lining up the flash just right so that the light bounces in a way that will strike your subject. Fortunately, this isn't the case.

The flash on your T1i, or an external flash unit, emits light in a conical pattern. So, as the light travels farther away, it spreads out. If you point the light at the ceiling to use it as a big reflector, then by the time the light hits the ceiling, it will be fairly widely dispersed. The ceiling will reflect that light back down and create a light that's much more natural-looking, both because it will be coming from overhead and because it will be very diffuse, rather than the point light that your flash produces if you aim it directly at a subject.

Consequently, when you think about lighting, you shouldn't just think of the source; you should also think about the path of the light. If light is shining from a source directly onto your subject, then, yes, the light source is your source of illumination. But if the light is bouncing off something else, say, a reflector, then the reflector is your light source. This is an important distinction, because a reflector can change the characteristics of a light. It can alter its color or make it more diffuse.

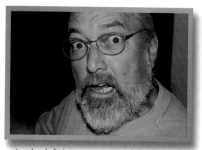 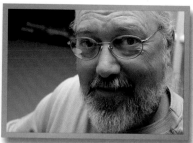

In the left image, we used the T1i's built-in flash. In the right image, we used an external flash pointed at the ceiling. Note that the bounced flash lights up a larger area, including the background, is more diffuse (there are no bright highlights on his face), and creates a very natural-looking overhead light.

With a Canon Speedlight like the 430EX II or 580EX II, you simply tilt the flash head up. The flash calculates the appropriate exposure for a good bounce and is usually very accurate in its calculations.

If you're dealing with an especially high ceiling, then you may want to tilt the flash forward a little so that the bounce goes directly over your subject.

Just as you can use flash exposure compensation to increase or decrease the amount of flash power in the built-in flash, when an external flash is connected, this same control will increase or decrease the output of the external unit.

As with the internal flash, check the camera's histogram to ensure you have a good exposure. If you see an overexposure, adjust flash exposure compensation and shoot again.

CHAPTER 11

Raw Shooting

USING RAW FORMAT TO GAIN MORE CONTROL
AND BETTER IMAGE QUALITY

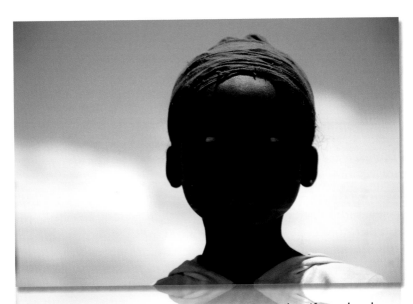

The Rebel T1i produces excellent JPEG images, but if you do a lot of image editing, want the absolute best color you can manage, or tend to shoot in extreme lighting situations that make exposure and white balance tricky, then you'll want to look at raw shooting. Shooting raw has its drawbacks, but by the end of this chapter, shooting in raw will probably become a regular part of your photographic life. In fact, don't be surprised if you eschew JPEG shooting altogether.

What Is Raw?

In Chapter 7, you saw how, with JPEGs, the camera takes the data off the image sensor and performs a number of processes to it, from white balance adjustment to gamma correction to a number of corrections and adjustments similar to what you might apply in an image editor. You also learned that one of the last things the camera does before saving a JPEG image is throw out a lot of color data so that the 14-bit image that the camera captured can be stored in the 8-bit space that the JPEG format specification dictates. Earlier, I also told you about JPEG compression and how it is a lossy compression scheme that can, when used aggressively, degrade your image.

Although the T1i's high-quality JPEG compression is very good (you'll be hard-pressed to find evidence of JPEG compression in an T1i file saved at high quality), if you later perform a few edits in your image editor and save the file *again* as a JPEG, then you might start seeing some blocky patterns. Similarly, though the camera has to toss out 6 bits of data per pixel when it saves to JPEG, you won't necessarily notice a lack of color in the JPEG files saved by the camera. However, once you start editing and begin to brighten or darken areas, you might notice that gradient areas of your image (skies or reflections on a curved surface, for example) start to look chunky as you push your edits further. This is a result of the camera having to jettison some of its color data to save the file as a JPEG.

When you shoot in raw format, the camera skips all these image-processing steps —including the bit-depth conversion and JPEG compression. Instead, the raw data that is captured by the image sensor is read and saved. No demosaicing or color conversion is performed. The data is saved, and *all* the processing that the camera normally would perform is skipped entirely. Instead, you will later use special software on your computer to perform the calculations that are necessary to turn the raw data into a usable image.

> **TIP:** Picture Styles and Raw Files
>
> If you're using a picture style, it's noted in the raw file, but picture styles affect the raw conversion of your image only if you use Canon's Digital Photo Professional (DPP) software. Other raw converters ignore these picture styles. So, if you're shooting raw and *not* using DPP, there's no reason to use picture styles, unless you're shooting Raw + JPEG, in which case the JPEG images will receive the picture style effects.

Why Use Raw?

Using raw has many advantages, and we've already mentioned two important ones—that the full bit depth of your image is preserved and that there's no JPEG compression—but there are other reasons.

Changing White Balance

As I explained in the previous section, when you shoot raw, *all* white balance adjustment functions are deferred until later and are performed on your computer. This means you can set the white balance to anything you want *after you've shot the image!* So, if you were shooting in an especially tricky white balance situation, you could simply perform the equivalent of a manual white balance while editing your image on your computer.

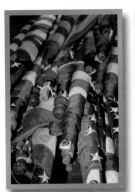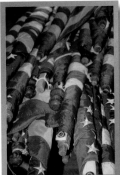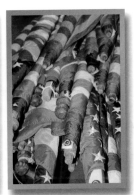

With a raw file, you can achieve radically different white balances after you shoot your image.

Highlight Recovery

Raw files also allow you to perform a seemingly magical type of edit. You've seen what happens to a JPEG image when you overexpose the highlights: they turn to complete white and lose all detail. No matter how you edit the image, that detail is gone, and those areas will remain white.

With a raw file, though, there's a good chance you'll be able to recover the lost detail in your overexposed highlights.

If recovering data from nothing seems impossible, know that an overexposed white area is not necessarily devoid of data. You've already learned that a pixel is composed of separate red, green, and blue elements. Sometimes when you overexpose an area in a scene, you don't overexpose all three color channels. Sometimes only one or two channels get clipped, and another channel is properly exposed.

In these instances, the raw conversion software you use on your computer can reconstruct the wrecked channels by analyzing the channel that's still intact and thus restore image data.

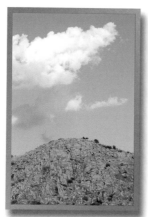 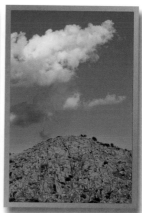

In the left image, notice that the bright parts of the clouds have been overexposed to complete white. If you were shooting JPEG, there'd be nothing you could do to repair this problem. Because the image is raw, though, you can recover the overexposed highlights to restore detail to those areas.

This means you can't recover *all* clipped highlights. Any highlight that is completely overexposed—that is, a highlight that has clipped all three channels—will be unrecoverable.

The ability to recover highlights doesn't mean you don't still need to be thoughtful about exposures, but it *does* give you a safety net for times when you—or your camera—choose an exposure that results in overexposed, blown-out highlights.

More Editing Latitude

Let's return for a moment to the 8-bit versus 14-bit issue and take a closer look at the raw file's bit depth advantage over JPEG files. Simply put, shooting with raw is like having a box of 64 crayons, rather than a wimpy box of 16 crayons. Straight out of the camera, you won't see a difference between a 14-bit processed raw file and an 8-bit JPEG file. But once you start editing, you'll find that raw files offer a lot more flexibility.

Smooth gradients and transitions are a critical component of quality color. While it's easy to think of the sky as simply "blue," the sky is a huge range of colors from dark blue up high to light blue near the horizon. Later in the day, you might see it go from blue to purple to red, all in a perfectly smooth gradient. Most objects and surfaces in the world have a similar variation in color because of multiple light sources, shadows, and reflections that strike the surface at various angles.

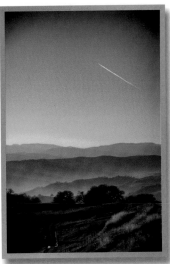

Smooth gradients are critical to an image like this, which has a sky that ranges from dark blue to orange. Gradients are also necessary to render the foggy portions. Chrome and reflections have similar requirements.

Because our visual world is composed largely of gradients and variations of colors, it's essential that your camera be able to produce a huge range of intermediate tones. For a gradient to appear realistic and smooth, you want it to be composed of as many colors as possible. Although an 8-bit JPEG file can render smooth gradients, when you begin to edit that file—brightening and darkening or changing colors—the smooth color transitions in your image may start to suffer.

Consider a staircase. If you need to build a staircase that rises 15 feet but you have only a small amount of wood, then you'll have to make very large steps to cover these 15 feet of rise. These steps will be strenuous to climb. But, if you need to build a staircase that rises 15 feet and you have an abundance of wood, then you can build refined steps that are the perfect height for most people's gait so that they're easily ascended. Gradients work the same way. If you have only a few colors to work with, it can be hard to build a gradient that looks smooth and natural.

JPEG images can create nice gradients, but once you start to edit them, things can quickly fall apart. For example, consider this nice smooth gradient that goes from dark gray to light gray:

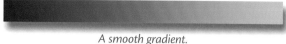

A smooth gradient.

Let's say we wanted to expand the contrast in this gradient. That is, we want to darken the dark tones and lighten the light tones so that the gradient stretches from full black to bright white. The problem with such an edit is that your image-editing software can't make up new tones. Computers simply aren't smart enough to figure out intermediate tones in a situation like this. Instead, it has to take the existing tones and brighten them or darken them. The result looks like this:

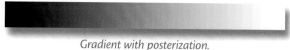

Gradient with posterization.

See the ugly banding patterns? That's called *posterization*, and it happens any time you try to expand a range of tones without adding new intermediate tones. Every edit you make to an image "uses up" some of the editing latitude that's inherent in the file, because each edit—whether it's a change in brightness or a change in color—shifts some tones around and introduces the risk of posterization.

With a raw file, though, you're starting with so much more color data than what you have in a JPEG file that you have much more editing latitude. You can perform more edits and push them much further before you see any posterization artifacts. If you do a lot of adjustment and editing, this is a critical reason to use raw.

A True Digital Negative

The fact that raw processing takes place in the computer and not in the camera has certain advantages. First, you're in control of it, so you can tailor the processing exactly to your taste. For example, you can choose to recover highlights, render some areas brighter, or change the white balance. Second, your camera is designed to perform as quickly as possible. It can't sit around all day meticulously processing an image, because it needs to be sure it's ready to shoot the next picture when you ask it to. Consequently, the processing employed inside the camera uses slightly less-sophisticated algorithms than what a desktop raw converter will use. This means you'll probably get better color out of your desktop raw converter than you will out of a JPEG file that's been processed by the camera. It's a slim chance, because the JPEG quality in the T1i is very good, but for a tricky image it can be important.

Finally, the raw file is truly like a negative. It's simply raw data, and the final image that results from that data depends on the software you use to process it. Raw conversion software is improving all the time as imaging engineers discover new algorithms and refine old ones. This means that years from now you might be able to reprocess the same raw files in a newer raw converter and get better results. In the short term, this also means you can process the same image in different ways to get very different results. For example, you might process the image one way to produce a very warm result and another way to produce something much cooler. By processing the raw file in different ways, you can achieve very different adjustments without using up any of your image-editing latitude.

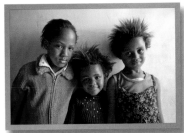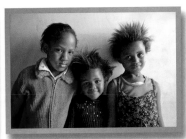

On the left is a fairly accurate representation of this scene; on the right is one that has been warmed up. Both were processed from the same raw file.

Easy Batch Processing

With a raw converter, it's easy to apply the same edits to multiple images. For example, if you come back from a shoot and find that the white balance is off on all your images and that they're all about half a stop underexposed, you can easily apply a white balance change and exposure adjustment to the entire batch at once. With JPEG files, you'd have to open each JPEG and apply the edits, being careful to save in a way that won't further degrade your image.

Raw Hassles (the Disadvantages)

I shoot exclusively raw on all the cameras that support raw format. But raw shooting does present some extra headaches that you won't find when shooting JPEG images. As software improves, these headaches are getting fewer and fewer, and it's easy enough to work around them. However, before you dive into the world of raw, you'll want to consider these caveats:

Raw files take up more space Raw files are larger than JPEG files—sometimes a lot larger. JPEG compression is very effective at squeezing the size of an image. On the Rebel T1i, you'll typically find that shooting in raw adds in excess of 10 MB to the size of *every image* you shoot.

On the Rebel T1i, you can fit about 174 JPEG files on a 1 GB card, but only about 56 raw files. (I say "about" because file size varies depending on the content of the file. For more information on file sizes and memory capacities, check out the chart on page 70 of the T1i Owner's Manual.) Obviously, this larger file size means you'll need more storage cards for your camera. But it also means you'll need more disk space for your postproduction work and more long-term storage for archiving—whether that's hard disks or recordable CDs and DVDs. Fortunately, storage of all kinds is cheap these days, so ramping up to a raw-worthy storage capacity is not too expensive.

Other people may not be able to read your files There's no standard for raw format images. Every camera maker uses a different raw format, and sometimes they even change formats from camera to camera. JPEGs are a standard, so it's easy to hand other people images straight out of your camera and know they'll be able to read them. With raw files, they'll need a raw converter that supports your camera.

Your software of choice may not support the T1i Because there's no standard for raw format, companies that make raw conversion software have to build custom raw profiles for every camera they want to support. When a new camera comes out, this often means you have to wait until your software of choice supports it.

Your workflow might be a little more complicated With JPEG files, you simply take the images out of the camera and look at them in any program that can read JPEGs. And there are a *lot* of programs that can read JPEGs. Your operating system probably shipped with a JPEG viewer, you can open them in any web browser, you can open them in almost any image-editing program, and your email program and cell phone can probably even read them!

With raw files, before you can even look at the file, you must pass it through a raw processor Windows Vista and Mac OS both have raw converters built into the operating system, which means you should at least be able to see a preview of the raw file (assuming you've installed an update that adds support for the Rebel T1i), but if you want to edit or create a file that you can give to someone else, then you'll have to first run the images through a raw converter.

This may sound like a hassle, but the process is actually not so bad. Raw-processing software has improved tremendously over the years, including Canon's Digital Photo Professional, which was bundled with your camera. You may have to learn one or two more steps, but once you do, you'll probably find that shooting raw is no more difficult than shooting JPEG and is well worth the extra control.

Shooting Raw with the Rebel T1i

Telling the T1i to shoot raw is very simple: you just select one of the raw options from the Quality menu in Shooting Menu 1 (you can also make this change from the Info screen). After all the JPEG options, you'll find two raw options. Raw tells the camera to save a raw file, whereas **RAW** + **◢L** tells the camera to save a raw file *and* a JPEG file. Why would you choose both? The advantage of **RAW** + **◢L** is that when you get home, you have a JPEG file that you can use right away, without hassling with any raw processing. After you select your raw format option of choice, you can start shooting normally.

> **TIP:** Raw + JPEG to Get Dual Advantages
>
> Some people, especially those on tight deadlines, shoot Raw + JPEG because they need to deliver only JPEG files to their client, and the T1i JPEGs are excellent quality. So, after a shoot, they can sort through their images, pull out the JPEG images they like, and send them on their way. If one of the files has bad white balance or a clipped highlight, then you have the raw file to use for correction. They can write out a better JPEG from the raw file and send that off later. Shooting Raw + JPEG takes more space and slows the camera down. If you need to shoot sustained bursts, then Raw + JPEG is probably not a good idea, especially if you have a slower media card. If you're not ready to commit completely to raw, then Raw + JPEG is a good intermediate step.

Picture Styles, White Balance, and Raw

Picture styles and white balance are functions that are performed by the camera during the image-processing steps that happen after you take a shot. Because raw files have no processing applied to them, picture styles and white balance choice are less significant. However, the white balance setting you choose is stored in the image's metadata. Later, your raw converter will read this setting and use it as the default white balance for that image. Because white balance in a raw file is completely editable after you shoot, you're free to change it any way you want.

When shooting raw, the white balance you set on the camera is simply a way to have a more convenient postproduction workflow. If you get white balance right in-camera, it will save you a couple of editing steps later. (As opposed to JPEG, where if you get white balance wrong, there's probably no way to correct it later.)

The picture style you choose is also embedded in the raw file. However, the only raw converter that reads this picture style data is Canon's Digital Photo Professional, which is included on the EOS Digital Solutions Disk. If you're not going to use DPP for your raw conversions, then there's no need to use picture styles when shooting raw. If you're shooting Raw + JPEG, then the white balance and picture style choices you make are more critical, because they will be applied to the JPEG file that is saved alongside the raw file. Similarly, if you shoot with Peripheral Illumination Correction active, this will also be noted in the raw file, and Digital Photo Professional will apply the appropriate correction when you process the file. However, just as when you're shooting JPEG with this feature, if your lens isn't supported, no correction will be applied. As with picture styles, Peripheral Illumination Correction doesn't get applied if you're using a raw converter other than Digital Photo Professional.

Processing Your Raw Files

When you're done shooting, copy your raw files to your computer using whatever technique you normally use for JPEGs. If you're using a version of Photoshop or Photoshop Elements, Aperture, Lightroom, or iPhoto, then you'll be able to work with your images just as if they were JPEGs. The browser functions built into these applications will be able to read the files (assuming they've been updated with T1i support) and display thumbnails. iPhoto, Aperture, and Lightroom let you use the same editing tools that you use for JPEG files when you edit a raw file. However, some of these tools, such as white balance, will have far more latitude on a raw file than they do on a JPEG. These editors will also provide additional tools when working with raw files, such as highlight recovery tools. Consult the documentation that came with your image editor to learn more about editing raw files.

> **TIP:** Canon's Digital Photo Professional Application
>
> The Digital Photo Professional application that's bundled with your T1i is a full-powered raw converter. While it's slower than many competing programs and lacks more advanced workflow features such as a good browser, it does let you process and save your raw files, and it provides support for picture styles—something no other raw converter offers.

CHAPTER 12

Customizing the T1i

CONFIGURING CUSTOM SETTINGS AND
ADDING LENSES AND ACCESSORIES

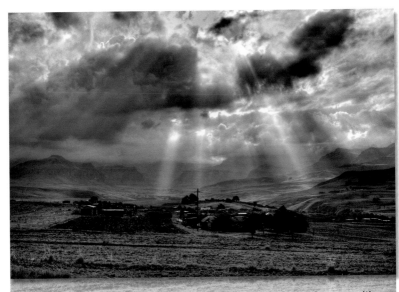

Personally, I find that the T1i interface makes a lot of sense. I like that I can drive the camera with one hand and access critical exposure features without taking my eyes from the viewfinder. Nevertheless, everyone has different needs and different ways of thinking, so the T1i allows you to customize many of its features. And, of course, you can further refine the T1i as a photographic tool by adding different lenses. In this chapter, we'll look at a number of ways to customize and tweak your camera.

My Menu

The T1i has a number of features spread across its six menus, but you'll probably use only a few of them regularly, and it can be a hassle to navigate to the exact feature you want. For this reason, the T1i provides a single customizable menu, called My Menu, that you can populate with only the commands you want. Depending on how many you use, you might be able to create a single My Menu page that contains all the functions you need.

Building My Menu

To add an item to the My Menu page, navigate to My Menu and then select "My Menu settings".

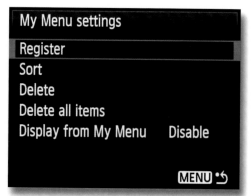

Choosing to register allows you to select commands that you want to include on the menu. Press Set to execute the Register command, and you'll be shown a complete list of commands.

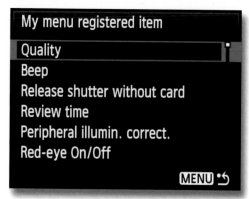

These are listed in the order they appear in the menu system, starting with the first shooting menu. Select an item you want to add, and hit the Set button. The T1i will ask you to verify that you want to add that item to the page:

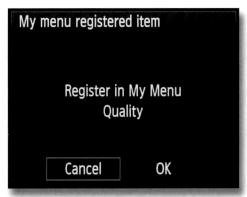

After you've added an item, it will return you to the list so that you can select another. You can add up to six items to My Menu. Like the other menus, My Menu doesn't scroll, so you can always see the entire contents of the menu. Note that after you've added six items, the My Menu settings option is still at the bottom. This is to ensure you always have a way to edit and adjust the menu.

What should you put in the menu? Here's what I usually include:

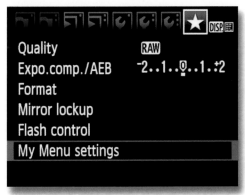

My particular My Menu choices.

I use autoexposure bracketing a lot, so I want that in there. I also want to be able to quickly format the card, and I like having flash exposure compensation when using the onboard flash. Because I do a lot of low-light landscape photography from a tripod, I like having mirror lockup easily accessible. Finally, though I shoot raw 99% of the time, for the few times when I want JPEG, it's nice to have easy access to the Quality menu.

If you're a flash shooter, you might want to consider adding Red-eye On/Off; if you regularly shoot tethered, you might want quick access to "Shoot w/o card". Or if you often shoot events in locations where you need to keep a low profile—concerts and weddings, for example—then Beep might be a good addition to your menu.

Organizing My Menu

Once you've populated My Menu with items, you can use the Sort command to put them in the order you like. Select Sort, and press Set. Navigate to an item whose position you want to change, and then press Set. Arrows will appear next to the item to indicate you can now move it using the up and down arrow buttons.

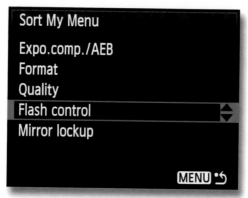

You can reposition your My Menu items to fit your preference.

Move it into position, and then press Set again to accept the new position. When you're done, press the Menu button to back out of the My Menu editing screen. Because the menu "wraps around," it's best to put your least-used items in the middle of the menu. You can quickly get to the top or bottom of the menu to access those items.

After pressing "My Menu settings", you can use the Delete command to delete individual My Menu items or use Delete All Items to clear the whole menu.

Make My Menu the Default

Finally, if you want My Menu to appear whenever you press the Menu button (rather than the last menu you selected), go to the "My Menu settings" page and set "Display from My Menu" to Enable.

Changing Screen Color

You've seen the T1i's default status screen color, but by using the "Screen color" command on the first tools page, you can select a different color scheme—one that might be easier to read in your current lighting conditions.

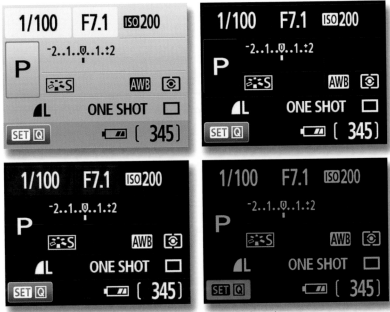

The T1i's four different interface color schemes.

Some screen colors will be easier to read in bright light, while some will be easier in low light or dark conditions. Experiment with each until you find something that's right for your current lighting conditions.

Beep and Power-Off

As you've already probably noticed, your T1i makes a beep any time you autofocus or use the self-timer. You can deactivate this feature by selecting Beep from the first shooting menu. Silencing your camera can be essential for shooting in auditoriums or museums.

By default, the camera shuts off after 30 seconds of inactivity. This helps conserve battery power, but there are times when it can be annoying. For example, if you're shooting a product setup or still life and have the camera mounted on a tripod, you might be spending time moving back and forth between your subject and your camera, refining positioning and lights. Portrait setups can also be like this. If the camera keeps dozing off, you'll have to keep waking it back up again. You can use the Auto Power Off command in the first shooting menu to tell it to wait longer before sleeping.

Adding Copyright Information

You've seen how your T1i embeds all essential exposure information—as well as the date and time the image was shot, and more—in the metadata of every image you take. In addition to all of this data, the T1i can also store a custom copyright message in your images. This is a great way to prove ownership of an image, especially if you plan on posting it to the Web.

You create a copyright message using the Canon EOS Utility. If you have already installed the software from the EOS Solutions Disk, then you're all set. If you don't have the software installed, consult the Software Instruction CD-ROM that came with the T1i.

To define a copyright message:

1. Plug the camera into your computer using a USB cable, and power on the camera.

2. Launch the EOS Utility.

3. From the first screen, click Camera Settings/Remote Shooting. A new window will open, which provides a number of controls, including the ability to remotely trigger and control the camera. These functions allow for tethered shooting, which can greatly speed certain types of in-studio shoots.

4. About halfway down the window, there are three buttons. Click on the tool button.

5. In the Set-Up Menu section, click on the Copyright Notice entry. An editable field will appear.

6. Enter your copyright information and click OK. (Note that you might also want to configure the Owner's Name field.)

7. To confirm that your copyright information has been set properly, press the Menu button on the T1i, and then navigate to the third tool menu and choose Clear Settings. Press the Disp button to display the camera's current copyright info.

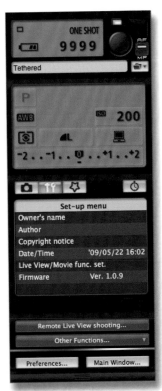

The EOS Utility can help you add copyright information.

Now you can quit the EOS Utility and unplug your camera. You can also use the Clear Settings menu to delete the current copyright information settings, or re-define them using the EOS Utility.

Any image editor or browser that can display EXIF information should allow you to view the copyright information of an image. If you shoot some images and go examine this data, you should see the message you defined.

Custom Functions

In Chapter 9, you got a glimpse of the T1i's custom functions when I discussed mirror lockup. Custom functions are special commands that you access through the Custom Functions command on the third tool menu. Although a few of these commands, such as Mirror Lockup, seem more like primary commands that should be in the normal menu system, the bulk of the custom functions are commands that let you tweak and alter the behavior of other commands.

To alter a custom function, choose custom function (C. Fn) from the third tool menu. Use the left and right arrows to select the function you want to edit, and then click Set. You can then use the up and down arrows to change the value of that function. Press Set when you've configured it as you want it. Here's what they do:

01 Exposure Level Increments This lets you change the increment used by exposure compensation, flash exposure compensation, and autoexposure bracketing. You can choose between a 1/3 stop (the default) or a 1/2 stop. Obviously, a 1/3 stop gives you a finer degree of exposure control, but a 1/2 stop is easier for some people to conceptualize.

02 ISO Expansion Enables ISO 6400 and 12,800, as discussed in Chapter 7.

03 Flash Sync Speed in Av (Aperture-priority AE) mode The shutter in the Rebel T1i is composed of two curtains: one opens to expose the sensor, and the other closes to obscure the sensor. On very fast shutter speeds, the second shutter starts moving to close off the sensor before the first shutter has completely opened. In other words, the sensor is never fully uncovered. Instead, the shutter creates a moving slit that passes very quickly in front of the image sensor. If you fire a flash while this slit is moving across, you'll get a single vertical streak of flash exposure. In other words, you want to use the flash only with a shutter speed that completely uncovers the sensor. In addition, you want the flash in sync with the shutter so that it fires when the shutter is completely open.

By default, when shooting in Aperture Priority mode, the camera will choose any shutter speed from 30 seconds to 1/200th of a second. These are all speeds that will work with the flash, because they all allow the sensor to be completely revealed. However, these longer speeds also mean you run the risk of camera shake. If you want, you can change this custom function to limit the choice of shutter speeds from 1/200th to 1/60th of a second. This will properly expose your subject and reduce camera shake, but will possibly result in the background being too dark. You can also fix the shutter speed at 1/200th, which will also help prevent camera shake, though the background will be even darker.

04 Long Exposure Noise Reduction We looked at this function in our discussion of night shooting in Chapter 10.

05 High ISO Speed Noise Reduction We also looked at this function in our night shooting discussion.

06 Highlight Tone Priority If you're shooting a scene with lots of bright details—people in white clothing, street shots with white buildings, polar bears in bright sunlight—then activating Highlight Tone Priority can help preserve more details in your highlight areas. If you shoot raw, you can get this same functionality through highlight recovery in your raw conversion software. Highlight Tone Priority provides this same type of highlight protection for JPEG shooters.

07 Auto Lighting Optimizer By default, when you shoot JPEG images in darker, lower-contrast situations, the T1i automatically brightens them to restore better contrast. You can increase the amount of brightening or deactivate this feature altogether using this custom function. In very low light, this feature can add additional noise to your images, so you might consider turning it off, to see if you get cleaner results. If you're shooting raw, your raw files will be tagged with Auto Lighting Optimizer data. Canon's Digital Photo Professional will read this data and correct your image.

08 AF-assist beam firing This allows you to tell the camera to not use its built-in pop-up flash for autofocus assist. You can independently toggle the use of both the built-in flash and external flashes.

09 Mirror Lockup We discussed mirror lockup in our discussion of night shooting in Chapter 10.

10 Shutter/AE Lock button This function offers four choices that let you change the functionality of the Exposure Lock button (✱). AF/AE Lock is the normal behavior that we've seen throughout this book. AE Lock/AF lets you lock exposure and focus separately, rather than having them both happen when you half-press the shutter button. With this option activated, pressing the Exposure Lock button (✱) causes the camera to autofocus, whereas half-pressing the shutter causes the camera to meter and lock exposure. The other two options affect the function of the AI Servo feature. See page 188 of the T1i owner's manual for details.

11 Assign Set Button You can assign one of five features to the Set button on the back of the camera. This provides you with quick access to either the Quick Control screen, Image Quality, Flash Exposure Compensation, turning the LCD monitor on and off, or displaying the menu.

12 LCD Display When Power On By default, the camera always activates the rear-panel LCD display when the camera is powered up. If you prefer, you can choose Retain Power Off Status so the camera remembers the state of the LCD screen when you power it off. If you're trying to conserve battery power or if you're shooting in a location where the bright light of the LCD screen is inappropriate, this can be a great feature.

13 Add Original Decision Data If you activate this custom function, the camera will embed special information in your image. When used in conjunction with the optional Original Data Security Kit, it can be possible to determine whether an image has been altered.

> **DEFINITION: Image Forensics**
>
> *Image forensics* is the science of trying to determine whether an image has been altered. For photographs used in legal cases, knowing whether an image has been altered can be critical.

Lenses

One of the great joys of working with an SLR is having the option to change lenses. If you're stepping up to the T1i from a point-and-shoot camera, then there's a whole world of new shooting possibilities for you to explore (and a whole new way to drain your wallet).

By changing the lens on your camera, you can:

- Shoot with different focal lengths, from super-wide to extremely telephoto.

- Get higher-quality images. A better lens can improve contrast, color, sharpness, and other, less definable characteristics of an image.

- Shoot in lower light. A faster lens—that is, one that can open to a wider aperture—will give you the option to shoot in much lower light. An f1.2 lens, for example, can make it possible to shoot at handheld shutter speeds in outright dark situations.

- Shoot with different effects. Fish-eye lenses, the Lensbaby, and other specialized lenses let you create effects that would be unattainable with other lenses and very difficult to produce with editing software.

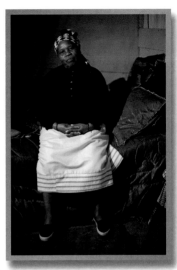

With an extremely fast lens—such as the Canon 50mm f1.2—you can shoot in extremely low light at faster shutter speeds, making it possible to capture images that would be impossible with a slower lens.

Choosing a Lens

Your first decision when choosing a lens is to determine what type of shooting you think you want to be able to do. The 18–55mm and 18–200mm lenses that ship with the T1i kits are great, general-purpose, "walk-around" lenses. They deliver good quality and are stabilized for easier low-light shooting. They also have a focal length range that's suitable for most everyday situations. So, what might you want in addition to one of these lenses? Think about the following questions:

- Do you often find you want to be able to zoom in closer than you can with the kit lens, or that you're regularly cropping your images to focus on a specific detail? If so, you should probably opt for a telephoto lens of some kind.

- Conversely, are you regularly frustrated by the 18mm end of things because you don't feel it's wide enough? Then you might be better served by a wide-angle lens.

- Do you shoot a lot in low light and find yourself unable to get sharp images because your shutter speeds are too slow? If so, you need a faster lens, one with a very wide maximum aperture (f2.8, 2, 1.8, 1.4, or 1.2).

- Do you find yourself frustrated with a lack of sharpness in your image or strange color fringes around certain high-contrast areas?

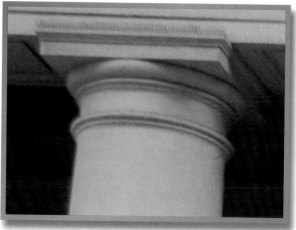

The purple and green fringes on the edge of this column are examples of chromatic aberration. These areas are places where the lens has not focused all of the wavelengths of light equally, leaving some out of registration with the others.

If you have this type of problem a lot, then you need a higher-quality lens. In addition to opting for better quality (which, yes, means more expensive), you'll still need to identify your focal length and speed needs.

Once you've zeroed in on the type of lens you're looking for, you'll be ready to start comparison shopping to find the specific model that's right for you.

Canon EF, EF-S, and L lenses

Canon makes three lines of lenses:

EF lenses are the most common and offer very good quality and a huge selection of focal length and speed options. They work on any EOS digital or film SLR.

EF-S lenses are lenses engineered *specifically* for EOS digital cameras that use an APS-sized sensor (at the time of this writing, this means every current EOS digital camera except for the 5D Mark II and the 1DS Mark III). Because they're engineered specifically for the T1i's smaller sensor, EF-S lenses can deliver tremendously high quality in a very small, light, (relatively) inexpensive package. EF-S lenses can't be used on EOS film cameras or cameras with a full-frame sensor.

L lenses are Canon's high-end line of lenses. These lenses use superior optics that often deliver better color and superior contrast (and occasionally better sharpness) while minimizing flares and other optical artifacts. L lenses are often very fast and are generally built to sturdier specifications than EF lenses. Some L lenses are white, some are black, but they all have a red ring around the end of the lens.

Now, here's the tricky part: There are some exceptional EF lenses that deliver quality as good as some L lenses. There are also some EF-S lenses that are actually L-quality glass but not labeled as such. And finally, some L lenses are unequivocally better than any of the competition. So, before you buy, you need to do a little research online. Check out some reviews, look at samples, and try to get your hands on the lenses in question.

Prime versus zoom

Prime lenses have a fixed focal length. So, a 50mm prime lens can shoot *only* at a 50mm focal length (on the T1i, this is equivalent to an 80mm lens on a 35mm film camera). Zoom lenses, as you have you've seen, have variable focal lengths. It used to be that prime lenses always offered better image quality than zoom lenses, but that's not always the case now. However, as you saw earlier, having a fixed focal length can be a very interesting way to shoot because it makes you compose and frame in a very specific way. So, you may find that you *like* not having the zooming options, especially if you're hungry for a fast lens.

Some Lens Suggestions

Here are my recommendations for currently available Canon lenses that fill the different lens categories we mentioned earlier.

Telephoto zoom

Canon EF-S 55-250 f4-5.6 IS Offering a direct extension of the focal length range provided by the 18–55, this lens extends your shooting range to the equivalent of a 400mm lens. Because it's an EF-S lens, the 55–250 is smaller than full-frame lenses that offer the same range. However, because it's only about $300, the 55–250 is definitely less sturdy than some alternatives. It has a plastic lens mount, which is easier to break, and a generally fragile feel. However, if you're careful with it, this lens will last you for the life of your camera. With a maximum aperture of f4, it's not super speedy, but the four stops of stabilization will help in low light.

Canon EF 70-300 f4-5.6 IS If you can afford about $650, this is a great mid-range telephoto that offers excellent image quality and a very sturdy build. With an equivalent focal length range of 112 to 480mm, this lens gives you a lot of reach. However, if your only other lens is the Canon 18–55, then you're going to be missing the range between 55 and 70.

Wide angle

Canon EF-S 10-22 f3.5-4.5 While the 18mm end of the T1i kit lens is pretty wide, if you like ultrawide lenses, then you won't do better than the Canon 10–22. This lens is branded as an EF-S (because it's engineered specifically for cropped sensor cameras), but it's actually L-quality glass. Razor sharp with great color and contrast and a sturdy build, this is a great lens for photographers who like to shoot wide.

Prime

Canon EF 50mm 1.8 II This is probably one of the best values in lenses for any camera in the world. Offering exceptional optics and a fast maximum aperture of 1.8, you can get this lens new for less than $100. Don't expect much in the way of physical quality—it's a cheap plastic lens, and it feels like it. But if you need to shoot in low light, this is a great lens. Remember, a 50mm on your T1i is going to be equivalent to 80mm on a 35mm camera. So, this lens ends up being a great portrait lens with a flattering focal length and a wide, background-blurring aperture.

Specialty lenses

EF 50mm f2.5 Compact Macro If you're interested in macro photography, this is a great alternative that offers very good quality in a small package.

EF 15mm f2.8 Fisheye Fisheye lenses aren't for everyday use, but if you're looking for an unusual perspective, they can be a lot of fun, and this lens offers great quality in a solid package.

> **TIP:** Third-Party Lenses
>
> Of course. Sigma and Tamron, among others, make some very good lenses that are compatible with your Rebel T1i, including models that compete with the lenses mentioned here. Do your research and see what other users are saying about their experiences with the particular models you're interested in.

T I P : Rent Lenses for Evaluation

A number of online lens rental services will rent you lenses by mail for very reasonable prices. This can be the best way to make a decision about a lens because you can shoot with the lens for a few days, on your own terms. Check out *www.rentglass.com* or google "lens rental".

Evaluating a Lens

Once you've picked a lens you think you're interested in, you'll want to get your hands on it and take it for a test-drive. If you have a local camera store that stocks these lenses, they should be able to answer any questions you have and may even let you try the lens in the store. Take your camera with you and shoot some images. When you get home, you can examine the results up close to try to assess quality. Presumably, by the time you're ready to test a lens, you will already have determined that it has a focal length range and maximum aperture that suits your needs. Consider these additional issues when evaluating a lens:

Sharpness Look at the fine detail in your sample shots. Does it hold up? Is it clearly rendered? Does the camera stay sharp throughout its aperture range? Shoot at wide open, then shoot again at f16 or f22. Is there a sharpness drop-off? If there is, that's not a deal breaker. Most cameras have a sharpness sweet spot that sits within a specific range of apertures. Ideally, you want this range to be as wide as possible.

Chromatic aberrations Are there weird purple, blue, or magenta fringes around high-contrast areas in your scene? This can be hard to test in a camera store, but if they'll let you step outside, try shooting through some trees against a bright sky or along telephone wires. You'll most likely find these issues on the edges of the frame. Also, try a range of apertures. Sometimes these colored fringes show up only at the extremes of the aperture range.

Distortion Does the image bow inward or outward at the edges of the frame? Wide angles will almost always have a little distortion, and you can usually correct it in a good image editor. Still, it's good to know whether the lens has these issues.

Vignetting This is a darkening of the corners that usually appears in wide-angle lenses and usually only with wider apertures. Although it can be corrected, it's something you'd rather avoid, so look carefully for any vignetting problems.

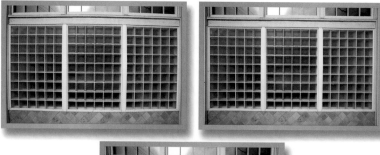

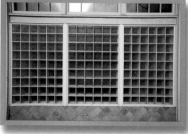

The upper-left image suffers from barrel distortion, which causes the lines to bow outward. The upper-right image is fairly distortion free, whereas the lower image has a problem with pincushion distortion, which causes its lines to bow inward.

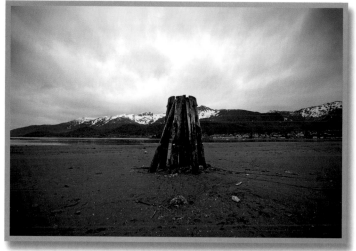

This image suffers from vignetting, a darkening of the corners. Vignetting isn't always bad, and in this image it serves to draw more attention to the center. However, you don't always want vignetting, so it's good to know ahead of time whether a lens has this tendency.

Index